Bridging Research and Policy in Development

Bridging Research and Policy in Development:
Evidence and the Change Process

Compiled and edited by
JULIUS COURT, INGIE HOVLAND and JOHN YOUNG

with

MARGIE BUCHANAN-SMITH
KARIN CHRISTIANSEN
EMMA CREWE
JULIUS KAJUME
SIMON MAXWELL
WILLIAM SOLESBURY
JACOB WANYAMA

Practical Action Publishing Ltd
25 Albert Street, Rugby, CV21 2SD, Warwickshire, UK
www.practicalactionpublishing.com

© Overseas Development Institute, 2005

First published 2005

ISBN 10: 1-85339-603-6
ISBN 13 Paperback: 9781853396038
ISBN Library Ebook: 9781780444598
Book DOI: https://doi.org/10.3362/9781780444598

All rights reserved. No part of this publication may be reprinted or reproduced or utilized in any form or by any electronic, mechanical, or other means, now known or hereafter invented, including photocopying and recording, or in any information storage or retrieval system, without the written permission of the publishers.

A catalogue record for this book is available from the British Library.

The authors, contributors and/or editors have asserted their rights under the Copyright Designs and Patents Act 1988 to be identified as authors of their respective contributions.

Designed and typeset by Christian Humphries

Since 1974, Practical Action Publishing has published and disseminated books and information in support of international development work throughout the world. Practical Action Publishing is a trading name of Practical Action Publishing Ltd (Company Reg. No. 01159018), the wholly owned publishing company of Practical Action. Practical Action Publishing trades only in support of its parent charity objectives and any profits are covenanted back to Practical Action (Charity Reg. No. 247257, Group VAT Registration No. 880 9924 76).

Reasonable efforts have been made to publish reliable data and information, but the author and publisher cannot assume responsibility for the validity of all materials or for the consequences of their use.

The manufacturer's authorised representative in the EU for product safety is Lightning Source France, 1 Av. Johannes Gutenberg, 78310 Maurepas, France. compliance@lightningsource.fr

Contents

List of boxes, figures and tables	vi
About the authors	vii
Foreword by Simon Maxwell	ix
Preface	xii
List of acronyms	xiv

Part I: Background and theoretical framework

1. Research and policy in international development: introduction — 3
   JULIUS COURT, INGIE HOVLAND and JOHN YOUNG

2. Context, evidence, links: a conceptual framework for understanding research–policy processes — 25
   EMMA CREWE, INGIE HOVLAND and JOHN YOUNG

Part II: Case studies

3. The PRSP initiative: multilateral policy change and the role of research — 51
   KARIN CHRISTIANSEN with INGIE HOVLAND

4. How the Sphere Project came into being: a case study of policy making in the humanitarian-aid sector and the relative influence of research — 79
   MARGIE BUCHANAN-SMITH

5. Animal healthcare in Kenya: the road to community-based animal health service delivery — 103
   JOHN YOUNG, JULIUS KAJUME and JACOB WANYAMA

6. Sustainable livelihoods: a case study of the evolution of DFID policy — 133
   WILLIAM SOLESBURY

Part III: Synthesis and conclusion

7. Crosscutting issues and implications: promoting more informed international development policy — 157
   JULIUS COURT, INGIE HOVLAND and JOHN YOUNG

Footnotes	179
Bibliography	187
Index	203

Boxes, figures and tables

Box 2.1	Why is research ignored?	27
Box 2.2	Pressures facing policy makers and researchers	33–34
Box 2.3	The 'woodfuel crisis': simple research messages used to rationalize flawed policies	37
Box 2.4	Using information to influence policy in Indonesia	38
Box 2.5	Grassroots research has a global impact on policy making	40
Box 2.6	The potential of information and communication technology	43
Box 2.7	Research–policy networks	45
Box 3.1	Schematic history of development cooperation	52
Figure 1.1	The RAPID framework: context, evidence, links	9
Figure 2.1	Adaptations of the 'context, evidence, links' framework	29
Figure 5.1	Opportunity for policy change	128
Figure 6.1	IDS's sustainable rural livelihoods framework	140
Figure 6.2	DFID's sustainable livelihoods framework	141
Figure 7.1	The RAPID framework	169
Table 7.1	Practical recommendations	176

About the authors

Margie Buchanan-Smith is an independent consultant and former head of the Humanitarian Policy Group at the Overseas Development Institute (ODI).

Karin Christiansen is a research fellow in the Poverty and Public Policy Group at the ODI.

Julius Court is a research fellow in the Research and Policy in Development (RAPID) programme at the ODI and is on the council of the Development Studies Association of the UK and Ireland.

Emma Crewe is an independent development consultant, formerly with Intermediate Technology Development Group (ITDG).

Ingie Hovland works on ethnography of development and organizational processes. She is currently completing a PhD at the School of Oriental and African Studies (SOAS), University of London.

Julius Kajume is a veterinarian working in the Department of Veterinary Services, Kenya.

Simon Maxwell is Director of the ODI and President of the Development Studies Association of the UK and Ireland.

William Solesbury is Associate Director of Networks in the UK Centre for Evidence-based Policy at Queen Mary, University of London.

Jacob Wanyama is a veterinarian who worked with the Department of Livestock Services in Kenya before joining ITDG in 1992.

John Young is a research fellow and head of the RAPID programme at the ODI.

Foreword
by Simon Maxwell

This book is for researchers, policy makers and practitioners in the field of international development. Though entering the field from different corners, these groups share a commitment to the shaping of a better world. That may seem an obvious statement, but it is not. Research, for example, can be an intellectual game, an abstract pastime pursued for its own sake or for the academic plaudits that elegant findings attract. Researchers in our field are no less passionate about ideas than others, and no less likely to be seduced by the blandishments of publishers or conference organizers. However, for the vast majority of researchers these factors are not their primary motivation. There are few who do not carry searing memories of personal encounters with the very poorest people in the world; very few whose lifetime work is not informed by a determination to understand and act against poverty. The same is surely true for policy makers and practitioners: it is no accident that the UK's Department for International Development (DFID) is the one of the top choices among graduates entering the civil service.

That level of commitment makes the field of development studies an exciting one, but it also imposes a special responsibility to write and implement policy to the highest standard. We expect researchers to be policy-relevant in their work and to make sure that their findings reach policy makers in a form that is accessible and useful. We expect policy makers to find research-based evidence, to think about it, and to use it.

Can we say, collectively, that we do those things? Sadly not, or at least we do not do those things well enough. We all know why. Researchers find it hard, often impossible, to abstract sufficiently from their case material to be useful, and to avoid equivocation. Policy makers find it hard, often impossible, either to read research or make it count in the political cauldron of policy formation. Both sides struggle with shortage of time, under-funding, information overload, poor channels of communication and competing priorities.

But we can do better, and at the Overseas Development Institute (ODI) that is our central purpose. Our mission statement describes us deliberately as a think-tank rather than a research institute, and goes on to explain what that might mean: our mission, it says, is to 'inspire and inform policy and practice which lead to the reduction of poverty, the alleviation of suffering and the achievement of sustainable livelihoods in developing countries. We do this by locking together high-quality applied research, practical policy advice and policy-focused dissemination and debate.'

The ODI mission statement recognizes that good research is the foundation of our enterprise, but also challenges us to carry research findings into the public domain and into dialogue with policy makers. A range of 'products' is needed to do that. ODI publishes two academic journals and a variety of research reports and working papers. It also publishes briefing papers and opinion pieces, arranges private briefings and public meetings, manages a busy website and participates in public debate through the press and other media. ODI staff are also much engaged in providing policy advice to governments and aid agencies across the world.

A typical project, then, certainly involves research: the reading, number crunching, interviews, fieldwork, thinking, that are the stuff of intellectual engagement. Our projects certainly also involve producing research for publication in professional outlets. But, in a way, that is the least of it. We also expect that a research project will generate concise briefing papers written for policy makers. We hope that there will be one or more public meetings for an audience of parliamentarians, parliamentary researchers, NGO policy staff, civil servants and the media. There might be an opinion piece, written for the op-ed page of a national newspaper. There might be a private briefing for senior policy staff in development agencies. And it is quite likely that the researcher will be asked to carry out advisory work somewhere in the world.

This diversity of activity certainly makes for a lively working week, but it also requires staff to make difficult choices about priorities, and to deploy a complex and demanding set of skills. For instance, is it best to write a journal article, briefing paper, or newspaper article? Or would it be better to spend the time on the telephone to an MP or to the clerk of a parliamentary select committee? Or perhaps the best course of action would be simply to travel to the relevant developing country and just conduct the research? If research findings challenge accepted policy, is it best to 'publish and be damned', or perhaps nuance the presentation of findings in order to win over the policy-making establishment? How does that decision affect the likelihood of funding for future work?

Being able to answer questions like these ought to be the key shared competence of all those who work in international development research – and to an extent it is. Some people are natural 'policy entrepreneurs': fluent, practical, well networked, and politically astute. Others have learned. Many, probably most of us, are learning.

On the other side of the fence, the same is true. Civil servants, for example, are increasingly judged by their success in delivering performance targets or development results. In agencies like DFID, what counts is not just managing aid projects successfully – indeed, there are few traditional projects in the DFID portfolio – but rather achieving change in the policies of developing countries or the policy and practice of international organizations. This 'influencing agenda' overlaps with the mission of the think-tanks, although civil servants and politicians with budgets at their command can easily out-gun researchers whose only weapon is the power of ideas. Similar questions arise, however, about how to use resources and how to induce change.

There is more to do. As the authors of this book point out, the science of international development policy making is still in its infancy. Policy making has been studied in developed countries, but there is much less literature in developing countries. Furthermore, there is precious little anywhere on policy change across national borders, when many actors are involved.

This book moves us forward. Naturally it provides a detailed literature review and a conceptual framework: this is a research report, after all. There are four case studies, which range from the local to the international and from theory to practice. The authors have synthesized the lessons learned. The power of the book lies in these case studies. They demonstrate the importance of cultures and structures, of people and places, of timing, of the interplay between strategy and serendipity. This is how policy making really is. But the actors – that's all of us – are not simply 'blowing about in the wind'. The point of the book is that there are things to do differently on Monday morning, both in analysing policy environments and in managing them more effectively.

This book is a staging point, not a conclusion. Research needs to continue, as the authors demonstrate. In addition, however, and in the spirit of the work on which the book reports, there is a need for briefing papers and opinion pieces, meetings and briefings, advisory work and training. ODI's RAPID programme is already much engaged in this kind of programme. There will be more.

Preface

How can policy makers best use research for evidence-based policy making? How can researchers best use their findings in order to influence policy? How can we improve the interaction between researchers and policy makers? Despite the substantial funds that go into research on international development and the usual contention that research informs policy change, there remains surprisingly little systematic understanding regarding the links between research and policy. Our aim is to provide a contribution towards filling this gap in the literature – and to suggest ways that researchers might have a greater impact on efforts to move towards evidence-based pro-poor policy.

This volume presents the first cohesive and consolidated reporting of the work carried out under the Research and Policy in Development (RAPID) programme at the Overseas Development Institute (ODI). The RAPID programme aims to improve the use of research and evidence in development policy and practice through research, advice and debate. The RAPID programme has four principal themes.

- The use of evidence in policy identification, development and implementation.
- Improving communication and information systems for development agencies.
- How better knowledge-management can enhance the impact of development agencies.
- Promotion and capacity building for evidence-based policy.

The volume draws, in particular, on a project entitled 'Bridging Research and Policy', funded by the UK's Department for International Development (DFID). The specific aim of the project was to improve understanding of the links between research and policy in international development through in-depth analysis of selected case studies. To guide this research, the project completed a literature review and developed a conceptual framework for understanding links between research and policy: the 'context, evidence, links' framework. The project then applied the framework to four detailed case studies of specific policy changes: the adoption of the Poverty Reduction Strategy Paper (PRSP) initiative; the impact of the Sphere Project on the performance of international humanitarian agencies; the spread of para-professional livestock services in Kenya; and the emergence and adoption of the Sustainable Livelihoods Approach (SLA) in DFID's 1997 White Paper.

We are extremely grateful to partners and colleagues around the world who have helped in developing the framework, undertaking the case studies and reviewing our work. Simon Maxwell and Diane Stone encouraged work in this area and have provided guidance throughout the various stages of the research. Conversations with Desmond McNeill were instrumental in developing the framework and we greatly appreciate his advice. We would also particularly like to thank the case study authors – Margie Buchanan-Smith, Karin Christiansen, Emma Crewe, Julius Kajume, William Solesbury and Jacob Wanyama – not only for the rigorous studies but also for their extensive comments during the project.

We are also grateful to many of our current and former colleagues at ODI who have helped shape our thinking. We would like to thank Tim Conway, David Booth, Elizabeth Cromwell, James Darcy, Ruth Driscoll, Cokro Leksmono, Andy Norton, Sheila Page, Amy Pollard, Ben Ramalingam, Keiko Suzuki, Frances Stevenson and Maja de Vibe.

The project ideas and draft papers have been discussed at various meetings and workshops involving other experts. Here we would particularly like to acknowledge the insights of Cari Aleta, Stuart Coupe, Suzanne Jaspars, Megan Lloyd-Laney, Sandra Nutley and Ian Scoones. Each of the case studies depended on interviews with key informants, and we would like to thank all those people for taking time to provide insights and comments.

We are grateful to DFID for funding this work and particularly to Paul Spray and Dylan Winder who provided substantive inputs at various stages of the project.

While we are indebted to all those who helped us along the way, we are ultimately responsible for the contents of the volume.

> Julius Court, Ingie Hovland and John Young

Acronyms

ACT	Action by Churches Together
AfDB	African Development Bank
Afrodad	African Forum and Network on Debt and Development
AHA	African Humanitarian Action
AHITI	Animal Health Training Institute
AHT	animal health technician
ALNAP	Active Learning Network for Accountability and Performance in Humanitarian Action
ASAL	arid and semi-arid lands
ASMP	Agriculture Sector Management Project
CAFOD	Catholic Fund for Overseas Development
CAHW	community animal health worker
CAS	Country Assistance Strategy (World Bank)
CDF	Comprehensive Development Framework (World Bank)
CSO	civil society organization
DAC	Development Assistance Committee (OECD)
DAH	decentralized animal health
DC	development committee
DELIVERI	Decentralized Livestock Services in the Eastern Regions of Indonesia Project
DFID	Department for International Development (UK)
DGLS	Directorate General of Livestock Services (Indonesia)
DRI	Debt Relief International
DVO	district veterinary officer
DVS	Department of Veterinary Services
EC	European Commission
ESAF	Enhanced Structural Adjustment Facility (IMF) (replaced by the PRGF)
ESCOR	Economic and Social Research programme (ODA)
ESRC	Economic and Social Research Council
EU	European Union
FAO	Food and Agriculture Organization (United Nations)
FAR	*Forces Armées Rwandaise*
FARM Africa	Food and Agriculture Research Mission for Africa
G7	Canada, France, Germany, Italy, Japan, USA, UK
G8	G7 and Russia
GDN	Global Development Network
GTZ	*Deutsche Gesellschaft für Technische Zusammenarbeit* (the international development agency of the German government)
HAP	Humanitarian Accountability Project
HIPC	heavily indebted poor countries
HIPC1	Heavily Indebted Poor Countries Initiative
HIPC2	Enhanced Heavily Indebted Poor Countries Initiative
IBRD	International Bank for Reconstruction and Development (World Bank Group)
ICRC	International Committee of the Red Cross
ICT	information and communication technology
ICVA	International Council of Voluntary Agencies
IDA	International Development Association (World Bank Group)
IDRC	International Development Research Centre (Canada)
IDS	Institute of Development Studies
IDT	international development target

IFAD	International Fund for Agricultural Development
IFI	international financial institution
IFPRI	International Food Policy Research Institute
IFRC	International Federation of Red Cross and Red Crescent Societies
IIED	International Institute for Environment and Development
IISD	International Institute for Sustainable Development (Canada)
IMF	International Monetary Fund
IMFC	International Monetary and Financial Committee
IPRSP	Interim PRSP
ITDG	Intermediate Technology Development Group
JEFF	Joint Evaluation Follow-up, Monitoring and Facilitation Network
JSA	joint staff assessment
KALT	Kenya Association of Livestock Technicians
KFC	Kamujini Farmers Centre
KVA	Kenya Veterinary Association
KVAPS	Kenya Veterinary Association Privatisation Scheme
KVB	Kenya Veterinary Board
LWF	Lutheran World Federation
MDG	Millennium Development Goals
MSF	*Medecins Sans Frontières*
NCDDR	National Center for the Dissemination of Disability Research
NGO	non-governmental organization
NORAD	Norwegian Agency for Development Cooperation
NRAC	Natural Resources Advisory Committee
NRPAD	Natural Resources Policy and Advisory Department
NSI	National Systems of Innovation
OAU/IBAR	Organisation of African Unity (became African Union in 1999) /International Bureau for Animal Resources
ODA	Overseas Development Administration (became DFID in 1997)
ODG	Overseas Development Group
ODI	Overseas Development Institute
OECD	Organisation for Economic Cooperation and Development
OFDA	United States' Office of Foreign Disaster Assistance (USAID)
PAF	Poverty Action Fund of the Ugandan Budget/PRSP
PARC	Pan Africa Rinderpest Campaign
PARC-VAC	participatory and community-based vaccination project
PDR	Policy Development and Review Department (IMF)
PE	public expenditure
PEAP	Poverty Eradication Action Plan (Uganda)
PFP	policy framework paper (IMF/World Bank)
PIP	policy institutions and processes
PPA	participatory poverty assessment
PREM	Poverty Reduction and Economic Management (World Bank)
PRGF	Poverty Reduction and Growth Facility (IMF)
PRSP	Poverty Reduction Strategy Paper
PVO	private voluntary organization
RAPID	Research and Policy in Development
RAWOO	*Raad voor het Wetenschappelijk Onderzoek in het kader van Ontwikkelingssamenwerking* (Netherlands' Development Assistance Research Council)
RPF	Rwandese Patriotic Front
RRN	Relief and Rehabilitation Network
SAP	Structural Adjustment Programme

SAPRI	Structural Adjustment Participatory Review Initiative
SAPRIN	Structural Adjustment Participatory Review International Network (formerly SAPRI)
SARN	South Asian Research Network
SCF-UK	Save the Children Fund UK
SCHR	Steering Committee for Humanitarian Response
SID	Society for International Development
SLA	sustainable livelihoods approach
SLRG	Sustainable Livelihoods Resource Group
SLSO	Sustainable Livelihoods Support Office
SNNPR	Southern Nations, Nationalities and Peoples Region (Ethiopia)
SNV	Netherlands Development Organization
SPA	Strategic Partnership with Africa
TRVTT	thermostable rinderpest vaccine technology transfer
UEA	University of East Anglia
UK DEL	UK delegation to the Boards of the IMF and World Bank
UN	United Nations
UNDAF	United Nations Development Assistance Framework
UN DHA	United Nations Department for Humanitarian Affairs
UNDP	United Nations Development Programme
UNHCHR	United Nations High Commissioner for Human Rights
UNHCR	United Nations High Commission for Refugees
UNICEF	United Nations Children's Fund
USAID	United States Agency for International Development
VOICE	Voluntary Organisations in Cooperation in Emergencies
VSF	*Veterinaires Sans Frontières*
WDR	World Development Report
WFP	World Food Programme
WHO	World Health Organization
WRI	World Resource Institute
WTO	World Trade Organization

Part I
Background and theoretical framework

Chapter One
Research and policy in international development: introduction
JULIUS COURT, INGIE HOVLAND and JOHN YOUNG

Background

The challenge of evidence-based policy making

Better utilization of research and evidence in development policy and practice can help save lives, reduce poverty and improve the quality of life. For instance, the results of household disease surveys informed processes of health service reform which contributed to 43 and 46 per cent reductions in infant mortality between 2000 and 2003 in two districts in rural Tanzania.[1] A recent study by the UK Department for International Development (DFID), as part of its effort to develop a new research policy, forcefully catalogues the value of research for development (Surr et al. 2002). However, researchers frequently do not see influencing activities as a priority once the research is completed. Policy makers and other stakeholders often do not know what research exists, which policies are most suitable, or how they can best be implemented in different contexts. Or, as is illustrated (with devastating consequences) by the lack of response to HIV/AIDS in some countries, policy makers may be unwilling to act on the evidence.

Major investment goes into research on international development – from stakeholders in the South (government and non-government) and from governments in the North and international agencies. While an exact figure is difficult to arrive at, we estimate that Northern and international sources provide around US$3 billion for international development research. If we are to reduce poverty in the South and meet the Millennium Development Goals (MDGs), the key questions are: When and why does development research make a difference? Why do some research findings influence policy and practice while others do not? And how can we promote more informed international development policy?

Despite the importance of research–policy questions in the international development sector, very little relevant academic work exists on the topic. Studies on evidence-based policy have mainly focused on policy processes in the OECD (Organisation for Economic Cooperation and Development) countries, paying particular attention to the national medical and educational sectors in these countries. In the USA, the 1980s has been termed the golden age of studies on knowledge utilization, following Weiss's (1977) seminal research on 'knowledge creep' and 'percolation'. In the UK, evidence-based policy is the central theme of the Centre for Management and Policy Studies, established by the

Cabinet Office in mid-1999. In the same year, the Economic and Social Research Council (ESRC) established the Evidence Based Policy and Practice Initiative, a collaborative network of seven research units aiming to bring social-science research nearer to the decision-making process.

Analytical reflection on the many different contexts and factors influencing research–policy processes in countries outside the OECD is much more rare.[2] This is no small challenge, as the massive diversity of cultural, economic and political contexts makes it especially difficult to draw valid generalizations and lessons from existing experience and theory. In addition, international actors have an exaggerated impact on research and policy processes in several countries in the South. Alongside these analytic gaps, there is a lack of relevant case-study material to illustrate and highlight successful and unsuccessful practices.

There has been some interest in these questions in the international development sector over the past few years. In 1998, the International Institute for Environment and Development (IIED) identified a six-point programme for improving the policy impact of research (Garrett and Islam 1998). The Overseas Development Institute (ODI) has been researching research–policy linkages since 1999, with an early report providing a 21-point checklist of what makes policies happen (Sutton 1999). Impact assessments by the International Food Policy Research Institute (IFPRI) have focused increasingly over the last few years on measuring the policy impact of its research programmes, and how it can be improved. The link between research and policy has been a key issue for the Global Development Network (GDN) since its inception in 1999. The International Development Research Centre (IDRC) (Canada) is currently completing a strategic evaluation of the influence of IDRC-supported research on public policy.

This volume aims to enhance understanding of how research can contribute to pro-poor policy and practice. We believe it is a useful contribution for a number of reasons. First, it presents a cohesive framework that can be used to understand and analyse research–policy linkages. Second, it provides evidence from four systematic and in-depth case studies. The approach is innovative in that each case details instances of policy change and then does a 'tracer' study backwards in time to chart the different factors – including research – that led to the policy shift. We believe the approach is valuable in that it highlights the range of factors that affect policy uptake of research. Third, through comparison across the four cases, we draw out themes that will be relevant to those involved in development research or policy and who wish to use evidence to contribute to pro-poor policy making. In particular, we provide suggestions for how researchers might enhance the policy impact of their work.

The global context

An understanding of research–policy linkages in international development needs to take into account both the wide range of different contexts that development policies appear in, and the key challenges of the macro-level political context. There are a number of notable global trends here.

Democratization has been one of the striking developments of the past decades. In 1901, there were no nations that could be considered democratic – even according to the most basic definition. Now there are estimated to be more than 121 electoral democracies (Freedom House 2003). From 1976 to 1999 the number of democratic regimes has more than doubled, from fewer than 40 to more than 80 (Gurr et al. 2001).[3] This provides new entry points to the policy-making process. It is thought that democratic contexts would better enable research to be conducted and communicated (due to freedoms), and that there would be greater incentives for policy makers to use research (due to accountability mechanisms).

But many developing countries remain undemocratic and many countries have deficits in these areas even if they are seen as democratic in form (Hyden et al. 2004). Political systems are less representative and have weaker structures for aggregating and arbitrating interests in society, even in countries seen as democratic (Grindle 1980; Hyden et al. 2004). Policy-making processes tend to be more centralized and thus often remote and inaccessible with limited scope for wider input or participation except at implementation stage (Grindle 1980: 15). Often political leaders may view input from civil society as illegitimate or inefficient. The result is to increase policy makers' power whilst simultaneously isolating them from society. Policy formulation becomes responsive to the needs of élites rather than the majority – or the poor.

Markets are spreading and economies are increasingly open. Twenty years ago, only 2.9 billion people lived in a market economy, compared to 5.7 billion people today.[4] What does this mean for research–policy linkages? Most obviously, it brings new actors into political processes. It also creates increased demand for research that can be accessed by those outside academia. There is demand for research by private companies; and there is demand for research by governments – so that they are able to cope with technical issues around economic policy formulation and regulation.

Civil society is generally thought to be blossoming in an increasing number of nations. The number of non-governmental organizations (NGOs) is growing. The role played by civil society (NGOs, the media, and think-tanks) in shaping national priorities is expanding. A theme common to many countries is the increasing importance of non-state organizations as actors in the governance realm (Edwards 2004). An apt example is the role played by civil society through consultations and follow-up in national Poverty Reduction Strategy Paper (PRSP) processes. Nevertheless, many challenges remain (Hyden et al. 2004). The input of civil society into public policy is still quite limited. Civil society and state often live rather separate lives, with governments continuing to set the policy agenda largely on their own. There is still a tendency for governments to arrest or intimidate citizens who propagate views different from those in power.

The rapid development of **information and communication technology (ICT)** has incredible potential to transform the generation and sharing of information. The poor are poor not just because they are marginalized in economic and political processes, but also because they are marginalized in information flows in society. Widespread dissemination through ICTs can make information accessible to a far wider audience than before, and this information can potentially act as a catalyst for action – even for groups that have traditionally been marginalized. However, ICTs are no miracle cure. The information gap is widening, and the need to be 'plugged in' to information networks in order to be able to influence policy may also exclude groups that fall outside the information society.

There is increasing concern that the '**war on terror**' is leading to an increased politicization of aid and is diverting attention from poverty reduction (Christian Aid 2004). It is too soon to confirm the implications for research–policy links, but it appears that there is less emphasis on ensuring freer political contexts (important for collecting and communicating evidence) and on using evidence to encourage pro-poor policies in developing countries. The worry is that progress may stall in terms of the increasingly favourable context for pro-poor policy making that was evolving in many countries over the past two decades. These factors provide a broad outline of the context in which we wish to situate this study.

Conceptual framework

This global context raises the question of research–policy linkages. How can we understand research and policy in international development today? In this section, we provide a brief introduction to our approach to these concepts, and the way we have used them in the conceptual framework that guided the case studies.

Definitions: research and policy

In preparing the case studies, the project decided to use relatively open definitions of research and policy. This was important given the preliminary nature of the work, the diversity and complexity of the study topics, and the relative lack of existing case studies.

Like others, we thought it was difficult, and often unhelpful, to provide an overly specific definition of research since the exact meaning will depend on the context. For the case studies in the Research and Policy in Development (RAPID) project we considered research as 'any systematic effort to increase the stock of knowledge'.[5] This included therefore any systematic process of critical investigation and evaluation, theory building, data collection, analysis and codification related to development policy and practice. It includes action research, self-reflection by practitioners oriented towards the enhancement of direct practice.

We suggest that policy is defined as a 'purposive course of action followed by an actor or set of actors' (Anderson 1975). Our suggestion is to focus on public policy with the understanding that policy is not restricted to government. International organizations, bilateral agencies and NGOs also all have policies. What makes policies public is not that they are adopted and implemented by government, but also that they affect the public or are visible to the public. The cases explored how research can influence policy makers' horizons, policy development, declared public policy regimes and policy implementation or practice (Lindquist 2001).

An integrated framework: context, evidence, links

Traditionally, the link between research and policy has been viewed as a linear process, whereby a set of research findings is shifted from the 'research sphere' over to the 'policy sphere', and then has some impact on policy makers' decisions. At least two of the assumptions underpinning this traditional view are now being questioned. First, the assumption that research influences policy in a one-way process (the linear model); second, the assumption that there is a clear divide between researchers and policy makers (the two-communities model).

Recent reviews of the literature on research–policy links move away from these assumptions, towards a more dynamic and complex view that emphasizes a two-way process between research and policy, shaped by multiple relations and reservoirs of knowledge (see, for example, Garrett and Islam 1998; Keeley and Scoones 2003; Lindquist 2001; Neilson 2001; RAWOO 2001; Stone 2001; Sutton 1999).

Following Weiss (1977), current research–policy reviews usually recognize that although research may not have direct impact on specific policies, the production of research may still exert a powerful indirect influence through introducing new terms and shaping the policy discourse. Weiss describes this as a process of 'percolation', in which research findings and concepts are gradually filtered through various policy networks. Thus, while the traditional question could be phrased: 'How can research be transported from the research to the policy sphere?', the new question to be addressed concerns research uptake pathways: 'Why are some of the ideas that circulate in the research–policy networks picked up and acted on, while others are ignored and disappear?' The answer to this seems to lie in a combination of several determining influences. The integrated framework developed by RAPID (Crewe and Young 2002) has broadly divided these influences into three areas, as illustrated in Figure 1.1 (see page 9).

First, research–policy linkages are shaped by **political context**. The policy process and the production of research are in themselves political processes: from the initial agenda-setting exercise through to the final negotiation involved in implementation. Political contestation, institutional pressures and vested interests matter greatly. So do the attitudes and incentives among officials, their room for manoeuvre, local history and power relations (Clay and Schaffer 1984; Kingdon 1984). In some cases the political strategies and power relations are obvious, and are tied to specific institutional pressures. In other cases the pressures are more vague, and are tied to broad discourses or paradigms that may exert a powerful influence over which ideas are noticed and which are ignored.

Second, the RAPID framework proposes that the nature of the **evidence** is important for policy uptake. The literature suggests that significant here are research approach and methodology, credibility of the evidence, simplicity of the message, how it is communicated and the degree it challenges received wisdom. The sources and conveyors of information may be as influential as the content; for example, people accept information more readily from those they trust. But it is our hypothesis that good-quality research, local involvement, accurate messages, and effective dissemination strategies are all important in aiming for more evidence-based policy making.

Another key set of issues concern how evidence is communicated. The way new messages are packaged (especially if they are couched in familiar terms) and targeted can make an enormous difference to how a policy document is perceived and utilized. For instance, marketing is based on the insight that packaging rather than content (in and of itself) often determines people's reaction to a new product or idea (Williamson 1996). The key message is that communication is an extremely demanding process and that it is most effective to take an interactive approach (Mattelart and Mattelart 1998). Continuous interaction leads to greater chances of successful communication than a simple or linear approach.

Third, the framework emphasizes the importance of **links** between communities, networks and intermediaries (for example, the media and campaigning groups) in affecting policy change. Some of the current literature focuses explicitly on various types of networks, such as policy communities (Pross 1986), epistemic communities (Haas 1991), and advocacy coalitions (Sabatier and Jenkins-Smith 1999). Issues of trust, legitimacy, openness and formalization of networks are important in relation to the speed and degree of research uptake. Existing theory appreciates the role of translators and communicators (Gladwell 2000), while it seems that there is often an lack of appreciation of the extent and ways that intermediary organizations and networks impact on formal policy guidance documents, which in turn influence officials.

The framework is examined in more detail in Chapter 2. We should note here that the framework is presented as a generic, perhaps ideal, model. It seeks to understand research–policy linkages by combining perspectives on the linkages from the three spheres as they appear in a given situation of policy change or stasis. In some cases there will not be much overlap between the different spheres, in other cases the overlap may vary considerably. In most cases, the historical changes that

Figure 1.1 The RAPID framework: context, evidence, links

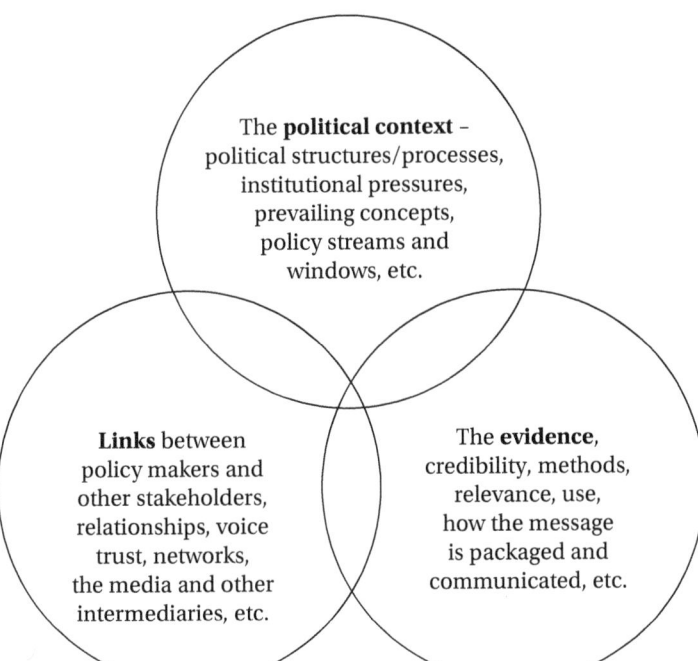

have occurred over time in each sphere will have an impact on the present situation. In addition, a set of factors emerged through the RAPID case studies that proved so important that they could justifiably be grouped as a fourth sphere in the framework, namely the set of factors that together make up 'external influences'. This additional conceptual dimension is discussed further in Chapter 7.

Research methodology

Research hypotheses

Building on the conceptual framework, the following hypotheses were tested through the four comparative case studies.

Research is more likely to contribute to evidence-based policy making that aims to reduce poverty, alleviate suffering or save lives if:

- it fits within the political and institutional limits and pressures of policy makers, and resonates with their ideological assumptions, or sufficient pressure is exerted to challenge those limits;
- outputs are based on local involvement and credible evidence, and are communicated via the most appropriate communicators, channels, style, format and timing;

- researchers and policy makers share particular kinds of networks and develop chains of legitimacy for particular policy areas.

Research approach

RAPID originally applied the framework and hypotheses to three case studies of policy change, within areas where ODI already has substantial research and policy experience PRSPs; humanitarian accountability; and animal health in Kenya). RAPID also worked with the Evidence Network to prepare the fourth case study (on sustainable livelihoods). Each author separately developed the case study, but the same basic process was followed in each case and there were regular meetings to report and discuss the findings.

Each case constructed an historical narrative leading up to the observed policy change in question. This involved creating a timeline of key policy decisions and practices, along with important documents and events, and identifying key actors. The next step was to explore how and why those policy decisions and practices took place, and to assess the relative role of research in that process by drawing on the framework. This was done through interviews with key actors, review of the literature, and cross-checking of conflicting narratives.

The construction of an historical narrative in this way is sometimes called a 'tracer study'. A tracer study is a distinct approach in current debates because it starts from the policy change, and then works backwards to assess the key issues that made a difference. The opposite would be an approach that takes a specific determining factor as its starting point – e.g. a particular piece of research – and then follows the various impacts of this factor forwards in time; much of the work of IFPRI takes this approach. The RAPID project decided to choose the tracer-study approach. The crucial advantage of using a tracer study is that the process of working backwards in time gives a more realistic view of the broad range of factors – other than research – that influence policy, while tracking forward probably overemphasizes the importance of research *vis-á-vis* other factors.

However, the tracer-study approach has drawbacks and limitations. Since policy processes are complex, multilayered and change through time, it is difficult to identify the key factors that caused policy to change (or not), and to isolate the impact of research. The standard challenge of unconscious selection of informants is common to case studies; the RAPID case studies sought to balance this by seeking the views of a wide range of informed stakeholders. Interviews with these stakeholders played a key part in the research process, but there is a certain risk that actors may 'rewrite history' after a time lapse of a few years, and in light of the perceived failure or success of the policy in question. The benefit of hindsight may also lead people to downplay the role of competing policy ideas that previously seemed important, but which have later been discarded. Hindsight may also induce people to claim credit for ideas that have proved potent, while in practice potent ideas may frequently have been noticed and applied by a number of people at the same time, influenced by the same generic conditions and the *Zeitgeist*.

Bearing these challenges in mind, substantial efforts were taken during the course of the research to triangulate and to verify the accuracy of the narrative. Actors with different stakes in the policy process critically reviewed various interpretations of the past, and conflicting narratives were cross-checked against documents and observations. The study authors reported that the approach allowed them to capture, in depth, the range of issues that mattered in the four cases. In addition, the challenges and findings of each case study were discussed in case-study workshops, which sought to facilitate iteration between the analysis of the specific case studies, the research questions for each of those, and the general research framework.

Research questions

Further building on the conceptual framework, key research questions were identified and used in each case study to ensure some consistency. With the overall goals of the study in mind, the interviews mainly used questions that addressed each of the three dimensions of the framework: context, evidence, and links. The list of questions below provided a guide, but there was also room for interviewees to list any additional factors they felt were important.

Context
To what extent is the impact of research on policy making shaped by political and institutional structures and ideological assumptions?

(a) How did the global, national and community-level political, social and economic structures and interests affect the room for manoeuvre of decision makers in particular policy areas? Which political, social or economic factors might have influenced the key decision makers? (These factors might, for instance, include: financial interests of international banks in relation to debt cancellation; socio-economic interests of vets in blocking the liberalization of regulations; or the impact of local political interests of warring factions on food distribution.)

(b) To what extent were decisions routine, incremental, fundamental or emergent, and who supported or resisted change? (Important factors might, for example, include: existing knowledge and values and the various actors; the old and new ideas underlying decisions; to what extent new policies might change the status quo; or who supported and resisted the changes and how.)

(c) How did applied and academic research influence the development of policy when being put into practice? How were the policies developed, adapted or distorted as they were put into practice? (Important factors might include actions taken and research used by project partners, 'street-level bureaucrats', and communities.)

Evidence
To what extent did local involvement, the quality of research and communication strategies affect the impact that research had on policy making in particular areas?

(a) How was information gathered and by whom? Who did the research – beneficiaries, NGO practitioners, activists, academics, consultants, or government researchers? Was it academic/applied and was it before/during/after/not part of a 'project' with non-research aims?

(b) What was perceived as credible evidence by different actors and why? What parts of the knowledge produced was valued, by whom, and how did they assess research quality?

(c) Did researchers segment their audience and if so, how, and did this have an impact on policy? Was information tailored for particular policy makers (according to organization, gender, discipline, policy area, etc.) and what impact did this have?

(d) How and why was information ignored, reinterpreted and/or distorted and by whom?

(e) What happened to the research findings within policy communities, and what type of information flows and patterns were apparent?

(f) Did the communicator, channel, format, style or timing of the communication play a role in influencing policy makers? How were the research findings communicated, at what stages, and by whom? What worked, what failed, when and why?

Links
To what extent is research used more effectively in policy processes if researchers and policy makers share particular kinds of networks, common goals and chains of legitimacy for particular policy areas?

(a) What roles were played by which kind of groups and individuals and what were the links between them? (Important information might include the types of relationships and networks between actors, such as epistemic communities, global public policy networks, issue groups, advocacy coalitions and citizen action groups, etc.)

(b) Which people had significant influence over the policy? Who were regarded as experts in the particular policy area? Who were the effective and ineffective policy entrepreneurs, connectors, mavens (experts) and salesmen? Were there any differences in impact according to gender, nationality, race or class?

(c) How did women and men researchers and advocates establish legitimacy, and did it make any difference to the policy outcomes? What were the chains of legitimacy between various stakeholders (for example, did Southern partners control the monitoring of action research, or to what degree were informants consulted about policy recommendations)? What was the influence of these chains of legitimacy on the quality of policy decisions?

Other factors
What else mattered?

Case studies

Chapters 3–6 present the four case studies in detail. The following section provides an introductory overview of each case, including the main findings in relation to research–policy linkages.

The PRSP initiative: multilateral policy change and the relative role of research

The case study in Chapter 3 (by Karin Christiansen with Ingie Hovland) traces the emergence of the Poverty Reduction Strategy Paper (PRSP) initiative and the various factors that contributed to its adoption in September 1999, including the role and relative influence of research in this process. A PRSP is a document that sets out an analysis of poverty in a country and defines the national strategy on how the government is going to reduce it. Preparation of a PRSP is an entry criterion for debt relief under the Heavily Indebted Poor Countries (HIPC) initiative, and is also an eligibility criterion for concessional lending from the International Development Association (IDA) of the World Bank and the Poverty Reduction Growth Facility (PRGF) programme of the International Monetary Fund (IMF).

Context
Probably the most important contextual factor that shaped the PRSP initiative was the major convergence of debates and controversies in the field of international development in the late 1990s. This led to a widespread sense of there being 'a problem' within the international development policy field, even though policy makers did not agree on the exact nature of the problem. The challenges that needed to be addressed, particularly by the World Bank and the IMF, included the following.

- The mandates of the IMF and the World Bank were called into question, due to factors such as the 1997 Asia Crisis and the commonly believed failure of structural adjustment programmes (SAPs) in sub-Saharan Africa.
- The fall into disuse of the Policy Framework Paper (PFP), which was meant to be the operational mechanism for cooperation between the IMF and the World Bank.
- The 1999 review of the HIPC initiative, which raised the question of how to link debt relief to poverty reduction. There was a backdrop of substantial external pressure building up around this issue, particularly from the NGO movement, such as Jubilee 2000.
- The need to operationalize the new conceptual framework for aid put forward by Wolfensohn's Comprehensive Development Framework (CDF) in early 1999, and to find a means of combining this with an explicit focus on poverty reduction. Poverty reduction had also become a central concern for DFID, led by Clare Short.

The PRSP initiative can be viewed as bringing together all these interlinked concerns, and providing answers, or at least partial solutions, to the issues that needed to be addressed. Many different parties, therefore, bought into it.

Evidence

Broadly speaking, two evidence fields influenced the emergence of the PRSP initiative. First, the broad field of academic development research contributed, albeit often indirectly, to the big shifts in international development discourse in the 1970s, 1980s and 1990s, towards poverty, participation and aid effectiveness. This research highlighted problems with existing practices within international development, setting the stage for the reviews of the 1990s.

Second, there is the field of applied policy research undertaken in the late 1990s, in particular the research related to the Enhanced Structural Adjustment Facility (ESAF) reviews, the HIPC review, the Strategic Partnership with Africa (SPA) Working Groups, and NGO research on debt relief. This evidence focused more on providing policy recommendations and operational solutions. It was considered most credible when it was commissioned by the international financial institutions (IFIs) or other donors, demonstrated analytical rigour, and was communicated in a language that was accessible and relevant to World Bank and IMF staff and other donor agencies.

Less directly related to research, but with an extremely powerful demonstration effect, was the positive experience of Uganda in drafting and giving policy prominence to a Poverty Eradication Action Plan (PEAP). This did much to convince policy makers of the feasibility and merits of the poverty-reduction strategy model.

Links

The PRSP story is characterized by a multitude of links between the various players, both policy makers and researchers. The discussion of the main institutional actors – the World Bank and IMF, SPA, the UK and US governments and the NGO movement – illustrates clearly the high level of contact between individuals in different institutions. It was also significant that individuals moved between institutions and thus carried ideas with them. As one interviewee put it, 'none of the players is more than two handshakes away from any of the others'. The formal and informal networks contributed to the speed with which the PRSP ideas were spread and accepted in international development policy.

The PRSP tipping point

The PRSP policy initiative can be viewed as a 'tipping point' in the international development field that drew together the concerns and thinking around poverty reduction, debt relief, World Bank and IMF lending to low-income countries, and aid effectiveness. In sum, the PRSP was an operational solution that solved several internal problems and provided an answer to external pressures, particularly for the IFIs but also within different bilateral organizations. The fact that an idea as potentially radical as the PRSP initiative was approved by the boards of the IMF and World Bank in September 1999 is due largely to the high level of ownership felt for the idea by various policy makers (including staff and management in the IFIs, bilateral donors and the NGO community). This in turn was due to its emergence in a variety of debates and places during the late 1990s.

How the Sphere Project came into being: a case study of policy making in the humanitarian aid sector and the relative influence of research

One of the most significant policy shifts in the international humanitarian aid sector in the last decade has been the move to strengthen the accountability of humanitarian agencies and to find ways of improving performance in humanitarian response. In 1996, the decision to launch the Sphere Project was one of the key policy initiatives associated with this shift. It resulted in the publication of a *Humanitarian Charter and Minimum Standards for Disaster Response* in 2000 (Sphere 2000). The case study in Chapter 4 (by Margie Buchanan-Smith) explores the process that led up to this policy initiative, and how buy-in and ownership were achieved (or, in some cases, not) during the first year of Sphere's existence.

Context
In the first half of the 1990s, the policy context within the international humanitarian aid sector was becoming increasingly conducive to an initiative such as Sphere. The days of unquestioning acceptance of the 'good work' of humanitarian agencies were over. As agencies entered more difficult conflict environments, they were subject to much more rigorous scrutiny and more sophisticated political analysis. There was a growing sense of unease among some agencies and individuals about the range of standards and performance to which different agencies operated.

Although these concerns created an atmosphere conducive to the Sphere Project, it was the scale and intensity of the humanitarian crisis in Rwanda in 1994 that determined the vigour, depth and direction of Sphere. The refugee crisis that unfolded and the unprecedented international humanitarian response, under the spotlight of the international media, publicly magnified the fault lines within the humanitarian aid system to an extraordinary degree. These were significant factors in creating the momentum for change, particularly among NGOs, and an increasing openness to countenance radical change. A few individuals (and agencies) capitalized upon this unprecedented window of opportunity in order to get their ideas accepted, eventually resulting in the Sphere initiative.

These ideas were given real impetus by the 'categoric, clear and well-documented'[6] report of Study 3 of the Joint Evaluation of

Emergency Assistance to Rwanda. Critical of the performance of some NGOs in the Rwanda crisis, it commended the embryonic NGO initiative to develop performance standards. (The Sphere Project developed out of two separate initiatives that pre-dated the Rwanda evaluation. In the USA, InterAction commenced a project to develop best practice for disaster work. Meanwhile in Europe, two individuals from Oxfam and the International Federation of Red Cross and Red Crescent Societies (IFRC) were developing a project to improve quality and accountability standards in humanitarian relief.) But Study 3 went further than any NGO in also recommending some form of self-managed regulation or accreditation of NGOs to monitor compliance. NGOs have consistently shied away from implementing this recommendation.

Study 3 of the Joint Evaluation had a real impact on policy makers. This well-resourced evaluation had high credibility; partly because of the composition of the team, who were seen to be objective, and combining research and operational experience. Study 3 was also seen to be a very thorough piece of work, more akin to a research project than a conventional consultancy. Its findings and recommendations were clearly presented, and were often targeted at particular groups of actors. Also, crucially, the structure for managing the evaluation proved critical to safeguarding the independence of the sometimes unpopular findings of the Study 3 team. The management group, comprising objective evaluators from a selection of donor agencies, was able to shield the evaluation team from undue pressure by the agencies and governments who were being evaluated, and who were represented on the evaluation steering committee.

Links
This case study supports the hypothesis that close links between researchers and policy makers greatly increase the likelihood of research influencing policy. Those links were, unusually, institutionalized by the structure put in place for the Rwanda Joint Evaluation. The evaluation was effectively commissioned by the respective evaluation departments of different donor agencies, represented on the evaluation management group. However this was done with the support and input of policy makers who were represented on the evaluation's steering committee. Thus, a critical and cooperative link was established at the outset between those who commissioned the 'research' and the policy makers at whom the findings were directed. Also, there was a clear synergy of interest between the evaluators and certain key policy makers; they were working to a similar agenda, to bring about change to improve NGO performance. The evaluation's endorsement of these early initiatives gave them real momentum. This inclusive experience of the Rwanda evaluation influenced the process put in place for Sphere. All the main NGO umbrella organizations, plus individual agencies, were given membership of the project committee. This highly inclusive process, designed to get maximum buy-in, was put in place in order to draft Sphere documents in its first year.

There were also certain key actors who played catalytic roles in Sphere's birth and in its infancy. Particularly noteworthy is the role of two 'policy entrepreneurs' – Peter Walker and Nick Stockton – who are most closely associated with the launch of Sphere. In Gladwell's (2000) terms they were 'connectors' (networkers) and 'salesmen' (persuasive, trusted and listened to). They were also 'innovators' and they spotted the policy window to take forward their ideas. Other individuals, such as Jim Bishop of InterAction and Susan Purdin, the first Sphere project manager, also played critical 'connector' roles.

Immediate but partial policy impact
In conclusion, this case study shows that the policy impact of Study 3 of the Rwanda evaluation, on finding ways of improving NGO performance, was more or less immediate in terms of the impetus it gave to the embryonic Sphere Project. However, the impact was also partial; the more challenging and radical recommendations around accreditation and regulation of NGOs were ducked.

Animal healthcare in Kenya: the road to community-based animal health service delivery

Chapter 5, by John Young, Julius Kajume and Jacob Wanyama, presents the results of a case study on livestock service reform in Kenya. Livestock services were among the first rural services targeted for privatization under structural adjustment programmes, particularly in sub-Saharan Africa. The veterinary profession has however been very slow to respond, and the increasing financial constraints effectively paralysed government services in the late 1980s and early 1990s. During this period, NGOs introduced a new model of community-based livestock services. Intermediate Technology Development Group (ITDG) was one of the early pioneers in the mid-1980s, and adopted an action research approach with a clear objective to use the results, if positive, to influence the policy environment to allow the approaches to be widely replicated. This case study explores the reasons why, despite the outstanding success of the new community-based decentralized animal healthcare (DAH) approaches, it took more than 15 years to convince policy makers to develop policies and legislation to allow this to happen – which still have not been formally adopted, despite the proliferation of community-based livestock services throughout the arid and semi-arid parts of Kenya.

Context
In 1986, ITDG arrived in Kenya with an explicit focus on developing and testing new approaches to livestock services. They quickly sought to influence the policy environment so that successful approaches could be implemented more widely. At the same time, Sessional Paper No. 1 of 1986 (Government of Kenya 1986), 'Economic Management for Renewed Growth', set the stage for structural adjustment and privatization of

public services, thus creating a favourable macro-policy context for the reform of livestock services. However, Dr Wamukoya's appointment as Director of Veterinary Services, and his emphasis on veterinary professionalism and ethics, reversed an emerging interest in policy reform that had been driven by contracting government budgets and emerging evidence of the value of the alternative decentralized animal health (DAH) model. The policy context for DAH approaches to livestock services dramatically improved when Dr Kimanzi, a vet with substantial practical experience of field services in arid and semi-arid land areas and a more open-minded attitude towards new approaches, took over as Director of Veterinary Services in 1994, and appointed Dr Kajume as Deputy Director.

From 1994 to 1997, there was a quiet proliferation of agencies training community animal-health workers (CAHWs). Eventually, the gradual spread of the approach led to the publication of a letter by the Kenya Veterinary Board (KVB) in 1998 threatening to punish livestock owners and veterinarians involved in DAH programmes in an attempt to stop what they regarded as a dangerous approach. The letter had the opposite effect. Far from stopping DAH programmes, it forced all stakeholders together into a policy network to try to find a solution to the problem. The crisis caused by the KVB letter was clearly a tipping point. Supporters in the government used the crisis to launch a multi-stakeholder study (known widely as the Hübl study), which significantly increased the weight of evidence in favour of the approach.

In 1999, a multi-stakeholder workshop (based on ITDG's vets' workshops) in Meru, central Kenya, provided a clear signal from policy makers that they were interested in finding a solution, which improved the political climate for change still further. The political climate could not have been better while Julius Kajume was acting Director of Veterinary Services in 1999, but deteriorated with the appointment of the more conservative Dr Chong in 2000. In 2001, increasing opposition to the new policies from the Kenya Veterinary Association (KVA) both undermined the policy coalition, reducing the link between researchers/practitioners and policy makers, and complicated and worsened the political climate.

Evidence
Although some of the external NGOs promoting the approach had been influenced by emerging ideas in the development discourse, formal research seems to have contributed relatively little to the policy process in Kenya, and research reports even less so (with the exception of the Hübl study). Evidence generated by operational CAHW schemes, communicated directly to visitors by livestock owners and the animal-health staff directly involved in them, seems to have been much more important. Early on, this evidence contributed to the rising popularity of DAH programmes with donors and field veterinarians, and in the mid-1990s, albeit second hand, to the alarm of the KVB resulting in the publication of their letter in the national press.

Links
ITDG organized the first vets' workshop in 1988, which brought together DAH practitioners from several projects around the country. This marked a significant increase in interactions between researchers/practitioners and policy makers. In 1992 the establishment of bilateral DAH projects added weight to the DAH approaches, and ITDG's international DAH workshop strengthened the emerging network of practitioners and links between policy makers and practitioners. The attendance of Dr Kajume, then Provincial Director of Veterinary Services for Eastern Province, at the 1993 vets' workshop marked a further improvement in linkages between researchers/practitioners and policy makers.

Could the process have been accelerated?
With the benefit of hindsight, distance and the results of this study, it is possible to suggest some changes in what was done that might have accelerated the process of adopting DAH approaches to livestock services in Kenya. These include:

- greater effort to understand the political context – the legal and policy framework, the key actors, their attitudes and influences, and other reform processes;
- greater effort, earlier on, to get government staff, especially those opposed to the idea, to visit working CAHW schemes and learn about them first-hand;
- an effort to generate interest among non-veterinary members of staff and parliamentarians;
- a clearer communication strategy to influence government vets and government policy;
- more effort to get to know the key actors – the director and deputy directors of veterinary services in Nairobi – and figure out how best to influence them;
- more effort to understand the policy process in Kenya, how new ideas become incorporated into policy, and how new legislation is enacted.

It is also evident that working with local communities to develop effective and sustainable examples of new approaches is essential to prove their effectiveness and acquire the legitimacy to advocate for change. That takes time, and the early pioneers of the approach in Kenya deserve recognition for the efforts they have made over the past 17 years.

Sustainable livelihoods: a case study of the evolution of DFID policy

Chapter 6, by William Solesbury, is a case study of the influence of research on a particular shift in policy for DFID. In the 1997 White Paper on international development, DFID made the 'sustainable livelihoods approach' (or SLA) a core principle of its strategy for pro-poor policy making. The concept of SLA had first appeared in research literature in the 1980s, and its inclusion in the White Paper marked its transfer to the policy domain.

Context
In a number of ways, the emergence of the SLA was well aligned with the political and institutional context. First, the SLA was in tune with wider shifts in approaches to development through the 1980s and 1990s; towards a focus on human well-being and sustainability rather than economic growth. Crystallized in the Brundtland Commission Report in 1987 and the first UNDP Human Development Report in 1990, NGOs and supportive researchers had negotiated this shift over the preceding decades. The new perspective was welcomed in the mid-1990s by DFID as it strove to redefine its role and mark the change of government in 1997 with a distinctive and timely approach to international development. The SLA succeeded in winning the attention of key policy makers in donor institutions in the mid-1990s, most notably in the Natural Resources Department of DFID in 1997. This attempt succeeded because of the collision of two factors: a broad international climate that favoured people-centred approaches, and a specific need to mark out a new phase of development practice in DFID.

Evidence
In the decade before the 1997 White Paper, researchers and practitioners (in dialogue with each other) had tested the concept of SLA both intellectually and empirically. Evidence with these qualities was particularly attractive to DFID, who were not persuaded by a single campaigning group but through their interactions with diverse sources and media. The numerous strands to SLA, and the fact that it was communicated many times by many agents, lent resilience to SLA as a core concept, which would not be undermined by a single piece of counter-evidence or failed argument. The very personal means by which SLA was transferred between colleagues, often through face-to-face discussions, also fostered resilience as the concept could be tailored to engage with the expertise and interests of specific individuals. However, of equal importance to the multifaceted nature of SLA was its clarity and ability to be recognized and referred to. Since Chambers and Conway (1992) coined the phrase in their seminal research paper *Sustainable Rural Livelihoods: Practical Concepts for the 21st Century*, 'sustainable livelihoods' has expressed a complex set of relationships and ideas with great economy. The Sustainable Livelihoods Support Office produced a collection of literature for both lay and political audiences that presented the SLA clearly, with a range of case studies and practitioner guides. These have provided a centre of gravity around which more diffuse and wide-ranging debates around SLA can revolve, and have ensured that – whilst being worked on from many angles – the concept remained coherent.

Links
A number of individuals worked as testers, developers, champions, communicators, interpreters and advocates of SLA to facilitate its adoption within DFID. More often than not, a person fulfilled more than one of these roles, and several people performed many of these roles. In the development of SLA, core researchers, policy makers and practitioners tended to know, or at least know of, each other. This was especially true within DFID, which fostered mutual respect, awareness and trust and eased the quality of ideas' exchanges and the path of SLA. The creation of the Sustainable Livelihoods Resource Group boosted the development of this community on an international level. Flows of ideas between individuals were reinforced by flows of individuals themselves, as critical agents moved jobs and took their expertise and perspectives from one organization to the next. The flow of individuals such as Conway between Imperial College, IIED, Ford Foundation, Sussex University and the Rockefeller Foundation, illustrate the non-linear trajectory of research, policy and practice in the development of SLA.

Refining the context/evidence/links framework
In the SLA case, the conventional view of research informing policy which in turn frames practice (research–policy–practice) could be better represented as a triangle where all components inform each other.

Moreover, there are two elements of the case of SLA that fall outside the integrated framework (context/evidence/links): time and chance. In terms of **time**, a decade passed between the conceptual formation of SLA and its adoption in the 1997 White Paper. This time was necessary, in part, for the conjunctions of context we have outlined, but also in a less perceptible way for ideas to be internalized and embedded. The context/evidence/links framework falls short of tracking this process. As for **chance**, a number of lucky encounters, overlapping diaries and external decisions set up the chronology of SLA. Arguably, the web of relationships that characterizes the community of policy makers, researchers and practitioners was sufficiently close and well-developed that had these incidents not taken place others would have emerged in their place, but this cannot of course be verified.

Thus, in order to counter the potential for determinism from the context/evidence/links framework we must recognize a separation between necessary and sufficient conditions. Without necessary conditions there would be no chance of a successful impact of research on policy, but these conditions do not guarantee change on their own. Sufficient conditions lead to actual impact. In the case of SLA, these sufficient conditions were time and chance encounters. In other instances of research influencing policy, the conditions may be very different.

Synthesis and implications

In the final chapter, we will draw conclusions from the research exercise in order to reflect on the question posed at the outset: Why are some of the ideas that circulate in the research–policy networks picked up and acted on, while others are ignored and disappear? Drawing on a synthesis of crosscutting issues from the case studies, central factors are highlighted and discussed. The findings on the whole confirm the three hypotheses presented above, and elaborate on these. Comparison across the four cases suggests that the political institutional context is the most important arena affecting the uptake of research into policy. Political contestation, institutional pressures and vested interests matter greatly. Policy influence tends to be enhanced where the research is relevant, credible, and provides useful solutions to policy problems. Continuous interaction, where an idea is passed back and forth within networks and between researchers and policy makers, leads to greater chances of successful uptake into policy.

The final chapter also discusses various issues that emerged through the research process; these emerging issues provide an opportunity to reflect on the possibilities and limitations of the integrated framework and on the nature of research–policy linkages in general. When comparing the four case studies it becomes obvious that the relationship between the three spheres in the framework varies according to the case. For example, the PRSP case presents a great overlap between the links sphere and a political context where similar sets of problems and ideas were emerging from various actors simultaneously. In contrast, in the case of livestock services in Kenya the links between livestock owners and veterinarians on the ground were far removed from the political context of policy processes. The analytical framework, then, should be adapted to each particular context, and could therefore be viewed as a trio of floating spheres of variable size and degree of overlap.

In all four case studies, a set of factors that could be labelled 'external influences' – including, for example, donor actions and international lending instruments – proved to have a decisive influence on research–policy linkages. The role of such external influences is so vital – especially in relation to research–policy linkages in Southern and international development processes – that in the final chapter this set of factors is regarded as a fourth dimension of the framework. Given the importance of external influences on Southern policy contexts, a pertinent question becomes how much impact Southern research and civil society institutions have on international policy processes. Northern-based institutions undertake much of the research on development issues. These institutions also have more ready access than their Southern counterparts to knowledge about international development policy processes and access to international research–policy networks.

Finally, the last chapter draws out implications that this comparative exercise may have for researchers, practitioners, policy makers and others who wish to be aware of and contribute to improved research–policy linkages through their own work. We hope that this initial effort will spur further research on how research–policy linkages can be improved. Even more important perhaps, we hope that the findings will resonate with researchers, policy makers and practitioners in international development and that the ideas will be tested and, where useful, promoted further. We believe the findings are particularly robust in making suggestions for ways that researchers can enhance the policy impact of their work.

However, as is evident throughout this discussion, there are several analytical concepts that both clarify the nature of research–policy linkages and provide stepping-stones for drawing out the implications of this. Before moving on to the case study chapters, therefore, the next chapter presents a detailed discussion of the analytical concepts used, and the way they complement each other within the integrated context/evidence/links framework .

Chapter Two
Context, evidence, links: a conceptual framework for understanding research–policy processes

EMMA CREWE, INGIE HOVLAND and JOHN YOUNG

Introduction

Research could have a greater impact on international development policy than it has had to date. The first step is to understand more about the context within which researchers, policy makers and stakeholders are working, and the relationships between them. In this chapter we hope to take the investigation into research–policy linkages further by explaining the problem, offering an historical, contextual and comparative approach for making sense of the dynamic between research and policy, and making suggestions about how further research could test our hypotheses. The following section of this chapter examines the perceived problem – 'power without knowledge' – while the third section provides a detailed presentation of each of the three dimensions of the integrated framework: context, evidence, and links.

The problem: power without knowledge

Although much research has been driven by the aim to influence policy in the field of international development, the underemployment of cutting-edge knowledge by decision makers puzzles academic and applied researchers alike. It is evident that research is often ignored; according to one study of 70 000 research projects undertaken on education, only 70 had a significant influence on education policy and practice (Molas et al. 2000). Initially, one might posit a range of causes for this state of affairs (see Box 2.1, page 27).

While some claim that research is being underemployed, others argue that it has neglected the concerns of the poor and been top down (Chambers 1983), or that the research that does make an impact is misleading. Research that benefits the poor is so under-funded or undervalued that 90 per cent of the world's disease burden is the subject of less than 10 per cent of all international research on health (DFID 2000e). To promote evidence-based policy making that responds to the demands of poor or marginalized people, we need a deeper understanding of the relationship between research and particular policy areas.

The nature of the relationship between research and policy making has become a well-established topic of inquiry for social scientists. The linear model, pioneered by Lasswell in the 1950s and portraying the policy making process as a series of stages during which policy makers rationally consider information, has been under attack for 30 years.

Caplan, for example, pointed out that the different worldviews of researchers and policy makers gave shape to a cultural gap between the two communities, thus preventing adequate use of research (Neilson 2001). Clay and Schaffer's (1984) claim that 'policy is a chaos of purposes and accidents' is more realistic, but probably should not be taken literally; the decision-making process may not be simple, but it is not completely chaotic either. We will argue in this chapter, along the lines of Keeley and Scoones' (1999: 32–33) suggestions, that it is structured by a complex interplay between political interests, competing discourses and the agency of multiple actors.

This interplay is hard to describe. According to Stone (n.d.), taking account of different policy environments, institutional structures and political arrangements renders the construction of a single explanatory model impossible. Processes of globalization – including fewer trade restrictions, the rise of transnational corporations and social movements, and the information communication technology (ICT) revolution – as well as shifts in institutional power away from the state in some countries, appear to have accelerated the rate of change and compound the problem of analysis. Furthermore, making generalizations about how knowledge is disseminated and used involves a struggle with the diversity between policy areas. As examples, advocacy coalitions have worked in some contexts, epistemic communities in others; science dominates some areas, the law is more important to others.

Consensus on how policy makers use research, or indeed whether they use it at all, eludes researchers in part because they define 'research', 'use' and 'policy' differently. Research and policy defy neat separation. Researchers, policy makers and practitioners are not discrete groups; one individual can easily be in all three categories in different contexts or over a period of time. However, research and policy can be conceptually distinguished by their goals and methods.

- **Research** aims to investigate, learn and produce knowledge by gathering information, contemplation, trial, and/or synthesis. In an international development context, this may involve action research or academic study ranging, as examples, from a pilot project to a laboratory experiment, a consultation exercise, a quantitative survey, a literature review, participant observation or a participatory evaluation. Beneficiaries, development practitioners or academics from scientific and social science disciplines might lead research.

- **Policy** aims for continuity or change of a practice, including plans and their evolution when put into practice (that is, the 'how' as well as the 'what' of decisions; Shankland 2000). 'Public' policy is usually led by policy makers and practitioners within different types of institutions and organizations, and is what we are concerned with in this volume, rather than private policies negotiated at the level of communities or households.

> **Box 2.1** *Why is research ignored?*
>
> ▶ Inadequate supply of, and access to, relevant information
> ▶ Researchers' poor comprehension of policy process and unrealistic recommendations
> ▶ Ineffective communication of research
> ▶ Ignorance or anti-intellectualism of politicians or bureaucrats
> ▶ Inadequate capacity among policy makers
> ▶ Politicization of research, using it selectively to legitimise political decisions
> ▶ Gaps in understanding between researchers, policy makers and public
> ▶ Time-lag between dissemination of research and impact on policy
> ▶ Research is deemed unimportant, censored or controlled
> ▶ Some 'ways of knowing' are seen as more valid than others
>
> *Source:* Stone (n.d.)

These broad categorizations of research and policy – including action research and the implementation of policy, both of which are often left out – achieve some clarity but also broaden the context of both domains. More processes, organizations and actors are drawn into the arena, that is, the interface between research and policy, than might be with a narrower definition. On the other hand, we are posing a relatively focused question about the relationship between the two: how can policy makers and researchers make better use of research to contribute to more evidence-based policies that reduce poverty, alleviate suffering and save lives? We are not asking, therefore, what impact research has on policy in an undifferentiated sense. Rather, taking particular policy shifts within particular sectors, we suggest that understanding the differences between them, and accounting for the role played by research in particular cases, might extend our analysis of how research influences policy. This comparative approach could lead to more specific findings about how particular policy processes and sectors work.

An integrated approach

What are the limits of existing models of policy making? While the linear model, whereby knowledge feeds into a logical sequence of decision-making phases, has few defenders anymore, other rational models continue to hold sway. Incrementalism – derived from Lindblom's idea that policy makers muddle through making little reforms rather than sudden, dramatic changes – is still based on a rational assessment of self-interest (Neilson 2001). The interactive model proposed by

Grindle and Thomas (1991) takes better account of the political context by proposing that decision makers are responding to pressure exerted by interested parties and economic conditions, but still relies on the idea that individual actors calculate losses and gains. Such an approach cannot take account of the relative consistency of behaviour between people with competing interests within a particular culture. Keeley and Scoones (1999) offer one way to move beyond polarized debates about rational agency by synthesizing different ways of looking at policy change, including:

- interactions between various different groups with differing political interests;
- actor-oriented approaches, such as policy communities and networks, interfaces, actor networks, epistemic communities, entrepreneurs/saboteurs;
- discourse, which is an ensemble of ideas communicated through practices via coalitions, narratives or rhetoric.

They fuse all three, taking account of political interests, formations of actors, and ideas, by arguing that 'structure and agency continuously and recursively interact' (Keeley and Scoones 1999: 28). Still more experience and ideas might, however, be usefully incorporated into such an approach. The general assumption in Keeley and Scoones that policy is determined by élites underemphasizes: (a) the role played by wider civil society, through citizen action or grassroots groups, as examples, and (b) resistance, adaption and development of policy making when put into practice. The political models of policy making – which Keeley and Scoones rely on quite heavily – have emerged from a focus on policy makers in Europe and the USA, with the consequence that the differences between and within other regions are obscured.

We decided to make use of a framework consisting of three dimensions to investigate research and policy, namely what we have called 'context', 'evidence' and 'links' between actors. Kitson et al. (1998)[7] have also suggested a three-dimensional approach; they argue that research utilization should be looked at on the assumption that $SI = f(E,C,F)$ where successful implement (SI) is a function (f) of the relation between E (evidence), C (context) and F (facilitation). This is useful, although each category is narrower than the dimensions proposed in our paper and, as defined by Kitson et al., more appropriate to the UK setting.

Before we outline our three-dimensional approach it might be worth mentioning how it could be used. It is clear that measuring the impact of specific research findings on policy, as if linear causality between the two prevails, would be extremely difficult. As Weiss (1977) has pointed out, research is not usually directly relevant to specific policy decisions. It may achieve influence in other important ways, namely by altering the language and perceptions of policy makers and their advisers, but such change occurs less decisively and over time, as a process of

Figure 2.1 Adaptations of the 'context, evidence, links' framework

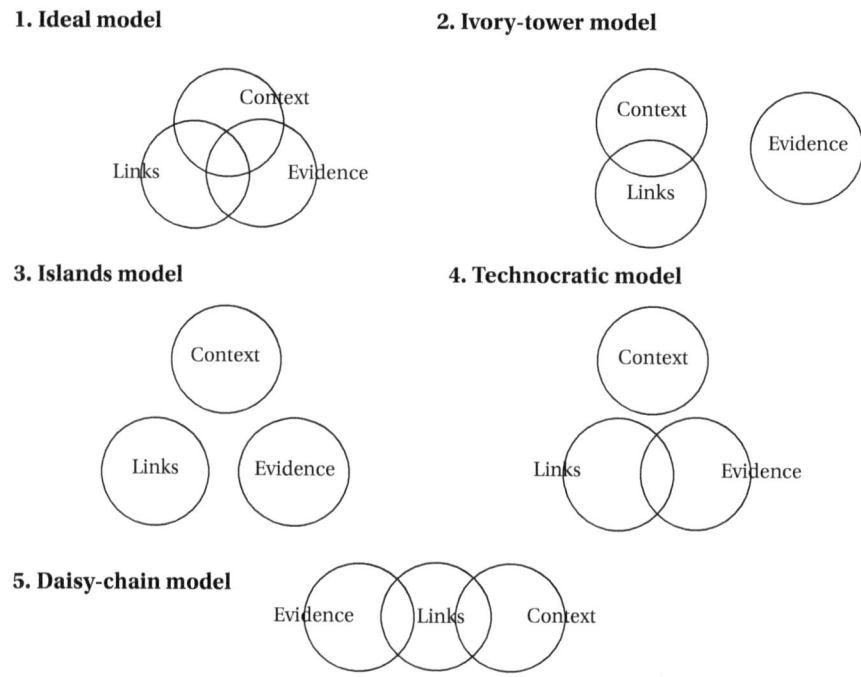

what she calls 'enlightenment'. This works by the circulation and 'percolation' of ideas and concepts, as opposed to timely, hard facts and robust theories to decisively guide policy interventions. Research knowledge 'creeps' into policy deliberations, and policy accretes rather than follows brisk decisions. Therefore, taking a piece of research and assessing its impact on policy would be unlikely to capture the whole picture. The opposite approach seems more fruitful; namely to identify a policy change and then trace the contributing factors towards it. We suggest that such a tracer study might begin to elucidate how structures, actors and knowledge operate within different international development policy areas – where research is only one among a range of potentially influential factors, directly and indirectly.

A synthesis of ideas from existing literature reviews, and the material in ODI's annotated bibliography on the subject (De Vibe et al. 2002), has led us to conclude that the most important dimensions when looking at the possible impact of research on policy in this fashion are threefold.

- **Context: politics and institutions** To analyse how the context shapes research and policy making it is necessary to take account of the political and institutional structures. The most important variables are likely to be: the interests of key policy makers and researchers, structures and ideologies they are limitedby, whether the policy changes are reformist or radical,

how organizational pressures operate, and to what extent policies are adapted, developed or distorted when put into practice.
- **Evidence: credibility and communication** Investigating the impact of research findings raises questions about the credibility of the research that makes an impact (how it is gathered, who gathers it, and whether it is perceived as accurate), and how it is communicated to policy makers.
- **Links: influence and legitimacy** While we often find significant information flows within the policy and research communities, these two communities are typically poorly connected. When assessing how research and researchers influence policy, it is important to identity the key actors and the informal networks they are part of; as well as assess issues such as the formal mechanisms for linking communities and relations with the media.

The factors within these three clusters stand in a dynamic relationship to each other, and will gain or lose importance in the interplay with other factors (see Figure 2.1, page 29). Strictly speaking, therefore, each of the three dimensions should be understood in relation to the other two and cannot be seen in isolation. However, to avoid complication, we will discuss each of the three dimensions in turn below – always bearing in mind, however, that the point of the exercise is to be able to bring the three dimensions together in an integrated framework.

Context: politics and institutions

Much of the literature on knowledge utilization and policy making is concerned with the UK or USA. When researchers work within their own countries, the context can be taken for granted to some extent. However, when considering the arena of international development policy, the institutional, cultural and structural dimensions become fantastically diverse. In any given context, different macro-level institutions (state, market, civil society) and meso-level institutions (for example, government departments, business corporations, NGOs) operate in different modes (for example, coordination, competition, cooperation) (Robinson et al. 1999) in a variety of different combinations. Even within one institution, it is not always easy to pinpoint one set of specific policies. For example, DFID's aims are expressed rhetorically in the White Papers, and where money is spent reveals a great deal, but like any organization different parts of it follow different, and sometimes conflicting, principles. Therefore, rather than trying to describe the political and institutional context of international development, we will merely highlight some of the political and institutional structures that shape (and are in turn shaped by) policy making and research.

Institutional settings
How the macro-political and macro-economic systems impinge on particular policy structures and processes is likely to be a part of any

policy analysis. It is a challenge to keep up with the pace of change in this field. An assumption that the state is the most significant policy-making institution still holds sway in much development discourse. Ferguson's (1990) argument that the 'development apparatus' in Lesotho is a machine for reinforcing and expanding the exercise of bureaucratic state power is still often quoted. At the same time, it is becoming clear that the power of the state is receding in some countries while civil and corporate agencies are gaining ground. Understanding the relative power of different institutions, and how it shifts over time and in different contexts, is important when: (a) piecing together how political context shapes policy making, and (b) identifying the key policy makers. It might also be worth considering what impact advocates or researchers can have on the policy context themselves. For example, leapfrogging the nation-state, and directly approaching international institutions when trying to influence policy makers may have an immediate impact on policy while at the same time reducing the future impact of democratic policy processes (Rai 2002).

Having assumed the importance of policy makers, we must also, ironically, point out that 'policy makers' are elusive as a category. For a start, all but those in the most senior positions tend to deny they are 'policy makers'; more often than not staff are trying to influence someone higher up. Also, policy makers in one context, Nigerian government ministers for example, become advocates in another, trying to influence the World Bank or IMF. Donors at international and national levels are making important policies, but they also try to influence each other. And influential policy makers are not only found in donor agencies, but in financial institutions, NGOs, businesses and so on.

Another elusive category is the group that policy is made for, namely 'the public'. International public bodies, civil society organizations (CSOs) and multinational corporations all have complicated and dynamic relationships with the public, with public opinion, and with the public good. Needless to say, the public is such a diverse group that any given policy will never be received in only one way; this observation reinforces the difficulty – and the value – of trying to understand the different institutional settings of the political context.

The importance of wider institutional settings for research–policy linkages has probably been discussed most thoroughly by the National Systems of Innovation (NSI) school. The NSI perspective argues that the research process and policy change must be seen as part of a wider context (Surr et al. 2002). Systems of innovation – also referred to as 'knowledge systems' – are embedded in institutional, political and economic environments. The effectiveness and impact of research will be a function of a large number of other elements of the system being in place. In particular, the nature of governance and other elements of the enabling environment are crucial to the returns that may be expected from investments in research. There are many countries where the wider context is adverse, and where, in consequence, investment in research will not have its full potential impact on pro-poor policy change.

Room for manoeuvre
Policy makers and researchers are not only limited by political, social and economic structures, but also the assumptions that underlie them, even if they push these limits on occasions (Clay and Schaffer 1984). They may take actions and use ideas that attract least criticism or the ones that they are most accustomed to and that help to make sense of their reality. These structural constraints influence the context of policy making on all levels – as examples:

- international financial institutions make assumptions about the likely impact of debt cancellation on future lending practices;
- at the national level, the liberalization of para-vet services in Kenya has been obstructed by government policies driven by the economic interests of vets;
- local politics jeopardized the distribution of food aid in Goma (then in eastern Zaïre) when it was appropriated by some of the perpetrators of genocide in order to attempt further attacks on Rwanda.

How power structures and powerful interests impinge on particular policy areas will be a matter of debate if not controversy. Rarely, however, will one policy or interest be so dominating that everyone else has to conform completely; usually agents at different levels will have – or will create for themselves – some 'room for manoeuvre' in relation to the political context.

The room for manoeuvre of policy makers, researchers or 'the public' is an uneven experience. To take an obvious example; in many contexts, the room for manoeuvre is gendered. For example, social science research undertaken by Latin American intelligentsia has largely been occupied with public space and modern production, both traditionally associated with masculinity – which has led to greater room for manoeuvre for male researchers (Franco 1994). The dominance of male policy makers in many policy sectors may partly account for the tokenistic aspect that may sometimes be attached to gender policy, which again affects the room for manoeuvre of different groups of women and men.

The degree of room for manoeuvre experienced by policy makers and researchers is often linked to institutional pressures (see Box 2.2, pages 33–34). The way they manage to negotiate these pressures will influence research–policy linkages.

Reform or revolution?
It might be revealing to look at policy decisions in terms of whether they are routine, incremental, fundamental or emergent, as Lindquist (2001: 19–21) suggests:

- **Routine** decision making adapts existing programmes to new situations and entails the least scrutiny and debate;

Box 2.2 *Pressures facing policy makers and researchers*

▶   The urge to simplify' is overwhelming for policy makers, as Sutton (1999: 29) points out. Shortage of time and money frequently makes it impossible for policy makers to take account of diversity, nuance and contextualization – all prized by most academic researchers. It is simpler and quicker for policy makers to devise 'blueprints' with standardized ingredients for all contexts – based on unequivocal assumptions about what causes poverty, for example – rather than allowing for decentralized or contextual decision making and more nuanced or equivocal assumptions. In recognition of this bureaucratic pressure, lobbyists also simplify complex issues and present them as 'development narratives' (Roe 1991). These narratives, such as the 'tragedy of the commons' or the 'woodfuel crisis', are taken up by policy makers and persist in their simple form even when evidence to the contrary calls into question their universal validity. For this reason, research that questions received wisdom may have to be presented as counter-narratives if it is to have any impact (for the dangers inherent in this, see the 'Quality of research' section below; Neilson 2001: 32).

▶   'Giantism' is a pressure that affects almost all policy makers due to organizational rules about how power bases are established. In many agencies, the bigger the budget of a project, the greater the status conferred upon its manager. (Assumptions about economies of scale mean that big projects may be attractive for other reasons as well.) Individual policy makers will be partly drawn towards large-scale projects to improve their own power position within the organization. Any researchers that stress the need for smaller projects that respond to local problems and solutions may meet the barrier of giantism.

▶   Long-term project planning is considered essential for all agencies seeking funding. Donors especially pressurize development agencies for explicit, long-range strategic plans. In reality, development practitioners know that formal strategy is not a 'magic bullet' because they work in volatile environments where conflicts between people mean that trade-offs between processes and individuals are necessary (Hailey and Smillie 2001). In this situation, the ways plans and policies are presented (for example, in project proposals) become more like fictions devised to deal with bureaucratic pressures than real strategies for dealing with reality (Mosse 2003).

> **Box 2.2** *Pressures facing policy makers and researchers*
> (continued)
>
> ▶ Fierce competition for funding discourages both NGO and academic researchers from collaborative research.
> Researchers from different academic disciplines may find it difficult to obtain funding for interdisciplinary projects. In some cases, these factors can hinder the production and publication of applied research. In addition, scholars can be fearful of making tangible recommendations – and even when they do so, these recommendations may not be disseminated, as it is often the communication aims of projects that first suffer cuts during funding shortages.

- **Incremental** decisions are made about selective issues as they emerge, but there is no comprehensive attempt to deal with all constituent issues associated with the policy domain;
- **Fundamental** decisions occur when relatively infrequent opportunities to rethink the policy approach arise, usually as the result of a crisis, a change of governments, or as a knock-on effect from fundamental decisions in neighbouring policy areas;
- **Emergent**: at the other end of the spectrum, there are decisions that go beyond a questioning of underlying assumptions to a broad new vision.

Each of these types of process has different implications for the uptake of research. Most policy decisions are routine (merely modifying previous decisions) and there is little scope for research uptake. Incremental decision making deals with selective issues as they arise, may make use of whatever analysis is close at hand, but is unlikely to involve a comprehensive review of all the associated issues. When fundamental or emergent decisions are being made, there may be more scope for comprehensive reviews of research.

We can hypothesize quite easily that staff within bureaucracies resist fundamental and emergent challenges, with their expensive and time-consuming debates and potential conflict, more vigorously than proposals for incremental change. Many researchers in academia and NGOs, on the other hand, see themselves as championing radical causes and challenging the status quo. Pross (1986) distinguishes between 'subgovernment' and the 'attentive public' within policy communities, whereby the former usually has a vested interest in the existing order while the latter tends towards criticism, creative ideas and novel approaches. Change can be inconvenient to bureaucracies and so challenges may be treated dismissively (Pross 1986). As Chomsky points out, policies can consist within what he calls a 'framework of possible thought' with various tacit doctrines that render dissent, or even debate, unthinkable. Dissident views on US foreign policy can be dismissed as anti-peace or anti-security, for example (Chomsky 1987).

If this is the case, why do fundamental paradigm shifts happen at all? The philosophy of science sheds light on this. Kuhn has portrayed the history of science as a series of revolutions. A scientific paradigm bumbles along quite happily making sense of the world, until the puzzles it cannot solve become so numerous that it causes a crisis. A new worldview, or paradigm (most recently Einsteinian), does a better job of explaining the puzzles and so replaces (or occasionally runs alongside) the old one (Kuhn 1970). These shifts in worldview – where an explanatory model meets a crisis and is replaced by an alternative – may take place at different levels of development discourse as well.

Intellectual revolutions are not the only kind of potential radicalism; pressure from below has achieved fundamental shifts in policy. The campaigns of citizen action that have met with relative success, dealing with issues like debt and landmines, have been based on a high degree of consensus within coalitions (Edwards 2001: 6). Gaventa (2001) has gone as far as suggesting that civil-society actors have challenged power relationships at all levels, influenced the World Bank, the IMF, the WTO and even multinational corporations, and affected a range of treaties and conventions. Conflicting interests have held back other areas of campaigning such as trade, environmental protection and labour rights.

Policy in practice

The complexity of the context of policy making intensifies even further when the implementation of policy is seen as part of the process. In fact, to move beyond a linear view of project planning, it might be more useful to consider the statements of intent as well as the practices entailed in policymaking. Policy statements can be adapted to local conditions, modified to take account of new circumstances, or even ignored due to conflicting interests between planners and practitioners (or different agencies) when put into practice.

Lipsky (1980) argues that 'street-level bureaucrats' who implement policy are also largely responsible for shaping it. These bureaucrats are often constrained by limited resources, continuous negotiation to make sure they are meeting targets, and relationships with clients. They may be in courtrooms or schools or civil society organizations. They exercise considerable flexibility during implementation, often producing outcomes that may be quite different from those expected (Sutton 1999: 8), but this may work in different ways according to the context. Conflicting priorities between partner agencies, international NGOs and their local partners often result in gaps between what is agreed as policy, what happens in practice, and what is reported by fellow members of staff during reviews. The result can be that the funding agencies have little idea how much the supposedly agreed policy has been ignored or modified by local partner agencies. Local conditions and power relations within communities often shape the channelling of policy; sometimes it is more likely to be this, rather than technical problems or shortage of information, that accounts for the failure of policy implementation. This has been the case, for example, in much of the funding allocated for women groups in Africa, which has been controlled by women élites, by those with good political connections, or by groups of men (Crewe and Harrison 1998: 166–71).

What influences policy practices will also be influenced by different historical and cultural contexts. Keeley and Scoones (2000), in their study of environmental policy making in Ethiopia, show how the different administrative and political cultures in the Tigrayan region versus the Southern Nations, Nationalities and Peoples Region (SNNPR) account for quite different interpretation of discourses about participatory approaches. There was more political space for debate and bottom-up approaches in Tigray, partly because of the close connections between regional actors and the ruling party. In contrast, since the late 1800s SNNPR has been ruled in a more autocratic way by the centre, and has little experience of locally based forms of governance. This difference in political administration was enough to lead to different ways of implementing the same environmental policy.

Evidence: credibility and communication

We define research as broadly as possible, to include activities ranging from laboratory experiments to a monitoring consultation with stakeholders. Within this broad definition, the type of research that is seen as most credible by different actors varies widely. In general, the sources of information – and who conveys it – are probably as important as the content of the research; people accept information more readily from those they trust. Farmers will pay closer attention to each other's views than they will to experts (National Center for the Dissemination of Disability Research 1996); academics tend to take those in their own discipline more seriously than those outside it. Those NGOs who have established their own credibility – through chains of legitimacy (see 'Links: influence and legitimacy' below), a record of excellence in research, and long grassroots experience – will usually be able to use research to influence policy makers more effectively than those with a poor reputation.

Quality of research
Research often involves trade-offs between stakeholder interests and project objectives. Since time is at a premium, thoroughness may have to be compromised when ensuring that enough alternative voices are given a chance to speak. Pro-poor research implies adequate consultation with poorer people and this may have to take priority over doing an exhaustive literature review. Time and resource pressures again play a role. Too frequently, Harper (2001) reminds us, NGO advocates have leaped from the local to global, armed only with anecdotes rather than rigorous and substantiated analysis. It is easy for policy makers to ignore researchers if they get their figures wrong. Poor quality research – hurriedly or inadequately collected or analysed – also means that the foundations of the message will be flawed.

> **Box 2.3** *The 'woodfuel crisis': simple research messages used to rationalize flawed policies*
>
> ▶ **Policy change** Multilateral/bilateral donors invest in improved stove programmes to save trees during the 1980s, and then cut funding during the early 1990s when they decided that the link was false.
>
> ▶ **Political context** The rise in the price of oil, and emerging environmental movement, increased concern in Europe and America about deforestation and global pollution from the 1970s onwards. This was a marked contrast to the low commitment to gender and household (rather than to what was regarded as national or global) interests in most donor organizations.
>
> ▶ **Narratives used** In the 1980s energy analysts made simple deductions, based on observations of fuel use and deforestation, that fuel-efficient stoves could save trees. To justify the decision to cut funding, donors referred to: (a) observations that rural dwellers did not cut trees for fuelwood consumption, publicized in a short and simple book written by a British journalist; (b) some selective and anecdotal evidence that most stove programmes had a poor record; (c) time-use studies showing that when women saved time, it was not spent earning income. Impact studies of a very small number of stove programmes that showed huge potential health and quality of life benefits at the household level, as well as studies by local researchers about links between deforestation and biomass use in urban areas, were ignored.

But it is not only inaccurate information or analysis that can be misleading; a lack of local involvement in drawing conclusions from research can also result in worrying impacts. An oft-quoted example is the bid to ban child labour; children who were withdrawn from working in some industries in Asia instead turned to more abusive forms of work like street trading and prostitution. Another frequently quoted example is the 'woodfuel crisis' and the simplified and misleading 'narratives' (Roe 1991) that were used to justify policy shifts in this case. These stories were perceived as credible, despite their lack of serious research, largely because they seemed to fit with the political context and could quote spurious evidence (see Box 2.3 above).

To counter the use of misleading narratives as the basis of policy, Fine et al. (2000) advise researchers aiming to influence policy to:

> **Box 2.4** *Using information to influence policy in Indonesia*
>
> ▶ Decentralized Livestock Services in the Eastern Regions of Indonesia Project (DELIVERI) aimed to improve livestock services to poor Indonesian farmers by reforming the Government of Indonesia's Directorate General of Livestock Services (DGLS) and its provincial and district organs. It has piloted new approaches to service delivery in four districts of Indonesia and used the results to influence policy and regulatory changes. The project identified the critical importance of clear information reaching the right people at the right time. During efforts to improve flows of information they found that when people had faith that the research they produced would be well received, and that somebody would respond to it, they would gather good quality information and articulate it well. When people felt their voices would be ignored, or they were afraid to speak, the information was often poorly considered, or chosen so as to reduce offence.
>
> *Source*: See www.deliveri.org

- beware of 'great stories', such as the unusual, the exotic, the bizarre or the violent, and the search for information that merely confirms their own understandings;
- draw upon a range of methods, sources of information and theoretical perspectives in order to triangulate the findings: different research methods will reveal different versions of the story that the researcher is telling;
- be accountable: researchers should inform the research group of how the findings will be used, invite them to critically review them, strive to stay accountable to them, and further their cause as far as possible through channels that they have privileged access to;
- consider how the research might potentially be understood or misunderstood by policy makers from different political camps.

It is extremely likely that getting the message right requires considerable time and investment of resources. Harper advises North-based NGOs:

NGOs will have to increase their own involvement in research, build research capacity among their partners in the South, and develop more collaborative relationships with academics. In a world of highly contested and contestable evidence, NGOs must ensure that their messages carry weight and authority. (Harper 2001: 256)

In this respect, issues of expectations and trust become important, and may have a great impact on information produced (see Box 2:4 above).

Who are seen as experts?
The type of research that influences policy making will depend on the policy area and the geopolitical level. Scientific arguments are important in environmental policy making, lobbying has contributed to the campaign for debt cancellation (Shankland 2000), while economic analysis is required if working on energy matters. In Britain, independent inquiries will usually be made up of distinguished practitioners and a token academic, in the USA a reputable professor will often be charged with sorting out a policy problem, while researchers in Germany are often institutionalized into advisory roles and in China researchers rely on finding *guanxi* (social connections) when trying to influence policy makers (Stone 2001: 23).

Although there are differences between locations and disciplines, certain patterns about the perception of expertise appear to prevail. The knowledge that makes the greatest impact on international development policies tends to be produced by centralized North-based institutions and tends to be integrated in transnational knowledge processes. The marginalization of indigenous knowledge is acknowledged (Hobart 1993; Warren et al. 1995), and inclusion of different types of knowledge in international development policy processes remains difficult. Language barriers play a role, both literally and figuratively. Development policy processes create their own language, rules and methods, which in some cases may contribute to power imbalances between those who are fluent in this language and those who are not. There are, however, examples where these barriers have been overcome (see Box 2.5, page 40).

Communicating research findings
Policy makers are not blank slates on which it is possible to write new knowledge merely by making it available, regardless of how good the quality of the research in question might be. In order to understand research–policy linkages, we need to understand how information flows; how it is received, digested and acted upon in different contexts.

The first formal model within information theory was Shannon's mathematical model of communication, developed in the 1940s, which laid out a linear schema of production, transmission, channel, receiver and destination (Mattelart and Mattelart 1998). According to this model, information is 'sent' by one person and subsequently 'received' and 'processed' by another. In this framework, communication is not seen as a problem; once the information has been sent out it will automatically be processed at the other end. Although widely discredited in academic literature today, the basic schema of the linear model (sender–message–channel–recipient) still provides the implicit underpinning of many communication initiatives.

The interactive model of communication emerges out of the criticism of the linear model. While the linear model assumes that the message is passed unscathed from the sender, via the channel, to the recipient, the interactive model argues that in practice the message will

> **Box 2.5** *Grassroots research has a global impact on policy making*
>
> ▶ After a survey undertaken with pavement dwellers in Mumbai, India, women formed their own network of savings collectives and joined a national federation of grassroots organizations. Rather than merely submitting alternative policies to the state, they set new 'precedents' – to demonstrate how practice could be changed – and organized mass demonstrations of support. The women designed their own low-cost housing and set up an exhibition that led to the state government of Maharashtra including resettling of pavement dwellers in their new strategy. Lessons learned about their defence of housing rights and community-based savings schemes have even been shared through regional and international networks in Asia and Africa. The Shack/Slum Dwellers International has enabled local savings groups in both Zimbabwe and Cambodia to secure land and other resources from their local governments. The focus on local processes of change, accompanied by international support from other communities as well as international agencies, accounts for their success (Patel et al. 2001).

never remain exactly the same. First, the context of the message will to a large degree determine how it is interpreted. People in different cultural contexts and political climates will view the message through different lenses, and will extrapolate different meanings from it. Second, the message itself is accompanied by a number of 'silent messages' – for example, the implicit understandings of linguistic codes, time, ways of relating, ways of expressing agreement or disagreement, and ways of interpreting understatement or phrases that are left out (Watzlawick 1978). In addition, the recipients receive a message that has several added dimensions and gaps in it, and they will (consciously or subconsciously) interpret these and fill in the gaps themselves. In this way, the original meaning of the message can quickly be altered.

Based on these insights, the interactive model of communication would suggest that, if communication is to be successful, it is not enough to 'send off' a message and assume that the recipient will automatically understand it. Rather, communication is a more demanding process, where the sender needs to communicate the message, then find ways of checking with the recipient how the message has been interpreted and, based on this feedback, re-communicate the message. According to this model, such continuous interaction leads to greater chances of successful communication than the linear approach.

Stephens (cited by Berkout and Scoones 1999) identifies two interactive communication processes: 'snowballs' (the accumulation of research impacts within policy élites) and 'whispers' (the reinterpretation of research findings in broader constituencies). Others have described the process in terms of the limestone model (information trickles like water through porous rock), the gadfly model (information gets through because persistent communication is prioritized as much as research itself), and the insider model (researchers exploit links with policy makers; Saywell and Cotton 1999).

There is no shortage of ideas about other ways to help information make a mark or achieve what Gladwell (2000) calls the 'stickiness factor'. He points to psychological research that shows that most people can remember up to seven-digit numbers but no more, or that presenters make a bigger impression if they outline no more than three points. Others argue that the element of surprise can usefully attract people's attention, but not if the contents of the message are impossible for them to relate to their existing knowledge in any way. People relate more easily to stories than to abstract discussions, and they identify more readily with a person in another part of the world if they are given a name and a picture. Stories are also easier to remember and reproduce. Pictures can be even more effective. Those with little experience of, or alternative sources of information on a subject themselves, will be struck by visual images (Philo 1996); 'seeing is believing'.

The question 'What makes an idea stick?' is related to the central question in the literature related to marketing: 'What makes people buy products?' One of the answers given is that the buyer sees the product as the solution to a problem (Lambin 1996). Frequently, therefore, advertisements set out to convince potential consumers that there is a problem. The same dynamic, although in a modified form, applies to communication aimed at policy processes. Policy makers will be more likely to take note of and remember pieces of evidence if they are convinced that the evidence is actually addressing a specific problem. If, on the other hand, they are not aware of the problem, they are less likely to notice or use the information.

Marketing is based on the insight that people's reaction to a new product/idea is most often determined by the packaging rather than the content in and of itself (Williamson 1996). In other words, advertising experts have realized that people respond far more strongly to the associations of a product rather than the product itself, and therefore advertisements aim to sell associations, meanings, an image and the identity that comes with it. The implications for those trying to communicate policy ideas are significant. Not least, it highlights the need to know your audience in order to find the right packaging so that the idea can be taken note of and remembered.

Marketing approaches have become more sophisticated during the twentieth century precisely as they have shifted from broadcasting to narrowcasting in order to get to know their audience(s). This involved defining a niche market, segmentation of markets (isolating broad geographic, demographic, life cycle, gender, and income groups that make up a particular market), or micro-marketing (tailoring products to specific individuals and locations) (Kotler et al. 1999). This raises an interesting question about what kind of segmentation of policy makers, or of 'the public', might be useful. For example, the idea of social marketing within HIV/AIDS programmes is meant to be closely connected to the importance of developing target-group profiles and an understanding of which associations are most effective in reaching this particular group (Price 2001).

Another main principle in marketing is to aim to elicit a response from the target audience. Once a person or group responds to a product/idea, they are engaged in the communication process and are far more likely to remember and potentially buy the product/idea than if they had not responded. There are several factors that can be used to elicit a response from people. Kotler et al. (1999) divide these into rational (putting forward a cost/benefit analysis), emotional (stirring up positive or negative emotions), and moral factors (appealing to a sense of right and wrong). Advertisers have developed skill in drawing on these three types of appeals while tapping on the motivations that they see as driving human consumption: functional, pleasure, self-identity, image, admiration and altruism. If these are invoked in the right way, the target audience will respond and, following on from a response, they may start identifying with and using the new product/idea.

Achieving behaviour change in a target audience is dependent on a certain level of interaction. Today, marketing specialists frequently argue that communication must be seen as a social process where attitudes and/or behaviour are changed with tangible and intangible exchanges in social relationships. Traditional models may have targeted individuals as if they were passive, but more recent theories have pointed to the fact that identity, meaning and knowledge do not arise in an individual's mind in isolation of their environment. Contemporary marketing-communication theory focuses on the complex relationships between families, households and the media, and is premised on the assumption that meanings are not transferred or shared but jointly produced in social interaction (Varey 2002).

Social marketing has also involved theorizing about what causes behavioural change. The 'stages of change' model identifies ten processes that people have to move through if changing their behaviour, including consciousness raising, self-reevaluation, social liberation, and helping relationships. Since few people are ready for action-oriented programmes, time must be invested to allow for people to move through the earlier stages (Lefebvre 2001).

Assessing the effectiveness of particular communication strategies on particular audiences is a vital part of any attempt to change policy. It is highly likely that monitoring the effectiveness of communication strategies will improve researchers' impact in the long-term. However, this is no easy task as the time lag between research dissemination and policy change can be great. And, as illustrated in the case studies later in this book, different communication channels will work in different contexts. Research reports, newspaper articles, meetings, briefings, radio programmes, protest demonstrations or the internet can all be

> **Box 2.6** *The potential of information and communication technology*
>
> Information and communication technologies have huge possibilities for communication within networks and coalitions with the following reservations:
> - ICTs will not build coalitions on their own because face-to-face contact is necessary for building trust.
> - ICT systems are social systems and as such have to be developed along with investment in the people who are destined to use the systems.
> - Those who stand to lose power as information brokers have resisted the development and use of ICT systems.
> - ICT can accentuate exclusion; by improving access to information for some (mostly in the metropolitan core areas of the world) but failing to provide for others, it accentuates existing patterns of marginalization or even creates new ones.
> - The privatization of information means that it is becoming a commodity not a right, that research responds to the demands of the most powerful consumers, and that public space is being eroded.
>
> *Sources*: Castells (1993); Elliot (1995); Peterson (1998); Volkow (1998)

effective at different times and for different types of material. We will not discuss these in greater detail here, but will briefly touch on a communication channel that is much discussed within marketing, communication and international development studies, namely information and communication technology (ICT). ICT creates new opportunities for improving research–policy linkages, but also brings with it a series of challenges for international development (see Box 2.6).

Links: influence and legitimacy

The relationship between researchers and policy makers shapes the degree and nature of influence they have over each other. Part of our hypothesis is that when they initiate and maintain various types of links, with appropriate chains of legitimacy to those they represent, researchers should have more policy influence and policy makers could make better use of research.

Research–policy networks
Some authors would argue that policy networks, or various groupings of actors, explain how policy changes come about; it is through networks of actors that particular discourses are established or promoted (Keeley and Scoones 1999: 32–3). Networks usually share some common

values and outlooks and consciously work together to take advantage of particular policy 'spaces' and 'windows'. To understand how networks operate, Lindquist (2001), Neilson (2001), Stone (2001) and Sutton (1999), point to different ways of mapping the actors and their networks (see Box 2.7 opposite).

One of the key distinguishing features of different types of networks or coalitions is the position of their members in relation to the policy-making process: that is, are they, for example, policy makers, experts, street-level bureaucrats or outsider researchers? A key question for research about how particular policy shifts have come about in international development is the degree to which policy makers themselves were members of the networks that had an influence.

Other distinguishing features of successful networks – in terms of campaigns for policy impact – are listed by Chapman and Fisher (1999): a long period of time, analysis of each level (state, market, civil society), different strategies for different target groups, collaboration, legitimacy, a narrow focus, individual champions and grassroots support.

Brown and Fox (2001) offer a similar recipe but add that:

- power and communication gaps in civil society need bridges for people to work effectively;
- chains with relatively short links are stronger; that is, a few key individuals who are sufficiently close can bridge huge chasms;
- trust is vital to these links and the internet is not sufficient for building trust, face-to-face negotiation is often essential;
- being accountable to grassroots interests entails recognizing, or even building, structures that are genuinely representative of local constituencies.

Effective policy entrepreneurs – or champions – will make the most of networks by using connections and negotiating skills, and developing ideas, proposals and expertise well in advance of policy 'windows' – whether brought about because of a change in government, citizen action, or a swing in the national mood (Neilson 2001: 29). The range of entrepreneurial skills required is seldom found within one individual alone. The spread of ideas is more effectively achieved by the interaction of different types of people, according to Gladwell (2000). Three types all play a vital role in what he calls 'social epidemics', the rapid spread of an idea.

- **Connectors** are networkers, they know who to pass information to and are respected, so they will have influence on key players.
- **Mavens** are information specialists, they acquire information and then educate others – a personality type that is considered indispensable to marketing.
- **Salesmen** are powerful, charismatic and, most importantly, persuasive: they are trusted, believed and listened to, where others would be ignored.

Box 2.7 Research–policy networks

▶   **Policy communities**: actors with access to privileged information inside and outside government who are highly integrated with the policy-making process in specific fields, including journalists, researchers, policy analysts, elected officials, bureaucratic leaders and groups of 'experts' who share the same values (for example, the Asia-Pacific 'policy community' in Malaysia (Camroux, 1994); or the 'policy community' in Washington, D.C.).

▶   **Global public policy networks**: alliances of government agencies, international organizations, corporations and elements of civil society that operate between and above the nation state (for example, the Global Environment Facility).

▶   **Epistemic communities**: networks of experts who share beliefs and engagement with a policy enterprise; professional and educational standards act as a socio-political barrier to entering the groups (for example, Keynesian economists; or the Intergovernmental Panel on Climate Change).

▶   **Discourse coalitions**: groups of actors who share a social construct and seek to impose their own discourse on the debate in different policy domains. Discourse becomes institutionalized as it dominates modes of perception and reasoning within organizations (for example, Israeli water policy has been driven by a farming/military discourse coalition; Jagerskog 2002).

▶   **Advocacy coalitions**: groups that share beliefs – rather than interests – within a sector leading to policy subsystems. Battles of ideas between different coalitions – two to four in each policy community – can cause policy change, with the dominant one usually getting its way (for example, Jubilee 2000, or what has since become Jubilee Research).

▶   **Issue networks**: groups may have different values, conflicting interests and varied solutions to a problem but they come together because they have knowledge about a particular issue (for example, Development Alternatives with Women for a New Era (DAWN); International Forum for Rural Transport and Development).

Sources: Lindquist (2001); Neilson (2001); Stone (2001: 33–4) and Sutton (1999)

Chains of legitimacy
The poor benefit when civil society is engaged in shaping pro-poor policy, particularly when engagement is well informed and leads to evidence-based policy. Within current international development policy there is an emphasis on the crucial – and as yet not fully utilized – role of civil society organizations (CSOs) in poverty-reduction policy. Experience has shown that when CSOs are able to assemble and communicate information effectively, there is a significant and pro-poor impact on policy. At present, the role of civil society is especially relevant to the large-scale development efforts around democratization, where strong CSOs are among the 'drivers' for democratic change, and PRSPs, where CSOs can potentially play a vital part in the planning process and in the immediate response phase.

At the same time, Northern development and research institutions are adapting to changing roles. Donors require these institutions to update them not only on service provision and technical skills, but also on the way knowledge is distributed and used – especially in capacity-building efforts. Northern CSOs and institutions have a new role to play in supporting Southern CSOs in developing their capacity to engage with national and global research and decision-making processes. As the latest DFID Research Policy Paper points out: 'The evidence suggests that the capacity of developing countries to generate, acquire, assimilate and utilise knowledge will form a crucial part of their strategies to reduce poverty' (Surr et al. 2002: 5).

In addition, Northern development NGOs are increasingly called on to do analytical work in collaboration with Southern partners, and to add value to policy debates both nationally and internationally. International NGOs defend their right to take positions on issues of international development as long as they were developed through 'real dialogue' with Southern partners. Yet experience indicates that NGO programme managers and policy officers are under perennial pressure of time and funds to move quickly from concept to implementation, with less space than they would wish for undertaking comprehensive research to strengthen their evidence or analysis on how to influence policy effectively.

These identified gaps are closely tied to the issue of legitimacy, which may be an influential factor in effective research–policy linkages. Research may be more likely to have a useful impact if it can demonstrate that it contributes towards the connection between the 'voices of the poor' on the one hand and pro-poor policy on the other hand. For this reason, Hudson (2000) argues that NGOs (and other actors) would be advised to map out their chains of legitimacy: when legitimacy is claimed on the basis of representation, systems of accountability need to be in place; when legitimacy is claimed on the basis of experience, the relevance of Southern operational experience to Northern advocacy needs to be demonstrated.

Broad participation
The first paper in the Rockefeller Foundation's Communication for Social Change (CFSC) working paper series examines how communication, knowledge and decision-making processes might be used at a community level to bring about social change (Figueroa et al. 2002). Communication in this respect is defined as the act of people coming together to decide who they are, what they want, and how they will obtain what they want. The rationale behind CFSC is that social change will be more sustainable if the affected community owns not just the physical inputs and outputs, but also the process and content of the communication involved. The paper argues that if any external agents wish to contribute to the process of communication and social change, they should shift their approach away from persuasion and one-way transmission of information, and instead engage in broad participation through dialogue and discussion with members of the community.

Chapman and Fisher (1999), in their research on what makes a campaign effective, identify three structures of collaboration used by campaigns: 'pyramids', which aim to access top-level policy but which do not link with the grassroots; 'wheels', which work more slowly but are good for information exchange and developing expertise; and 'webs', which are similar to wheels but without a central NGO to act as the hub. Pyramids rely on upward links and a narrow but important range of contacts. Wheels and webs, on the other hand, rely on downward links and broad participation. Chapman and Fisher suggest that the narrow focus of the pyramid can be effective in initially pushing an issue. However, they go on to argue that if the campaign is not widened out at a later stage it is unlikely to achieve effective change. The broad participation generated through wheels and webs ensures that several different people, at several levels, have a stake in the campaign. Wheels and webs are also better at incorporating multiple aspects of an issue, and therefore have the potential to come up with more sustainable policy recommendations.

An integrated framework

Having discussed each of the three dimensions of the framework in turn, it is important to reiterate that they should not be understood in isolation from each other. The dimensions overlap to some degree, and in specific situations of policy-change the context, evidence and links spheres will continuously have an influence on each other. That is why we have chosen the term 'integrated' framework for the analytical structure presented here; the framework is meant to raise questions about the integration of factors from the three spheres – context, evidence and links – in the complex and dynamic interaction that forms around a process of policy change. The following four chapters present four case studies in which each of the spheres, and the relationship between them, have been investigated in detail.

Part II
Case studies

Chapter Three
The PRSP initiative: multilateral policy change and the role of research

KAREN CHRISTIANSEN with INGIE HOVLAND

Introduction

In September 1999 the Executive Boards of the World Bank and the IMF adopted a new piece of 'aid technology', the Poverty Reduction Strategy Paper or PRSP.[8] This marked a notable shift in policy by the two organizations, with implications for multilateral debt relief and concession lending as well as for policy processes on the ground in developing countries. This chapter examines how the idea of the PRSP came to be adopted and the relative role of research in that process.[9] It does not attempt to look at the impact, implication or value of this change in policy, but instead focuses on this as an example of new policy thinking being adopted at the highest levels.

The PRSP initiative

The policy event in September 1999
In September 1999, the events, ideas and processes outlined in this paper culminated in the submission and acceptance of two significant documents by the first-ever joint meeting of the International Monetary and Financial Committee (IMFC; comprising governors of the IMF, typically ministers of finance or central bank governors) and the Development Committee (DC; a joint committee of the governors of both the World Bank and the IMF). The first document outlined the new approach to lending set out by the World Bank's International Development Assistance (IDA), suggesting that the new approach to aid be called the Poverty Reduction Strategy Paper (World Bank, 1999). The second was a discussion of how the Enhanced Heavily Indebted Poor Countries Initiative (HIPC2) could operationalize the link between debt relief and poverty reduction as conceptualized in the PRSP. This was jointly drafted and authorized by the respective heads of the policy departments of the IMF and World Bank (IMF/World Bank 1999a). The two papers cross-referenced each other and were closely coordinated. A few months later, the operational issues papers added further detail in December.

The PRSP process and principles
A PRSP is a document that sets out an analysis of poverty in a country and defines a national strategy for reducing it. The PRSP is usually, but not always, the result of a process that starts with an Interim PRSP (IPRSP). This document is drafted by the national government, usually led by the ministry of finance, and usually with consultation and advice

> **Box 3.1** *Schematic history of development cooperation*
>
> **1960s** With donor support, newly independent governments in a hurry displace the private sector: national development plans, government-led industrialization, nationalization.
> **1970s** Donors in a hurry displace government: donor-driven projects with their own management structures outside government, integrated rural development.
> **1980s** Governments, responding to donor/IFI stipulations, return ownership to private sector: structural adjustment, privatization.
> **1990s** Donors begin to return ownership to government: sector programmes, direct budget support, 'partnership' rhetoric replaces conditionality.
> **2000s** Increased emphasis on accountability to domestic institutions: governance, participation, CDF, PRSPs.
>
> *Source*: Foster (2000), adapted from a presentation by Barry Ireton.

from the IFIs, other donors and civil society. The IPRSP then becomes a 'road map' to the drafting of the final PRSP. In the period between the formulations of these two documents, a participatory consultation process is undertaken and data on the nature and distribution of poverty are generated and analysed statistically and often also using a participatory poverty assessment (PPA). The World Bank and IMF specify that in the PRSP document there must be a description of the participatory process undertaken, a 'comprehensive poverty diagnostic', clear and costed priorities and targets, indicators, and a system of monitoring and evaluating progress.

The staff of the World Bank and IMF then review the PRSP, and if, or once, they consider the document acceptable, they generate a joint staff assessment (JSA). This assessment contains some comments on the document, and a recommendation to the Executive Boards of the World Bank and IMF that the PRSP is a sufficient basis for concessional lending or debt relief. This was a way around the problem of the PRSP itself being the basis of an IMF or World Bank decision. Countries must then generate an Annual Progress Report on Poverty Reduction Strategy giving an account of the progress of implementation. Although only a few countries have yet reached this point (for example, Uganda and Bolivia), the idea is that the process of generating a PRSP might be repeated every three years.[10]

There are five core principles that underlie PRSP development and implementation (IMF/World Bank 1999c). The poverty reduction strategies should be:[11] country driven (involving broad-based participation by civil society and the private sector in all operational steps); results oriented (focusing on outcomes that would benefit the poor); comprehensive (recognizing the multidimensional nature of poverty);

partnership oriented (involving coordinated participation of development partners – bilateral, multilateral, and non-governmental); and based on a long-term perspective for poverty reduction.

By July 2003, 66 countries had entered a PRSP process, of which 21 had completed their first PRSP and the World Bank and IMF JSA had gone to the Board.[12] Embarking on a PRSP process is now an entry criterion for accessing debt relief under HIPC and for accessing the low-income-country concessional lending streams of the IFIs (the World Bank's IDA and the IMF's Poverty Reduction and Growth Facility [PRGF]). The PRSP process can also be a reason for going 'off-track' with these programmes, and so can hinder loans from IDA/PRGF or delay completion point under HIPC. In March 2003, 26 countries were receiving debt relief under HIPC2, of which eight had reached completion point.[13]

The length, structure and content of the final PRSPs produced to date vary substantially, as does the degree to which they adhere to the five principles. The extent to which PRSPs have, or even can, achieve these core principles is the subject of much debate, and is not directly addressed in this chapter. There is an extensive literature developing on this subject.[14]

Backdrop, narratives and players

There is no single coherent narrative of how PRSPs emerged, because there does not seem to be a single or dominant 'critical pathway' that ended in the PRSP initiative. There are a large number of different actors, institutional structures and strands of history and thought that interweave in this story. The complexity of the accounts that these actors present, their internal and external political context, and some of the events and shifts in thought, all need to be explained. This section looks at the shifts in approach to development and how to do it, then goes on to discuss the actors in this story, and finally explores the set of specific issues and problems facing the IMF and World Bank at the time.

Shifts in international development policy discourse

The emergence of the PRSP approach in 1999 clearly owes much to changes in thinking around the development process that occurred in the decades that preceded it (as briefly indicated in Box 3.1 above). First, the changes in thinking on the meaning and causation of poverty and the shift in the aim of development assistance to **poverty reduction** were clearly central building blocks in the emergence of the PRSP approach. During the 1990s, the poverty agenda was changing. In particular, this was due to the ideas summarized in the World Bank's *World Development Report* (WDR) in 1990, and the further refinement of the ideas expressed in this report through internal operational documents in the World Bank in the early 1990s, and critiques of its limitations

(Lipton and Maxwell 1992), leading up to the WDR 2000/2001. As a result of this process, several particularly important themes in the poverty discourse can be broadly summarized as follows:[15]

- growing interest in vulnerability and social protection;
- changing perspectives on the role of, and relations between, different development actors, specifically the market, the state (particularly following the Asia crisis in 1997) and civil society;
- broader definitions and alternative measures of poverty were taken into use, where 'poverty' expanded from measures of private consumption to include assets, social consumption, security, and empowerment.

Second, over the course of the 1990s, **participation** came to occupy a very important position in the discourse about development policy – reflecting, in part, a build-up of applied research findings on the issue. Broadly speaking, there are two distinct, if complementary, definitions of, and arguments for, participation in a developmental context. The first is a fairly narrow, project-level perspective, and is based upon the argument that participation of the intended beneficiaries in problem analysis and policy making improves the quality of information available to policy makers and, therefore, the quality of the programmes and plans that result (Chambers 1983, 1994, 1997). The second strand relates to the quality of governance in a country, and how this affects development results, including poverty reduction. Officially legitimized participation, it is argued, helps both those who make policy and those whom it affects to think of policy makers as accountable for their performance.[16] Both of these arguments about participation run strongly through the PRSP story, and are emphasized in the 'basic principles', that the PRSP is to be written on the basis of broad participation, engaging civil society and the private sector in the debate about national development and public expenditure priorities.

Third, the PRSP approach can clearly be seen as emerging from the **aid-effectiveness** agenda, which set out to evaluate the role, impact and effectiveness of official international development assistance. This shift, and the academic research that contributed to it, was by far the most widely recognized within IMF and World Bank circles and was also the most commonly regarded as relevant to the PRSP initiative. The aid-effectiveness debate was tied in particular to issues of conditionality, ownership, projects/programmes, public expenditure management and donor coordination. By the late 1980s it was clear that, for whatever reason, the anticipated growth was not generally happening, particularly in sub-Saharan Africa, and that the crisis had not been alleviated by the 'right policies and the right support package' that structural adjustment provided.[17] The critiques of structural adjustment came from many different quarters, and there was growing concern about the outcome of policy-based lending.[18] The debate about the use of conditionality began to change when research economists moved into the debate, trying to assess its effectiveness more systematically and empirically.[19] Evaluations of the approaches of the 1980s began to emphasize the policy environment (Boone 1994a,b; Burnside and Dollar 1997), some going further to suggest that aid was being used for consumption and thus not augmenting growth (Boone 1994a,b) and that if the policies 'were not right' then aid reduced growth. The flip side of the conditionality coin was identified as the need for 'better government ownership'.[20] At the same time, during the second half of the 1990s, the International Development Targets (IDTs) had been formulated but progress towards them had generally been disappointing. This was also an issue for concern and the topic of applied policy research (e.g. Demery and Walton 1998).

Simultaneously, critiques of project financing were emerging over the 1980s and 1990s.[21] The main critical conclusions of evaluations of project aid can be summarized as follows.[22]

- High transactions costs from the multiplicity of different reporting and accounting requirements.
- Inefficient spending that is dictated by donor priorities and procurement arrangements.
- Extremely unpredictable funding levels.
- Undermining of state systems through the special staffing arrangements and parallel structures.
- Corrosion of democratic accountability as mechanisms are designed to satisfy donor rather than domestic constituencies.
- Corruption, fraud and rent-seeking were not overcome by their independence from government.

During the mid-1990s the donor community began to respond to these critiques in more tangible terms. DFID's 1997 White Paper is one of the most significant examples of this shift in donor approach that committed the government to working as far as possible through governments and normal budgetary processes. The consequence of such an approach is a shift toward a focus on governance issues, and particularly the transparency and accountability of public expenditure systems. Donor coordination, an old concern, became closely linked to the programme aid and public expenditure (PE) approach to aid and the 'failures' of conditionality and project aid. The Comprehensive Development Framework (CDF) invented by the World Bank in early 1999 was influential in drawing together ideas about donor coordination, among other things.[23]

Description of the players[24]

World Bank and IMF
The international financial institutions (IFIs) set up at Bretton Woods in 1944 played the central role in this story.[25] In this section, they are discussed together because it helps to highlight some of the areas of

important tensions, as well as their similarities in terms of leadership, mandates and their internal processes that reinforce each other.

James Wolfensohn's arrival as the World Bank's new president in 1995 initiated a rather different era within the Bank. Wolfensohn was concerned to promote a more open and less secretive culture, and attempted to respond to the external criticism being levelled at the Bank. On the other hand, Michel Camdessus, head of the IMF since 1987, had a greater stake in the past. He had been a central player in the era of structural adjustment, and largely rejected the critiques of ESAF and negative assessments of the impact of IMF policies on the poor. He was initially resistant to debt relief. However, while he may not have accepted the content of the critiques, there was certainly recognition that the IMF was facing a serious public relations challenge and that there was at least a need to repackage.

Both the World Bank and the IMF have, in rather different ways, been through a difficult period, in which both internal and external forces have questioned their mandate and the division of labour between the two organizations. The split between short-term macro-economic instability and longer term development and growth has become increasingly problematic over the last few decades. Much of the debate has focused on the role of the IMF in low-income countries, particularly the question of IMF lending over the long term rather than for short-term balance-of-payments problems.

There is a strong contrast between the way policy is made and implemented in the IMF and in the World Bank. The IMF can be broadly characterized as a traditional, hierarchical bureaucracy where decision making is a top-down activity, and where policies, once they have been made, are implemented. This means that once senior management has given their approval, the impetus this gives in the IMF is far more powerful than in the World Bank. In contrast, the World Bank's decision and policy making are, relatively speaking, more egalitarian and diffuse. It can be described as an internal market for ideas. Particular ideas in the World Bank are published under individual names, partly due to the structure of staff incentives. Implementation is, in some sense, limited to those who 'bought' the ideas in the first place, and these do not necessarily represent the official line.[26]

Despite differences between the two institutions, however, it is worth noting that they are more similar than different in terms of economic outlook, and they are both very rule-bound institutions. In both of them, the executive boards play a significant role in shaping policy. In terms of individual behaviour and incentives in both organizations, although perhaps more pronounced in the IMF, most staff operate within the same economic paradigm, perhaps due to similar educational backgrounds and also an element of self-selection. Both organizations, particularly in the past, have had a significant tendency towards insularity, and the reaction to external ideas and critiques is usually less than positive.

In June 1995, a group of NGOs invited Wolfensohn to engage civil society in a joint assessment of the impact of adjustment programmes.

Part of the backdrop, and perhaps also a consequence, was Wolfensohn's effort to build a dialogue with the NGO community, including some of its most vociferous members. Wolfensohn accepted the proposal, and this resulted in the Structural Adjustment Participatory Review Initiative (SAPRI) in 1997 (later to become the Structural Adjustment Participatory Review International Network; SAPRIN). While there was a series of problems on the nature of selection and representation, it was increasingly led by Southern NGOs, with the important feature that the committee had access to the Executive Board of the World Bank. However, other NGOs – including the US Development Gap – felt that the World Bank–NGO Committee was too close to the Bank.

It is also important to mention the attitudes to research. Both IFIs pride themselves on the academic credentials of their staff and their links to academia. Beyond their research department, however, it is notable how little research produced outside the institutions is actually used. Above all, there is a neglect of non-US or non-UK scholarship. This is associated with the time and operational pressures that staff are under, and the lack of explicit, policy-relevant recommendations in much academic work. Internally produced or commissioned research has a much higher profile, and is taken far more seriously. Although internal research is more likely to have an impact, that which fits with the prevailing view is taken more seriously than that which casts doubts on key tenets. During the 1990s, the strength of the research departments in both organizations seems to have increased or become more relevant to low-income countries.[27]

The role of the executive boards and the governors in both organizations is central. The governance of the IFI is dominated by the G5 (France, Germany, Japan, the United Kingdom and the United States) and usually staffed by ministers of finance (with a few exceptions such as Clare Short as a development minister). Consequently, they have historically been rather conservative bodies, whose focus is on the international financial system. This conservatism has permeated the organizations. Whether or not something will 'get through the Board' is a central concern of programming and policy, and there is a fair degree of self-censorship that occurs as a consequence.

The relationship between the two organizations has always been problematic. Joint mechanisms such as the Policy Framework Papers (PFP) have failed (as discussed below). The failure to work effectively together was a particular source of pressure on their executive boards. While the lack of clarity over mandates has no doubt contributed to this, perceptions of each other are not always positive. To caricature the opinions expressed, the World Bank is perceived as ineffective and confused, and the IMF as rigid and arrogant. The close relationships that developed between the two policy divisions in the late 1990s are an important part of the story of the PRSPs.

Strategic Partnership with Africa

In September 1987, the Strategic Partnership with Africa (SPA), then the Special Programme of Assistance for Africa, was established as an informal association of donors focusing on the low-income, highly indebted countries in sub-Saharan Africa. The World Bank and the IMF proposed this initiative, with the primary aim of stimulating support for development assistance and the structural adjustment process among bilateral donors. Support for the IFIs, and thus funding flows, were flagging rather dramatically at the time. Additional aims were to review donor practices in support of reform, monitor the impact of reform on the poor, and provide intellectual leadership on a range of development issues (Shepherd and Bird 2000). Member countries and organizations in the SPA select their own representatives, who meet twice a year. Plenary meetings are informal and decisions are agreed upon through consensus without any formal voting.[28]

The SPA's ability to have a direct influence on World Bank policy seems to have been limited (Shepherd and Bird 2000). However, it appears to have played an important indirect role as a forum for discussion where key individuals were exposed to a range of ideas while they were still in 'draft' form, and commented on them – including the ESAF review and the World Bank's 2000/01 *World Development Report*. There were debates following the World Bank initiative 'The Social Dimensions of Adjustment', and issues ranging from partnership to public expenditure were discussed. The presence of many senior members of important bilaterals in the SPA also meant that it was influential on the bilaterals' own positions, and thus indirectly through their ministers of finance on the positions of the World Bank and the IMF. From a UK perspective, for example, SPA papers were circulated within DFID, SPA representatives contributed to the development of the DFID White Paper in 1997 and DFID's views on debt, and the UK SPA representatives also briefed UK DEL (the UK delegation to the Boards of the IMF and World Bank). The forum certainly provided for greater policy cohesion among a key group of 'like-minded' donors, with the representatives of the Utstein Group countries at the core in recent years.[29]

The UK Government
The UK is an important actor in this story because it played the role of advocate of many of the ideas that merged into the PRSP initiative. In the wake of the 1997 election of the Labour government, the new Department for International Development (DFID) gained a Cabinet position. The institutional importance of DFID was reinforced by the political and personal influence of the new Secretary of State, Clare Short. Development issues also had the political support and the strong commitment of the Chancellor Gordon Brown. The level of activity and impact of the UK on the Boards of the Bank and IMF also increased considerably, particularly with Brown's acceptance of Chair of IMF Board in September 1999.

Central to the new agenda brought in by Clare Short was an emphasis on the impact of aid on poverty, which resulted in her strong support for the IDTs that laid the foundation for the Millennium Development

Goals (MDGs).[30] Initially however there was little enthusiasm for the debt-relief debate, which was seen as missing, and even distracting from, the main point, which was poverty reduction. In May 1998, a shift in DFID thinking occurred around the drafting of a speech at Queen Elizabeth House, Oxford (see Short 1998). The work, undertaken by Clare Short and Paul Spray (who had joined DFID from Christian Aid's policy department), served to establish DFID's position of linking deeper and faster debt relief to a programme of poverty reduction. The shift in position was probably reinforced by the hero's welcome that Clare Short received a few weeks later at the G7 summit in Birmingham. Within DFID, the bringing together of the debt relief and poverty reduction agendas is seen as the starting point of a concept that developed into the PRSP.[31]

The US Government
The USA is a significant player in the story of the PRSPs, largely because of their financial importance. While not a main proponent for the PRSP approach, the USA was nevertheless influential because it could potentially have blocked it. In the interviews conducted for this study, the attitude towards poverty in the US was identified as an important underlying influence on US policy. In the public perception, poverty is linked to effort and morality, resulting in a separation between the deserving and the undeserving poor. This extends beyond individuals to governments. The link between poverty reduction and HIPC, which meant a focus on Africa and 'the deserving' poor, helped keep the debate surrounding these issues on easier ground for US politics. However, while the people of sub-Saharan Africa might be seen as 'deserving', their governments were regarded as less so. The sequences were largely about the need for conditionality to keep the benefits of debt relief out of reach of the undeserving. Demands for conditionality became a rallying point for the conservative, 'non-bleeding heart' Republicans and right-wing Democrats.

In 1999 an important Bill was introduced to approve US$435 million of bilateral debt cancellation. This happened shortly before the HIPC2 initiative went to the Boards of the World Bank and IMF. The political significance of the Clinton administration getting the Bill through should not be underestimated. It was unprecedented to get this amount of new money in an election year and with a Republican-led Congress. However, in the climate of generally limited support for the IFIs, the money came with substantial conditions attached. Notable among them was the 'Meltzer Commission' (or the International Financial Institution Advisory Commission), established in 1998 'to consider the future roles of seven international financial institutions', among them the IMF and World Bank.

The NGO movement
The increasing role of NGOs in the 1990s was instrumental in creating much of the political impetus and changing the nature of the debates

around debt relief. In the course of the 1990s, several NGOs became increasingly adept at presenting the problems related to poverty and debt, and the media was used very effectively to raise the profile of these issues. This facilitated the strong public pressure that enabled the NGO-led movements, particularly the 'Drop the Debt' campaign, to successfully pressurize policy makers.

The Jubilee 2000 movement was set up in the UK in April 1996, and in 1997 and 1998 extended across Europe, the US and Africa. The board of Jubilee 2000 rapidly became an important forum for discussion and idea-formation around the links between debt relief and poverty reduction. It also gradually became more coherent, overcoming the NGO factionalism of the early days. Increased coherence was accompanied by an improvement in technical capacity and focus. NGOs' own research, and the use of more academic researchers and other technical specialists to comment on their work, became an increasingly integrated part of their advocacy strategy. These efforts at greater analytical rigour were, however, largely limited to Jubilee 2000, Oxfam, CAFOD and Christian Aid.[32] A series of important technical skills acquired by this group of NGOs was transferred from Debt Relief International (DRI). Important linkages from this group seem to have extended into the IFIs, and an interesting chain of leaks associated with the development and critique of the first HIPC initiative worked through to Oxfam and the *Financial Times*.

The level and role of public support in the USA was much lower. The Jubilee movement in the USA ended quite quickly in stalemate, with a voting system which meant that more radical agendas could and did block decisions within the organization. The focus of activity in the USA thus shifted out of the Jubilee movement to a subset of largely Christian NGOs – the 'Debt Round Table' – who took their case directly to the US Administration and the Houses of Congress. Similarly to the UK actors, there was an increase in the sophistication of the movement's advocacy efforts, with rising staff numbers and dramatic increases in competency and expertise. This was an essential part of their success.

The Uganda experience
From the interviews conducted, it is clear that Southern governments' input into the gradual development of the PRSP initiative was minor. Other than some limited discussion at Executive Director-level of the World Bank and IMF, the contribution of Southern governments was largely indirect, through the demonstration effect of poverty-reduction programmes in practice. Countries named in this respect were Bolivia, Mozambique, Tanzania, and especially Uganda.

The Uganda experience is often cited as the model as well as the source of much of the PRSP concept. Events in Uganda during the late 1990s drew together a number of central strands.

- A shift in domestic political agenda toward poverty reduction, and the backing of other key members of the international community

against the traditional tickle-down approach the World Bank was proposing. This culminated in the Poverty Eradication Action Plan (PEAP) in 1997.[33]
- The establishment of the Poverty Action Fund or PAF, which identified priority programmes within the PEAP. This happened as a result of the initial confusions around HIPC1 in 1997, concerning debt relief and how the IMF would treat such relief.
- 'State of the art' public-expenditure management guidelines that were introduced in 1996 focussed on the need to integrate aid into the national budget and on the role of government as a coordinator of the process. Particular emphasis was placed on dropping 'earmarking' and introducing a greater 'results-based' orientation through the Medium Term Expenditure Framework. This was supported by a World Bank review in 1997 and the links between the budget and the PEAP solidified in 1998, reinforced in turn by the establishment of the PAF.
- The level of engagement and involvement of NGOs with the Ministry of Finance and the PEAP also set a precedent. Oxfam and the Ugandan government, in collaboration with a number of NGOs, initiated the first Participatory Poverty Assessment. This laid an important set of methodological foundations and set the precedent of the approaches proposed by the IFIs in the mid-1990s.
- Uganda's reduction in poverty from 56 per cent to 44 per cent, that was achieved from 1992 to 1997, was a significant factor in validating the approach and lent much credibility to the model that emerged (Appleton 2001).

IFI processes preceding the adoption of the PRSPs

By the late 1990s, the IFIs were under intense pressure. The G7 were pressing for 'delivery' and becoming increasingly frustrated with the wrangling between the IFIs. The conditionality and aid-effectiveness debates were becoming heated. Whether or not the critiques of conditionality and SAPs were considered fair, even the staunchest member of the World Bank and IMF staff recognized that they had a public relations problem that was being fuelled by the secretiveness of their operations. During the late 1990s within the World Bank and IMF, a number of specific processes and events took place that played a major role in establishing the conditions in which the PRSP idea developed and was accepted.

Failure of the policy framework paper
Camdessus introduced the policy framework papers (PFP) as a device to try and ensure coordination of the World Bank and the IMF at country level. While in theory PFPs were government documents, in practice governments had little sense of ownership over them. The document contained sections that required input from both IFIs and was then signed off by the recipient national government as part of a tripartite

agreement. By the 1990s, it was clear that this practice was only an IMF device. It was not an operational document for the World Bank, in the sense that it played no part in any World Bank procedures. While the IMF needed World Bank-input for the document, it was of no relevance to the World Bank's work. World Bank staff instead worked entirely through their Country Assistance Strategies (CAS). There was increasing recognition among staff in the IMF that this was a problem, and that a framework for collaboration needed to be established that was central to both institutions' operations, and could serve as a framework for both lending and debt relief. While this recognition was mounting among staff, Camdessus was more reluctant to consider abolition of the PFP. Thus the question of a credible replacement of the PFP became more pressing.

Wolfensohn's Comprehensive Development Framework
The Comprehensive Development Framework (CDF) launched in January 1999 was very closely identified with James Wolfensohn himself. The CDF laid out four principles that should govern the orientation and coordination of aid at the country level: (a) long term and holistic; (b) country ownership and participation; (c) results orientation; and (d) country-led partnership (Wolfensohn 1999). These principles embody a very high-level acknowledgement of the research-based critiques of aid in the past and an attempt to produce a solution. However, our interviews suggested that the CDF faced a problem in that there was little incentive to take it seriously within the World Bank because it was voluntary and had 'no operational content'. Its structure in practice mirrored the Bank's departments (each sub-pillar had a department), which meant that the staff did not actually have to change the way they operated.[34] However the CDF did play a vital role in preparing the ground for PRSPs, at least as a manifestation of a similar set of pressures. The CDF pulled together a large number of the strands of thought that the PRSP approach later built on.

The ESAF reviews
The review of the Enhanced Structural Adjustment Facility (ESAF) was another important process that prepared the ground for the PRSP's development and acceptance. The ESAF Review is usually used to refer to the External ESAF Review (IMF 1998a,b), but the fact that an internal ESAF review accompanied it is part of the reason that the review process had such a significant effect. The two review processes started in January 1997 and were both headed by Hugh Bredenkamp, then in the Policy Development and Review Department (PDR) of the IMF. The significance of the commissioning, and in large part acceptance by the IMF, of an independent review of their activities should not be underestimated. This in itself was a pioneering change in practice and played a role in opening the door of the IMF to greater public engagement and debate.

A central critique in both the reviews was the need to pay more attention to building government ownership and national consensus for reform and for better World Bank–IMF coordination, particularly on fiscal issues and *ex ante* social impact assessments and monitoring. The internal review went as far as proposing the piloting of new modes of collaboration between the World Bank and IMF in low-income countries, focusing on the two issues just mentioned, as well as speeding up public enterprise and financial sector reforms. The external review however went further than this, recommending the IMF to be more flexible and to address concerns about the control of agendas and negotiation processes. While accepting the general critique, the Executive Board was uncomfortable with the charge of 'inflexibility'.

There are a number of key issues around why the ESAF reviews had such an impact. First, they were IMF-commissioned, which was always likely to increase their palatability. Second, an internal review accompanied the external one and there was significant congruence on some key conclusions. Third, they did not question the basic policy content embodied in ESAF-supported programmes and, finally, the external experts were all highly regarded mainstream economists, which gave them high levels of credibility both within and outside the IMF.[35]

It should be noted that the external review was initially quite badly received by IMF staff. However, there was a significant shift in attitude over time. A key player in the change of perception was Tony Boote, then Division Chief of the Official Financing Operations Division (in the PDR), who took on the agenda that the reviews embodied and brought this forward positively within the organization. The person heading up the two projects, Hugh Bredenkamp, also had important connections to the HIPC review process and the SPA, which helped to cross-fertilize the experiences and ensure some of the coherence that developed between them. With time, there was an 'acceptance of bad collateral effects' of some of the elements of the approach, but it was emphasized by a number of interviewees that this was not a rejection of the economic model.

Debt relief and HIPC

In 1996 the World Bank and IMF launched the first HIPC initiative as an instrument to provide poor countries with a means of getting out of the debt trap. The initiative was a significant departure from previous practices of dealing with debt problems. The main feature was an attempt to move away from *ad hoc* efforts and instead to provide comprehensive debt relief to countries that established a good track record of implementing reforms.[36]

The scope and form of articulation of the critiques of HIPC1 varied, and they came from a range of sources, including NGOs, academics, religious leaders and organizations, a number of UN agencies, and increasingly bilaterals as well. The campaigning of the Jubilee movement and the 'Drop the Debt' campaign undoubtedly gave a great deal of political import to these critiques, which can be summarized as follows.

- **Broader – The criterion of debt sustainability** The definition was criticized because (a) it was set at a level that was too high and thus excluded many of the poorest countries, and (b) it used exports as the basis for calculation, rather than fiscal sustainability. The issue of sustainability was the focus of much detailed debate and wrangling.

- **Deeper – Not enough debt relief** The levels of relief being provided were not going to be sufficient to generate growth or poverty reduction.
- **Faster – The delivery of relief was too slow** The long periods between qualification and relief were attributed, among other things, to the level of complexity and lack of clarity about procedures, the extensive number of micro-conditions, and the need for a country to have graduated from two consecutive IMF programmes over a six-year period. Seven countries entered HIPC1, of which only three actually reached completion point.[37]
- **Better – The lack of a clear link to impact** This point includes a set of criticisms mainly related to the definition of what the money should be spent on, and the incentives for ensuring it had an impact. The definition was generally regarded as too narrowly focused on social sectors, with suggestions that it should be refocused on development or poverty reduction more generally – or even on the International Development Targets (IDTs). The incentives' issue was in part about ownership debates, including critiques of aid modalities such as social funds and arguments for programmatic approaches such as those set out in the DAC guidelines. However, there were also concerns about the increasing number of external specifications of how the money should be allocated.

With criticisms intensifying towards the end of 1998, members of staff responsible for HIPC1 were beginning to acknowledge the need for changes. Opinions varied as to whether this was implied acceptance of the actual content of the critiques or just a recognition that there was a public-relations problem. Throughout the period of the design of HIPC1, the level of leaks from within the World Bank and IMF had been very high,[38] suggesting perhaps that there was indeed some level of recognition of the validity of the critiques.

In early 1999 the World Bank and the IMF began a review of HIPC, with an external consultation process being launched in February.[39] The request was for comments and proposals on debt relief and HIPC including from member countries, multilateral creditors, NGOs, religious groups and other interested institutions. The focus, as they put it, was on the 'deeper, broader, faster' elements of improving the HIPC framework. This evolved into the first phase of a two-phase consultation process starting in February 1999. The first phase emphasized concerns and modifications to the current HIPC framework, including debt-sustainability targets, timing of decision and completion points, and performance under economic and social reform programmes. This culminated in a set of changes being discussed and agreed by the

Development and Interim Committees in April 1999. At this point, the ideas about the link between debt relief and its impact on poverty levels were largely concerned with applying more 'stroke of the pen' conditionality, which would ensure that debt relief was accompanied by increases in public expenditure on health and education.

The second phase of the HIPC review, in addition to taking further a number of issues from phase one, focused in more depth on the linking of debt relief to poverty reduction. The consultation process in phase two was also more extensive and proactive. It included a crucial consultation meeting in Addis Ababa in late July 1999, which is discussed further below.

On 23 July 1999, the joint staff finalized their suggested changes to HIPC for an informal meeting of both sets of directors on 3 August. This document (IMF/World Bank 1999b; see also IMF 1999; MacArthur and Trotsenberg 1999) proposed lower sustainability targets, calculations based on decision-point data instead of the completion point, interim assistance between decision and completion points, floating completion points, and 'front-loading' of debt relief after completion point.

The last few months

The impetus and activities that were to lead to the PRSP initiative accelerated dramatically around mid-1999. The number of Jubilee 2000 debt-relief demonstrations and events was mounting. The G7 Cologne Summit of June 1999 provided a great deal of momentum. The need to announce something concrete at the event was precipitated by Chancellor Schröder's launch of the Cologne Initiative in January 1999. Schröder had promised this would provide 'radical debt relief'. The announcement made in June was of an 'enhanced' HIPC with a reduced debt-to-export ratio of 150 per cent and the fiscal indicator set at 250 per cent. More importantly for this case study, there was also an endorsement for this relief to be provided for countries that demonstrated 'commitment to reform and poverty reduction'.

We have seen how the linking of debt relief and what became the PRSP was prepared by the IFIs' HIPC review process. It was also during mid-1999 that two important papers were written: 'Heavily Indebted Poor Countries (HIPC) initiative – Strengthening the link between debt relief and poverty reduction' (IMF/World Bank 1999a)[40], and 'Building poverty reduction strategies in developing countries' (World Bank, 1999).[41] This work was mainly, if not exclusively, undertaken by the respective policy departments of the World Bank and IMF, who at this point were under strong pressure from the G7 finance ministers and G8 heads of state to limit institutional turf battles and to work together towards some common goals. HIPC was seen as an example of successful collaboration, and there were increasing expectations that the IFIs would take HIPC forward and deliver on the poverty and debt concerns.

Despite the strong focus on the link to HIPC, there was limited consultation or engagement with even the Africa departments of the two institutions, let alone other departments. Within the IMF, the work concentrated on the HIPC review, which was run in the IMF by Tony Boote. Within the World Bank, there were three groups working on these issues. The first came together around 'the PRSP paper', led by Jeni Klugman, and the second consisted of the World Bank members of the HIPC team, particularly Peter Fallen. The third group that contributed was the team that had formed around the *World Development Report 2000/2001* on poverty, which was led by Ravi Kanbur until he resigned in June 2002.[42] Masood Ahmed, then head of PREM in the World Bank, was central in making the connections and drawing together the work of these three groups.

In June 1999, there was an SPA meeting in Washington. This was identified as playing an important role particularly for the further mobilization of DFID's ideas. Nick Amin from DFID commissioned a set of papers that developed the notion of linking relief and poverty reduction, with a little more emphasis on the consequences. This set included the last-minute papers put together by John Healey (Foster et al. 1999) and Tony Burdon (Oxfam, 1999a).

In July 1999, there were two further conferences that continued to develop the linkage and build the momentum. The first was a conference entitled 'Making the link between debt relief and poverty reduction', hosted by the US Executive Directors of the World Bank and IMF. It was also held in Washington and attended by NGOs, religious groups, poverty experts and representatives from governments and the Washington-based IFIs.

The second, a particularly pivotal event, was the conclusion of the second phase of the HIPC review consultations. The last of a series of meetings was held in Addis Ababa on 29–30 July 1999, which was chaired by the UN Economic Commission for Africa. Participants included a range of NGOs and religious organizations (for example, Oxfam, Afrodad, World Vision, Christian Aid, Jesuits for Debt Relief and Development), international organizations (for example, UNDP, UNICEF, EU, AfDB) and both debtor and creditor countries including Uganda, Canada, the Netherlands and the UK. The consultation and submissions made to the conference were collected in a two-volume compendium that was forwarded to the Executive Board (HIPC Debt Initiative 1999a,b).[43]

The conference in Addis was identified as the place where the implementation of the linkage between HIPC and poverty reduction, and mechanisms to achieve this such as the PRSP, were worked out. Masood Ahmed (head of the World Bank's policy department) and Tony Boote (one of the division chiefs in the IMF's policy department and head of the HIPC review team) are said to have discussed and fleshed out several of the ideas and possible approaches at this point.

The backdrop within both of the IFIs was resistance in some quarters to the emerging proposals. Ideas that had been discussed earlier in the HIPC review process, such as adding some 'stroke of the pen' poverty conditionality to lending, were easier to accept. Stroke of the pen conditionality would largely centre on specifying increases in spending on education and health, and perhaps add some further specification about primary provision.

On 5 August 1999, the Enhanced HIPC Initiative was reviewed by the Board of the IMF, overcoming the concerns particularly of Japan, the USA and Germany about how relief would be spent, whether the poor would benefit, and the moral hazard that would result from bailing out the most indebted countries. The exact nature of the relationship between HIPC, PRSPs and IDA and IMF adjustment lending was not entirely clear at this point. Although there were overlaps and similar eligibility criteria for the low-income-country lending streams of the World Bank (lending through IDA) and the IMF (lending through ESAF), they were not exactly the same.[44] More importantly however, a large number of IDA- or ESAF-eligible countries did not have access to HIPC debt relief, and it was unclear what the status of these countries would be in relation to the PRSP initiative once it was linked to HIPC. As the PRSP paper that went to the Joint Boards in September stated: 'It is envisaged that PRSP will gradually be done for all ESAF/IDA eligible countries.' What this meant in practice, however, was only worked out much later.

The Joint Board meeting in September 1999 received two papers, one on PRSPs and one on the link between PRSPs and HIPC. The meeting was controversial and there was a great deal of debate. Even the naming of the new IMF facility that was to replace ESAF took up several hours (the new facility was institutionalized as the Poverty Reduction and Growth Facility (PRGF) two months later, in November 1999). Though much was left unclarified, the meeting did make the crucial and formal link between the use of PRSPs and eligibility for HIPC, IDA and ESAF/PRGF flows.

Epilogue

In October 1999, Mick Foster and Andy Norton were asked to come to the World Bank to present their ideas on a number of PRSP-related issues that were identified by the World Bank as needing clarification. These issues included government ownership, initiative overload, who would assess PRSPs and with what criteria, timing and country variation. In a hugely overcrowded room, it became clear that many World Bank staff were totally unaware of the implications of the shift being made. A set of anxieties emerged about ability to control this process, fear that the Board would reject the documents, and timetable pressures due to HIPC that might undermine any institutionalization of the process. The concerns in the IMF seem to have receded more rapidly, in part because the PRSP initiative would make IMF staff jobs easier in the narrow sense, opening up their concerns to wider debate. The fears that remained were largely concerned with their increased reliance on the World Bank, and concerns that their efficiency would be reduced by that dependence.

Partial solutions to these problems were developed in the December 1999 operational issues papers. The idea of an interim PRSP, or IPRSP, was introduced. IPRSPs served as a means to preserve the link between the PRSP approach and PRGF lending, while not delaying access to PRGF resources given the likely time horizon to produce a full PRSP. IPRSPs also established a means to ease the pressure on getting countries into HIPC2, as did the World Bank and IMF Joint Staff Assessment (JSA) mechanism. This mechanism allowed the IFIs to skirt the potentially problematic issue of their endorsing or authorizing a sovereign government's domestic policy.

Analysis and reflection

The discussion and analysis in this section is structured around the framework of three interlinked domains: context, evidence, links.

Policy context: politics and institutions

The political and economic structures and interests that opened up the space in which the PRSP initiative came to be adopted can be seen at different levels: at a global level, relating to various – research-based – problem streams within international development that had built up during the late 1990s; at an institutional level within the IFIs themselves; and at a national level, relating to pressures within a number of individual board members' countries – particularly the USA, the UK and the rest of Europe. Each of these levels will be discussed in turn.

The problem environment and convergence around HIPC2
Around the late 1990s, there was a major convergence of factors that led to a widespread sense of there being 'a problem' within the field of international development policy. These factors were both economic and political, and related to structures and interests both inside and outside the IFIs. A new set of problems was being faced by policy makers at a global level in the context of a major shift provided by the end of the Cold War, which meant that aid could move away from being regarded largely as a geopolitical strategic tool. In addition, the Asia crisis and the lacklustre economic performance of sub-Saharan Africa posed serious challenges. Questions about the efficacy of the policy framework focused on the nature and sequencing of economic reforms and the use of policy conditionality.

In relation to the IFIs there was also a specific set of problems that began to converge. These clustered around the issues of coordination (represented by the failure of the PFP), debt relief (represented by the HIPC review), and structural adjustment lending and policy content (represented by the ESAF reviews). Pressure was building to find solutions. Perceptions differed as to exactly what the problems were: some groups thought there were substantive content and operational problems, while others thought it was mainly a public relations problem.

However, most actors adopted the common policy narrative that there was a serious perception of the 'failure' of structural adjustment. This case supports the ideas of Roe (1991) that 'policy narratives', whether accurate or not, are powerful influences on decision making.

Due to the above set of issues that converged during the late 1990s, a policy window was opening in the international development field. Policy windows occur when there is an opening for new views to enter the policy domain and inform policy decisions (Kingdon 1984). While policy makers may not have agreed on the exact nature of the problem in the late 1990s, there was a sense that there were serious challenges that needed to be addressed. Among a significant number of influential policy makers, practitioners and academics, there was therefore a search for new conceptual frameworks that could provide credible answers and operational implications.

Against this background, the HIPC review in 1999 can be seen as a trigger for the PRSP tipping point in the field of international development policy. As Gladwell (2000) argues, social change is brought about by tipping points, or a relatively minor occurrence that suddenly triggers large changes and which may galvanize trends that have been building up beneath the surface. These trends are often problem streams, a set of interlinked issues that may not necessarily have been previously regarded as problematic, but which at a certain point come to be seen as significant challenges within a policy domain (Kingdon 1984). The most important problem streams that were brought together around HIPC2 were:

- problems related to the first round of debt relief through HIPC, including how to ensure that debt relief is spent wisely and benefits the poor; how to ensure implementation through higher levels of government ownership; and better coordination between the World Bank and IMF;
- the need to operationalize the ideas expressed in the CDF about long-term, holistic, owned, participatory, results-oriented and country-led policy frameworks.

The need to rethink HIPC became a trigger that the diverse problem streams latched on to, and the formulation of the PRSP initiative, initially for HIPC and then for wider purposes, became a vehicle for attempting to address these concerns.

Within the IFIs
The internal context within the IFIs played a large part in the uptake of the research-based ideas, and the various processes that eventually merged into the PRSP initiative. As outlined earlier, the boards of the IMF and World Bank have a bias towards ministers of finance and representatives of central banks, and are therefore generally more interested in global financial issues than in development questions. The conservatism of the boards has traditionally permeated the institutions, as members

of staff use self-censorship to be certain that programmes and policies will 'get through the Board'. This means that the room for manoeuvre in terms of policy issues is at least perceived to be limited within the institutions. According to Clay and Schaffer (1984), the room for manoeuvre within policy processes refers to the degree of leeway that members of staff have when they are interpreting and implementing policies. Staff will usually form an opinion about how limited this room is and adapt their behaviour accordingly.

As discussed earlier, there are significant differences between the World Bank and IMF. The IMF's hierarchical structure means that both research and policy processes tend to be more conservative and slightly more rigid than in the World Bank. Within the World Bank, on the other hand, the less hierarchical nature of the institution and the internal competition of ideas mean that there is generally room for more junior staff – the World Bank's 'street-level bureaucrats' – to interpret and reinterpret policies. Street-level bureaucrats are the employees of an institution who are responsible for implementation, and who – according to Lipsky (1980) – ultimately decide how policy is to be translated into practice. The role of street-level bureaucrats seems more prominent in the World Bank than in the IMF.

Nevertheless there was increased room for manoeuvre within the IMF around the late 1990s. This was mainly due to the perceived failure of the PFP as an operational tool in the World Bank, and the IMF's acceptance of the failure because *de facto* it was clear that the Bank no longer bought into it. This generated a search for new solutions that the PRSP provided, at least in theory. There was also a sense in the IMF of being under siege, especially over the questions of their role in low-income countries and their legitimacy in the light of the 1997 Asia crisis, and the critiques that developed around the external ESAF review in 1998. The PRSP initiative presented an opportunity for the IMF to reformulate ESAF and to show that they were trying to address some of these problems.

In early 1999, Wolfensohn's CDF created a significant change in the policy environment. The CDF presented a significantly new framework of principles, and as such it can be argued that it was a 'fundamental policy decision' at a conceptual level, a decision that significantly altered the existing grounds for decision making (Lindquist 1988). However, there were no financial arrangements attached to the CDF. This contributed to the perception that there was a need to link the CDF concepts to both financial and bureaucratic systems within the World Bank. Later in 1999, the formulation of the PRSP initiative combined the CDF principles with an explicit objective of poverty reduction and the background work on poverty that was leading up to the *World Development Report 2000/2001*. The PRSP initiative also brought together conceptual and operational concerns, particularly through its link to HIPC2.

The challenges that the IFIs were facing meant that many of the policy and review decisions immediately preceding the PRSP were of an 'incremental' nature, and taken on an *ad hoc* basis as each problem became pressing (Lindquist 1988). These included the need to solve the PFP and IFI coordination problems; the challenge of making debt relief 'broader, deeper, faster, better' and ensuring that resources freed up by debt relief would be well spent; and, lastly, how to operationalize the explicit focus on poverty reduction and the CDF principles. If the PRSP initiative is viewed as the grouping of all these issues, it could surely be seen as an 'emergent' policy decision, i.e. a decision based on a broad new vision (Lindquist 1988).

Leading national actors
In the UK, the Labour government was elected in 1997, and DFID was established as a separate ministry with a strong alliance between Clare Short in DFID and Gordon Brown in the Treasury. These changes created a major new player on the international scene with a strong agenda of poverty reduction, which changed the policy environment.

At the same time, Jubilee 2000 gathered momentum both in the UK and in other European countries and was able to mobilize considerable public pressure, often in collaboration with faith-based organizations and other groups. Jubilee 2000 strongly contributed to the sense that there were serious challenges that needed to be addressed. This put pressure on national governments in Europe (and also on the IFIs) to be seen to be making positive steps towards increased debt relief for the Third World.

The US role in the PRSP story is, in general, about possible obstacles they might pose rather than their contribution to new frameworks. The fact remains that the USA is a vital member of the international decision-making community that needs to be appeased. This was particularly pertinent in a US context in the 1990s, characterized by lower levels of public interest in development issues, and political concerns about the need to replenish the funds of the IMF at the same time as the role of the IMF was raising problematic questions. There were also abolitionist tendencies in NGOs, which had some influence through lobbying activities. In general, the Clinton administration increased the room for manoeuvre to make 'progressive' changes by the World Bank and IMF – especially through the work of Larry Summers (former Chief Economist to the World Bank) as Secretary of the Treasury and the intense lobbying by the NGOs in the Debt Round Table. However, this space was dramatically reduced by the election of a Republican-led Senate and Congress. Thus the legislation that included increased financial contribution for HIPC involved 'cutting a deal' that resulted in setting up the Meltzer Commission.

Evidence: credibility and communication

In general terms, the evidence that contributed to the emergence of the PRSP initiative can be divided into two types. The first is the more academic development research that fed into the shifts towards poverty, participation and aid effectiveness over the course of the 1970s, 1980s and 1990s. This was an important contribution to problematizing the approaches that preceded the PRSP. The second is a set of more specific policy-oriented pieces of research, largely undertaken in the late 1990s. This included submissions to parts of the ESAF review, the review of HIPC, the outputs of the SPA working groups, and NGO work on debt relief – especially the work by Jubilee 2000, Oxfam and CAFOD, which in turn drew on studies by Debt Relief International (DRI) as one of their information sources.

Development research and shifts to poverty, participation and aid effectiveness
The contextual shift provided by the end of the Cold War in 1989 and the wave of democratization in the early 1990s set the stage for a new focus within development. A new framework of possible thought was adopted as the emphasis shifted away from geopolitical and security concerns. A 'framework of possible thought' comprises a set of views that seem persuasive in the current context and which gradually come to seem self-evident (Chomsky 1987). Thus new research on the issues of poverty, participation and aid effectiveness within international development gained importance and credibility during the 1990s, and set the stage for operational models that would follow up the views in practice. The most important influence of this body of work was its indirect shaping of the policy discourse through its critiques of historical practices. The process might be seen as an example of the 'percolation' model described by Weiss (1977), who suggests that the most important impact of research is achieved as new research concepts and interpretations gradually filter through various policy networks and contribute to the general framework.

On the whole, the general space that was opened up for and by development research during the 1990s was perhaps due to both the quantity of the work in these areas and the large number of highly credible academics undertaking it. Within the World Bank and the IMF, the most recognized strand of development research was the one concerned with aid effectiveness, conditionality and the question of why development expenditures were not going to plan. Well-known and respected economists, such as Collier and Dollar in-house and Killick externally, largely produced this research. Their research was presented in an economic discourse that was readily accessible to IMF and World Bank staff, and their conclusions were also regarded as being validated by the field experience of members of staff. These factors could all be seen to contribute to the credibility that their development research was perceived to have within the IFIs.

Applied policy research
In contrast to the more academic research referred to above, applied policy research focuses far more on policy recommendations and on providing workable solutions. Much of the policy research discussed in this section gained credibility and influence partly because of factors

that could be compared to good marketing strategies (see for example, Lambin 1996). For example, the applied research frequently formulated concrete solutions, found the right packaging for the recommendations, and was developed through interaction with the target group.

The fact that the policy makers in the IFIs directly commissioned the research was one of the key sources of the credibility of much of this research. In very general terms, both IFIs regard external research as less credible than internally produced or commissioned research. The least credible research is that which questions the paradigm, and which is not written in a language that is accessible or relevant to IFI staff. Thus the internal ESAF review was in general terms regarded as more credible by IMF staff than the external review. Nevertheless, in the end the IMF largely accepted the external review, as the review did not question the content of structural adjustment. While the World Bank is probably more open to external ideas, many of the same issues apply.

Much of the applied research on debt relief was carried out by NGOs, especially the Jubilee 2000 coalition. In the beginning, research and dissemination by some NGOs was fairly emotive and distorting, and ignored the complexity of the situation. Partly because of this, and partly because of ingrained perceptions about the lack of rigour and credibility of NGO research in general, NGO evidence was not taken seriously by the mainstream of many of the government institutions and IFIs. However, a substantial increase in credibility occurred. This was mainly due to a shift undertaken by the NGOs themselves in the type of research being produced, resulting in a marked improvement in the quality of their analyses and attempts to package the findings in language that was more palatable to policy makers. Oxfam became particularly adept at this, building on both country evidence and economic analysis in their papers on debt, and members of staff within the IFIs read Oxfam's policy briefs. Another important factor seems to have been the links developed between NGO researchers and key people inside donor institutions. The importance of linkages between actors is discussed more fully below.

Finally, the role of the Uganda model did much to lend credibility to many of the policy research recommendations surrounding national poverty-reduction programmes. The Uganda PEAP served as a successful 'pilot' case and was quite powerful in convincing policy makers of the feasibility and merits of the PRSP initiative. This reinforces the view that action research has considerable potential to influence wider policy if it feeds directly into the current policy context (Patel in RAWOO 2001). It also brings to mind the theory often expounded in communication and media studies that 'seeing is believing' (Philo 1996) and the relevance of this view to policy processes.

Links: influence and legitimacy

The role of formal and informal contacts between institutions, within various networks, and between individuals is very important in the

PRSP story. Such contacts played a central role both in the development of the ideas and in their adoption in the form of the PRSP initiative. The literature on advocacy coalitions and policy communities is relevant here (see for example, Sabatier and Jenkins-Smith 1999). This suggests that ideas are more likely to have an impact on policy if they are discussed and refined within groups that either have a similar outlook, or are willing to compromise in order to support the same strategy. Policy coalitions and communities are especially influential if they also manage to maintain links with a few prominent individuals and politicians.

Perhaps the most vital of the links in relation to the emergence of the PRSPs was the connection that developed between the World Bank and IMF policy departments in the late 1990s. A central component of this was the HIPC review, which was carried out by a joint team of both IMF and World Bank staff. The new and powerful connection between the IFIs, while partly due to new joint modalities, was also in large part made possible because the individuals concerned had sympathy for each other's approaches and worked well together.

At a political level, another important network was formed by the Utstein Group, which brought together some of the more influential bilateral European development ministers, and coordinated their approaches on poverty reduction issues *vis-à-vis* the IFIs. In many respects, the Utstein Group can be regarded as a policy community, a network of actors who had a stake in a particular policy area and who perhaps had an interest in acting together to change it (Pross 1986). The ESAF review teams, the DAC and the SPA working groups also facilitated significant formal forums for researcher–policy maker links. The working groups were influential because they managed to forge links between strategically placed policy makers in the IFIs and some of the key bilaterals. In this respect, they too functioned as a policy community. In addition, the SPA and its working groups generated a high level of commitment to the PRSP idea by functioning as an epistemic community, as a network of colleagues who shared a similar approach and whose connections with each other created a valuable discussion forum, and an informal basis from which to make public pronouncements (Haas 1991).

Similarly, the influence of Jubilee 2000 was based on a network between influential actors, especially within the Jubilee Steering Committee. This was an important forum where many debates and ideas were shared. One of Jubilee's main achievements was the development of a global network that brought together a large number of individuals and groups across different contexts. In this respect, Jubilee 2000 was an effective advocacy coalition, that is a coalition between actors who are different in many ways but who share a similar perspective on a particular issue, and who are willing to cooperate on the basis of this shared perspective (Sabatier and Jenkins-Smith 1999).

The above groups were formal entities. However, informal links also played a part in the PRSP initiative. One example of an informal network is the rather unholy alliance for debt relief that emerged between

President Bill Clinton, Bono of the rock group U2, Christian NGOs and right-wing senators in the USA. Another interesting set of informal links formed around HIPC, as documents were leaked to Oxfam UK, and then passed on to the *Financial Times* and *The Economist* with Oxfam's commentary on them. This chain of links had an interesting impact on moves to increase transparency later on in the HIPC review process. Important informal links were also evident in the loose network of people that had been involved in the Uganda experience. These included figures such as Mick Foster, Allister Moon, Marcus Manuel and Tony Burdon. Their familiarity with the Ugandan model and its success was transferred with them to a variety of institutions, most notably Oxfam, DFID and the World Bank.

The emergence of the PRSP initiative is not only characterized by groups and networks, but also to a remarkable extent by the input of specific individuals. There were 'policy champions' and 'entrepreneurs' at various levels that did much to move the PRSP agenda forward. Most prominent among these was perhaps Masood Ahmed, as well as Jack Boorman (heads of the World Bank and IMF policy departments, respectively), Tony Boote (IMF policy department), Stan Fischer (Deputy Managing Director IMF) and Clare Short (Secretary of State, DFID). In Gladwell's (2000) terms, these individuals can be described as both 'connectors' – networkers who know who to pass information to and who are respected – and 'salesmen' – powerful and persuasive individuals who are listened to where others might be ignored.

In summary, one of the central features of the PRSP policy change is the fact that there is no single source or single narrative that captures how the policy change came about. Similar sets of pressures, critiques and ideas were being addressed in different contexts, and different elements of what became labelled as the PRSP initiative emerged simultaneously in a number of places during the late 1990s. This led to a broad feeling of ownership of the PRSP idea within various different groups, which undoubtedly strengthened commitment to the initiative and was instrumental in the speed of its adoption.

Conclusion

The previous section has outlined an analysis of how the idea of the PRSP came to be adopted, and the relative contribution of research to that process. In summary, the PRSP was an operational solution that solved several internal problems and provided an answer to external pressures, particularly for the IFIs but also within different bilateral organizations. The simultaneous recognition of similar sets of problems and similar ideas for solutions by various actors in the international development field in the late 1990s is probably the reason why the PRSP idea, which was a substantial challenge to current practice, took hold relatively easily and rapidly. In other words, the fact that an idea as potentially radical as the PRSP initiative got through the boards of the IMF and World Bank in September 1999 is in significant part due to the level of ownership felt for the idea from its emergence in a variety of debates and places over the late 1990s. It was influenced indirectly by academic research within the international development field and directly by applied policy research, particularly policy-oriented research undertaken in relation to the ESAF and HIPC reviews, poverty reduction strategies, and debt relief.

In conclusion, what does this tell us about linkages between research and policy? The case study has tested the conceptual framework that was presented in Chapter 2. On the whole the three-dimensional framework – context, evidence, links – has proved to be useful. The PRSP case study has also highlighted a few additional points that are not captured in the initial hypotheses (as set out in Chapter 2). We suggest that the PRSP case study supports a slightly different set of four propositions, as follows.

1. Researchers are more likely to be influential if they interact with policy makers and understand their constraints and agendas

This case study of the PRSP initiative suggests that the first hypothesis is valid, that researchers are more likely to directly influence policy making if they engage with the political and institutional pressures facing the policy makers. As confirmed by the PRSP story, research commissioned by policy makers who are asking genuine questions, or which involves direct interaction with policy staff, is most likely to have an influence. Applied policy-oriented research or evidence that translates academic findings into the policy context is more useful for policy makers than pure academic research.

2. Research is more likely to be influential when it is regarded as rigorous

The second hypothesis seems to be partly valid; the channels and formats used to present research do make a difference. However, as can be seen in the increased credibility gained by NGO research, it is important to note that the rigour of the analysis itself is also a decisive factor; it is not just a matter of the language and formats used. On the whole, research was considered most credible when it was commissioned by the IFIs themselves or other donors, demonstrated analytical rigour, and was communicated in a language that was accessible and relevant to World Bank and IMF staff and other donor agencies. The degree of local involvement, on the other hand, is not directly relevant to this case study. If local involvement is taken to mean involvement by Southern governments or civil society actors, then such involvement in the process leading up to the PRSP was largely limited to the demonstration effect of changes in practice – as in the case of Uganda – while direct input was limited.

3. Researchers are likely to have an indirect influence through networks

The third hypothesis, on the importance of networks, seems to be more relevant. Those researchers who were involved in one of the networks around HIPC, ESAF, SPA, PREM or debt relief were more likely to have an impact than researchers outside these circles. There was a high degree of interaction between individuals within different institutions. As one of the interviewees put it, 'none of the players is more than two handshakes away from any of the others'. The dynamic between informal networks and formal institutions was particularly important, as it meant that ideas emerged in multiple places at the same time. A high level of ownership of ideas across various institutions increased the impact and speed of research uptake.

4. Evidence can change the policy context

While most literature on the bridging of research and policy assumes that it is very difficult to change the context, the PRSP case study shows how evidence can, to some degree, bring about change in the context, even when it challenges policy makers and fuels conflict. The NGO campaigns on debt relief drew on research that spoke the language of policy makers but which strongly challenged their viewpoints. This generated conflict but brought about significant change. The conflict that was created was effective because it altered the domestic political environment in a number of countries, and put pressure on the G7 to insist on changes in debt-relief policy. Those changes in turn triggered further initiatives that together have made a substantial difference to the context in which future policy debates will take place.

Chapter Four
How the Sphere Project came into being: a case study of policy making in the humanitarian aid sector and the relative influence of research

MARGIE BUCHANAN-SMITH

Introduction

One of the most significant policy shifts in the international humanitarian sector in the last decade has been the move to strengthen the accountability of humanitarian agencies and to find ways of improving performance in humanitarian response. In 1996, the decision to launch the Sphere Project was one of the key policy initiatives associated with this shift. It resulted in the publication of the *Humanitarian Charter and Minimum Standards for Disaster Response* in 2000 (Sphere 2000). This case study explores the process that led up to this policy initiative, and how buy-in and ownership were achieved (or, in some cases, not) during the first year of Sphere's existence, in order to learn more about the linkages between research and policy.

The launch of the Sphere Project was, essentially, a policy decision to strengthen the quality of work of humanitarian agencies, in particular non-governmental organizations (NGOs), and their accountability – especially their accountability to those affected by emergencies. Concerns about improving the professionalism of humanitarian aid work had been around since the late 1980s. The high-profile and publicly criticized international humanitarian response to the Rwanda crisis, beginning in 1994, meant that these concerns became much more widespread, with a greater sense of urgency that they needed to be addressed. The Sphere Project was one of a number of initiatives that aimed to do just that.[45]

Sphere is probably best known for developing minimum standards in five sectors that cover the basic and most common life-saving relief interventions required in many humanitarian emergencies: water supply and sanitation, nutrition, food aid, shelter and site planning, and health services. The Sphere Project also developed the *Humanitarian Charter*, regarded as 'the cornerstone' of Sphere, although referred to less frequently by agencies using Sphere.

> Based on the principles and provisions of international humanitarian law, international human-rights law, refugee law, and the Code of Conduct for the International Red Cross and Red Crescent Movement and NGOs in Disaster Relief, *the Charter describes the core principles that govern humanitarian action and asserts the right of populations to protection and assistance.* (Sphere 2000: 1).

The Sphere Project is intended to be relevant to the entire humanitarian sector, although it is mainly an NGO initiative. The extent to which there has been widespread buy-in is impressive. However it has also provoked significant controversy, and there have been strong critics of Sphere, particularly from a number of Francophone NGOs who have rejected Sphere (and in some cases begun to explore alternatives, for example the Quality Platform developed by some French NGOs). It has been a largely 'Northern'-driven policy initiative, although there are many agencies and institutions in the 'South' who are now strong supporters of Sphere and who have played a role in the piloting of Sphere.

There are two stories to tell when exploring the origins of Sphere.[46] The first story is about how Sphere was born. This is about understanding the different factors that led to the decision to launch Sphere, and in particular the relative influence of the 'Joint Evaluation of Emergency Assistance to Rwanda'. Study 3 of this evaluation reviewed the performance of humanitarian agencies in responding to the Rwanda crisis (Borton et al. 1996). Its findings were critical, and highlighted the need for NGOs to improve their performance. It recommended that there be some form of self-regulation or accreditation, and that systems for accountability needed to be strengthened. This seminal evaluation is often described as a piece of policy research,[47] and is considered as such in this project about bridging research and policy.

The second story, which of course is linked, is about how the Sphere Project developed in its first year of existence, particularly in terms of how buy-in and ownership were achieved (or, in some cases, not). This story throws up interesting and important lessons – for both researchers and policy makers – about the policy process, especially when success depends upon buy-in from a range of different actors.

The story of Sphere's origins

The overall context – the end of the Cold War and the changing face of humanitarianism

The end of the Cold War marked a turning point in the way that humanitarian emergencies were perceived, and in how the international humanitarian response was organized. The political causes of many emergencies were more widely and openly acknowledged,[48] as by proxy some wars came to an end, and as conflict became predominantly intra-state. The term 'complex political emergency' was coined, and has been used to describe many of the most serious humanitarian crises during the 1990s: the Kurdish crisis in 1991, the Rwanda crisis in the middle of the decade, and the Kosovo crisis at the end of the decade. There was a willingness to undertake military intervention in civil-war situations, ostensibly for humanitarian objectives, for example: to create safe havens for the Kurdish population in northern Iraq; in Somalia in 1992; and at the end of the decade in Kosovo. But this has been a very selective strategy and a controversial one (see for example Woodward (2001) and Macrae and Leader (2000)).

Humanitarian aid flows rose sharply and have doubled or even tripled during the 1990s compared with the previous decade. The number of international NGOs engaged in humanitarian work has increased substantially during the 1990s, particularly evident in the high-profile Rwanda and Kosovo crises. The amount of donor funding channelled through NGOs has also risen significantly, to around 25 per cent of their humanitarian aid flows by the end of the decade (Macrae 2002). Indeed, from the early 1990s onwards, humanitarian aid began to penetrate ever more difficult and contested environments, as humanitarian space[49] 'opened up' after the end of the Cold War.

Associated with this change in political context, and with the growth of the 'humanitarian industry', has been much more rigorous scrutiny and analysis. This was evident in the growing number of evaluations of humanitarian operations, commissioned by NGOs, by donor governments and by UN agencies. It was also evident in the increasingly sophisticated analysis of the causes and consequences of humanitarian emergencies, and in particular of the political/humanitarian interface (see for example Keen (1994)). This heralded a much more critical approach to emergency relief work, as it became apparent how the relief industry could become co-opted into the dynamics of violent conflict (see for example De Waal (1997)).

Early concerns about behaviour, standards and performance

The opening up of humanitarian space propelled agencies into ever more difficult conflict environments. As a result, they were faced with the day-to-day challenges and dilemmas of how to operate as an independent and impartial humanitarian actor – challenges that were familiar to agencies such as the International Committee of the Red Cross (ICRC), but less so to many NGOs, particularly those whose roots were in development rather than humanitarian work. Agencies began to grapple with the concept of humanitarian principles, **and** with the implications of inconsistency, where different agencies were working to different approaches and frameworks.

This also gave rise to concerns about agency performance. Staff within some of the more established humanitarian agencies became increasingly uneasy about the range of practice – and bad practice – among some NGOs, and about breakdown in cooperation at field level. For some, this uneasiness began during the widespread food crises and famines in sub-Saharan Africa in the mid-1980s, when they witnessed a range of undesirable emergency aid practices. Also, there was now more competition for donor funding as a subcontracting culture became more established, and as the number of NGOs increased. As NGOs began to 'globalize', differences in approach between NGOs originating in different countries became more apparent, for example in fundraising practices and in their use of the media.[50]

As the humanitarian industry grew in size and prominence, a number of initiatives were triggered within different agencies and in different parts of the world to codify and to develop some kind of written rules about how humanitarian agencies should work, to 're-establish' some of the basic principles. The French Red Cross Society proposed such an initiative to the International Federation of Red Cross and Red Crescent Societies (IFRC). At about the same time, the Emergencies Coordinator in Oxfam (Tony Vaux) decided that it was time to codify and put down in writing some of the basic, so far unwritten, principles to guide Oxfam staff in emergencies.[51] These efforts were combined under the auspices of the Steering Committee for Humanitarian Response (SCHR).[52] The Head of the IFRC's Disaster Policy Department (Peter Walker) worked with Oxfam's Emergencies Coordinator to produce the *Code of Conduct for the International Red Cross and Red Crescent Movement and NGOs in Disaster Relief* (RRN 1994). This sets out 10 basic principles of behaviour for agencies and their staff, and outlines what, in turn, agencies expect from the state. In 1994 ODI's Relief and Rehabilitation Network published the Code in a Network Paper (RRN 1994). However, there was no communications strategy to promote the code. Instead, it was 'lodged' with the IFRC, which kept a record of all the agencies that voluntarily signed up to the Code and reported on this in the annual World Disasters Report. Although the Code was widely welcomed, there was no means of verifying whether agencies were adhering to it or not, hampered by the very general nature of the principles outlined in the Code.

Meanwhile, on the other side of the Atlantic the relatively new Humanitarianism and War project was also grappling with the challenges of doing humanitarian work in conflict situations. It came up with the Providence principles and a code of conduct for practitioners, as 'fundamental objectives towards which humanitarian action should be oriented ... benchmarks against which performance can be measured and (to) help prevent energetic pragmatism from degenerating into unprincipled opportunism' (Minear and Weiss 1993: 5-6). It built upon an earlier piece of work by Minear (1988), commissioned by InterAction, on professionalism in US voluntary humanitarian assistance.

These are all indicative of a trend within the sector to clarify how best to work in situations of conflict (and, to a lesser extent, natural disasters), and how to achieve some kind of consensus and consistency, and to professionalize. On this latter point, it is worth noting another initiative in the early 1990s: to establish minimum standards and best practice in the recruitment and support of emergency staff. This was proposed by four British-based agencies in 1994, and eventually resulted in the *People in Aid Code of Best Practice*, published in 1997.[53] In many ways, the humanitarian system was 'coming of age'.[54]

The Rwanda crisis[55]

Against this backdrop, the Rwanda crisis happened in 1994. For at least three years beforehand, there had been fighting between the Rwandese

Patriotic Front (RPF) and the Government of Rwanda, causing the internal displacement of up to 900 000 people. Large-scale relief operations were launched in response. But it was the shooting down of President Habyarimana's plane on 6 April 1994 that triggered one of the worst humanitarian crises of the twentieth century. At the heart of the crisis was a genocide of horrifying magnitude: between 500 000 and 800 000 people were violently killed in a three- to four-month period.

The crisis was also associated with an unprecedented refugee movement. As the RPF gained control of more of the country, capturing the towns of Kigali, Butare and Ruhengeri by the middle of July, a massive exodus was triggered of around 850 000 people into Goma, then in eastern Zaïre (now DR Congo), over a four-day period between 14 and 18 July 1994. Almost all of those fleeing Rwanda were Hutu – civilians and the Force Armee Rwandaise (FAR). This huge refugee population arrived in a terrain of waterless lava fields, precipitating a sudden and massive humanitarian crisis. Within a few days cholera had broken out, claiming the lives of around 30 000 people within barely two weeks – the highest mortality rate ever recorded in a humanitarian emergency. Overall, the combination of cholera, dysentery, dehydration and violence claimed around 80 000 refugee lives. A total of about 1.5 million refugees fled Rwanda to neighbouring countries as the RPF took over government in Kigali.

The international humanitarian response to the Rwanda crisis, and the critique

The largest-ever international humanitarian operation was launched in response to the Rwanda crisis, specifically to the refugee movements outside the country.[56] It cost an estimated US$1.4 billion between April and December 1994 alone, and involved about 250 NGOs (Borton et al. 1996). It was also one of the most high-profile humanitarian response operations. The Public Information Officer for the United Nations High Commission for Refugees (UNHCR) in Goma estimated that there were around 500 journalists and media technicians in the Goma area by the end of July 1994 (quoted in Borton et al. 1996). This high-profile media coverage undoubtedly fuelled the massive response by governments and the public around the world.

Overall, according to Borton et al. (1996: 10),

the response contained many highly commendable efforts ... [including] the courage and commitment shown by UN, ICRC and NGO personnel in extremely difficult and often dangerous situations ... Given the magnitude and scale of the population movements and the distance of the beneficiary populations from coastal ports, this was a substantial achievement.

Despite this huge investment of resources, the failure to prevent the highest mortality rates ever recorded in a refugee population – in Goma in late July – haunted many organizations and their staff for years to come. The Rwanda evaluation concluded that:

there was frequently an imbalance in resource provision between preparedness and capacity-increasing measures, on the one hand, and response measures in the face of a pressing humanitarian need on the other, particularly where such needs were well covered by the media. (Borton et al. 1996: 157).

After this initial catastrophe, when mortality rates were eventually brought under control, agencies were still faced with the massive task of servicing the huge refugee camps along the Rwanda/Zaïre border in inhospitable volcanic terrain. Numerous agencies were involved, working under the media spotlight. Fault lines that already existed in the international humanitarian community were magnified dramatically in this hothouse of a relief operation. For example, the divergence of standards and experience between NGOs quickly became apparent, as much to the agencies themselves as to external observers and critics. According to the Rwanda evaluation:

Whilst many NGOs performed impressively, providing a high quality of care and services, a number performed in an unprofessional and irresponsible manner that resulted not only in duplication and wasted resources but may also have contributed to an unnecessary loss of life. (Borton et al. 1996: 161).

The media, particularly in Britain, vociferously picked up on the critique of humanitarian agencies, mainly focused on NGOs. The critique focused not only on poor performance of NGOs, but also, and more controversially, on the appropriate role and mandate of international NGOs (see, for example, African Rights (1994)). They were accused of indiscriminately feeding the killers, the '*genocidaires*', and thus fuelling violence and conflict in the region. The debate was heated, widespread and often soul-searching. It took place in a number of different forums:

- within and among NGOs, where there was a lot of questioning and self-criticism;
- in the media, as mentioned above;
- within and amongst donor and other (e.g. UN) agencies, partly triggering the decision to launch the Joint Evaluation of Emergency Assistance to Rwanda.

Key issues raised in the debate, and relevant to this present case study, included:

- the poor performance of some NGOs and the general lack of professionalism;
- the proliferation of NGOs and lack of regulation;

- appropriate demarcation of responsibility and roles between humanitarian agencies and politicians, that is who was responsible for separating the '*genocidaires*' from the bona fide refugees;
- the rights of those affected by the emergency (although this was articulated explicitly by only a few people, it was implicit in much of the ongoing debate).

Rwanda evaluation

In October 1994, six months after the genocide began, the head of Danida's Evaluation Secretariat (Niels Dabelstein) presented a proposal to the Development Assistance Committee's (DAC) Expert Group on Aid Evaluation to carry out an evaluation of the international response to the Rwanda crisis. Although a number of members of the group were enthusiastic, others were not. No consensus decision was reached. However, Dabelstein continued to pursue the idea, initially in an unofficial meeting after the DAC Expert Group meeting, and subsequently, a month later in Copenhagen, with a much broader group of agencies, including bilateral donors, UN agencies, international organizations and NGOs. All had a stake in the response to the Rwanda crisis and thus in the evaluation. An ambitious, multi-stakeholder process was the result.

A comprehensive structure for the evaluation was put in place, which proved to be very effective (see 'Discussion' below). A Steering Committee was established, representing 38 agencies and organizations.[57] NGOs were represented by umbrella organizations such as InterAction, SCHR and Voluntary Organisations in Cooperation in Emergencies (VOICE), and a Management Group was established, comprising members of the evaluation departments of five donor agencies (from Sweden, Norway, Denmark, the UK and the USA). The chair of the Steering Committee (Niels Dabelstein) was also the chair of the evaluation's Management Group.

The members of the evaluation's Management Group played a key role in drafting the terms of reference for the evaluation, which were broadened out at an early stage from a narrow (and conventional) focus on efficiency and effectiveness to include, explicitly, political and conflict-management issues. In the words of Niels Dabelstein: 'The terms of reference were comprehensive, and the special interests of the agencies were largely accommodated' (Dabelstein 1996: 4).

The speed at which this international multi-stakeholder evaluation got off the ground is remarkable. In December 1994, the Steering Committee of the Joint Evaluation met for the first time in Washington, and approved the final terms of reference. By January 1995, the evaluation teams had been appointed and started work.

ODI was awarded the contract for Study 3 of the evaluation, the largest study, on 'Humanitarian Aid and Effects'. A 20-person team was put together, led by John Borton. The 'usual' evaluation approach was used in gathering information, albeit on a huge scale. For example, the database of documentation collected for the evaluation eventually exceeded more than 2500 catalogued items, and 620 individuals were interviewed. A total of 1122 days' work (or four person years) were put into the evaluation by the team members. Two field trips were made to the region: a 20-day reconnaissance mission, and then substantial fieldwork over a two-month period.

In mid-October 1995, the first draft of Study 3's findings was submitted to the evaluation's Management Group and subsequently to the Steering Committee. More than 100 pages of comments were received and responded to. The final report of the Rwanda evaluation was published in March 1996 (Borton et al. 1996).

Study 3 made two sets of recommendations specifically targeted at NGOs. The first set of recommendations was to do with improving NGO performance. Having noted the unprofessional, and at times dangerous, performance of some NGOs, Study 3 commended the NGO initiative to develop a set of standards (the embryonic Sphere Project), and recommended that there be some form of regulation or enforcement, either through self-managed regulation, or through an international accreditation system. It also recommended that donor organizations give greater support to NGO emergency-training and lesson-learning activities. The second, and related, set of recommendations was to do with improving accountability. The availability and quality of performance data and reporting by NGOs (and other agencies) was found to be highly variable, and often incomparable. This gave further weight to the recommendation that there be some means of enforcing standards and codes of conduct. Alternatively it was recommended that a unit within the UN's Department for Humanitarian Affairs (UN DHA) should play a monitoring or even an ombudsman function, or an independent organization be appointed as ombudsman (Borton et al. 1996).

After such a momentous evaluation of the response to such a major crisis, a formal process of follow-up seemed important to the team leaders of the different evaluation studies, and to the evaluation's Management Group. It was agreed that the Steering Committee of the Rwanda evaluation should meet again, one year after publication, to review its impact. So a formal follow-up group, known as JEFF (Joint Evaluation Follow-up, Monitoring and Facilitation Network) was established in May 1996, comprising 11 members drawn from the Management Group, from the study team leaders and from the Steering Committee. JEFF's principal objective was to monitor the discussion and follow-up action on the Rwanda evaluation, in as many forums as possible. It was also involved in disseminating the findings and recommendations from the Joint Evaluation. Its members made more than 20 separate formal presentations, including at a two-day conference in Kigali. JEFF's findings were presented to the Steering Committee in early 1997. They focussed principally on the extent to which the evaluation's 64 recommendations, contained in the synthesis report (Eriksson 1996), had been taken up. JEFF's final report was printed in June 1997, although it was not formally published (JEFF 1997). The report noted the SCHR/InterAction initiative to establish 'a major project to develop a set of common minimum standards for humanitarian response, based on the rights of beneficiaries' (JEFF 1997: 39). It awarded category 'D' to the response to the recommendation of 'Self-regulation through improved agency coordination and standards within NGO community'. Category D meant that the recommendation had been formally discussed and resolution reached and/or action taken.

The beginnings of Sphere

Sphere's origins date from before the publication of the Rwanda evaluation findings, stemming from two different initiatives on either side of the Atlantic.

In June 1995, InterAction – the umbrella body for US development and humanitarian NGOs – submitted a proposal to the US Office of Foreign Disaster Assistance (OFDA) for the 'Development of training for PVOs in complex emergencies', specifically to improve their response capability in the wake of the Rwanda crisis. Three months later, InterAction held a PVO (Private Voluntary Organization) conference on disaster response. Commitment to best practice and defining minimum standards for operational response were both seen as important ways of improving operational effectiveness. InterAction subsequently secured funding from the Ford Foundation to develop an NGO Field Cooperation Protocol, and to develop best practice for disaster work. This was seen as 'an integral part of our community's wider effort to enhance performance and professionalism in disaster response'.[58]

A few months later, on the European side of the Atlantic, Peter Walker of IFRC, and Nick Stockton, the new Oxfam Emergencies Coordinator, had come together in various meetings in the wake of the Rwanda crisis, and had agreed that something needed to be done to improve the quality and accountability of NGO emergency work. Both individuals were also members of the Steering Committee of the Joint Rwanda Evaluation, representing IFRC and SCHR respectively. In February 1996, they submitted a proposal to SCHR for a project entitled 'Towards quality and accountability standards in humanitarian relief'. They proposed establishing a set of technical standards in four sectors, based on the rights of those affected by emergencies.

Shortly afterwards, in April 1996, discussions began between InterAction and the authors of the SCHR proposal. In early October 1996, SCHR hosted a meeting in Geneva to discuss all ongoing work on best practice. This was attended by representatives of all the main NGO umbrella organizations – InterAction, the International Council of Voluntary Agencies (ICVA), VOICE, Action by Churches Together (ACT) – and by representatives of a number of individual NGOs such as *Medecins Sans Frontières* (MSF) and CARE International. This was the critical meeting that brought together the two initiatives that had started on either side of the Atlantic. It resulted in an agreement to consolidate all work on standards and best practice within the framework of the SCHR project, which was now called 'Quality and accountability standards in humanitarian relief'.[59] At this point the governance structure for the project was agreed upon, which incorporated two InterAction members into the Project Committee.

Also in October 1996, fundraising for Sphere began in earnest. Recruitment for the first project manager also commenced. Susan Purdin was appointed and took up her post in Geneva in July 1997. When she joined, the title of the 'Sphere Project' was coined, and the first one-year project officially began.

Sphere gets off the ground

The Sphere Project came into being very quickly. It is useful to trace how this happened, and in particular how buy-in was achieved.

Having recently experienced the inclusive process of the Joint Rwanda Evaluation, Peter Walker and Nick Stockton proposed an inclusive process for managing (and for funding) Sphere. The Project Committee (as it was then called) initially comprised all SCHR member agencies. When this became a collaborative venture with InterAction, two InterAction members joined the committee. ICRC, ICVA and VOICE all became observer members (until 2001 when ICRC joined SCHR). Thus, all the main NGO umbrella organizations were involved. A number of UN agencies indicated their interest in, and desire to get involved in Sphere, but in early 1997 a policy decision was made to keep this as an NGO initiative, although UN agencies did contribute to the drafting of the minimum standards.

With the arrival of the project manager, Phase 1 of Sphere got off the ground. Four SCHR agencies and one InterAction agency were identified to lead each of the five sectors. A staff member from each of those agencies was seconded to Sphere for a period of six months, to lead a working group of sectoral experts and to put together a first draft of the proposed minimum standards. This was also a very inclusive process, involving more than 700 people and over 200 agencies. For most of the sectors there was a small core group of experts who provided most input. This was supplemented by e-mail discussion, open to anyone, which enabled large numbers to participate, albeit sometimes very briefly. There were regular meetings of all the sector managers, appropriately held in different cities in Europe or the USA, and very regular communication and updates between the project manager and the respective sector managers. The short time period allocated for drafting the sectoral standards put a lot of pressure on the sector managers, but also meant that Sphere took shape very quickly, and could not get bogged down in too much detail.

A few months later, in early 1998, a working group was established to draft the Humanitarian Charter, revising an earlier draft prepared by the Sphere project manager in August 1997.[60] This addressed the rights-based component of Sphere. In the wake of the Rwanda crisis, how could a stronger basis for the 'right to life with dignity' be established? Also mindful of the recent Rwanda experience, the distinction between combatants and non-combatants was restated, as well as the principle of non-refoulement. This was the more controversial part of Sphere, particularly with InterAction representing US NGOs, who feared the litigation implications of a rights-based charter, and therefore preferred to focus on the technical standards to improve quality.[61] Oxfam, IFRC, ICRC, InterAction and Save the Children Fund-UK (SCF-UK) were involved in drafting the charter. In May 1998, after much discussion, the Sphere Management Committee finally completed and approved the charter. But this was too late to feed into, or to influence the minimum standards part of the project; in April, editing had begun on the first draft of the minimum standards document. Also, conceptual understanding of what a rights-based approach meant in practice, and therefore its implications for setting technical standards, was rather unclear. The debate about a rights-based approach was still in its infancy at this stage and five years later the sector is still grappling with many of these issues.

Explanation

The policy context: politics and institutions

Political, social and economic structures and interests
In the first half of the 1990s, the policy context was becoming ever more conducive to an initiative such as Sphere. As described under 'Evidence' below, humanitarian agencies were faced with increasingly challenging operational issues – for example, how to operate when there was no state, how to operate in close conjunction with the military, and how to ensure humanitarian aid did not fuel conflict. As the analysis and discourse became increasingly politicized and sophisticated, the days of unquestioning acceptance of the 'good work' of humanitarian agencies were over. The sense of discomfort felt by some agencies and individuals about the range of standards and performance to which different agencies operated, and the moral and political dilemmas of providing humanitarian assistance within war zones were becoming more evident and familiar as more agencies entered the fray.

Although impossible to prove, in the early 1990s it seems unlikely that these concerns alone would have been strong enough to trigger an initiative on the scale of the Sphere Project. Instead, it was the unprecedented scale and intensity of the refugee crisis in Rwanda, and the unparalleled international humanitarian response, under the spotlight of the international media, that magnified the fault lines within the humanitarian system to an extraordinary degree, and did so very publicly. That was a major factor in creating the momentum for change, and openness to radical change. That momentum was particularly strong within the NGO community, which was the most visible part of the much-criticized international humanitarian system. Indeed, in the words of one of the members of the Joint Rwanda Evaluation team, 'the donors got off lightly'. A widely accepted and oft-repeated message reverberating within the NGO community was the mantra: 'we have to get our act together'. Some donor representatives reinforced this mantra in strong messages such as: 'if you don't do it, we (the donors) will'. And this message was forcefully communicated in a number of meetings following publication of the Joint Rwanda Evaluation. The Rwanda evaluation was seen by many in the NGO sector to have opened up the possibility of external regulation.[62]

In short, there were strong push factors to do something to improve NGO performance. Few individuals (and agencies) capitalized upon that in order to get their ideas accepted and eventually to launch the Sphere initiative.

Assumptions and attitudes

Most humanitarian actors involved in the response to the crisis in Rwanda shared a common analysis that performance by some NGOs had been poor, that lives had been lost as a result, and that something had to be done to raise the quality of humanitarian (in particular relief) assistance. Thereafter, the analysis started to diverge. For example, was it a problem of too many NGOs, of poor coordination, or of lack of regulation? Hence, there was some divergence of view about an appropriate solution and, in the words of some commentators, there was a lack of vision about what to do. However, when performance standards were proposed, it transpired that the majority of NGOs (on both sides of the Atlantic) were in favour.

Indeed, within SCHR, the two initiators of Sphere, who knew how critical the forthcoming Rwanda evaluation was going to be about NGO performance, used the threat of heavy-handed donor action to generate support within SCHR for their quality and accountability proposal. Similarly, within InterAction the threat of external regulation provided an impetus to develop the 'Field Cooperation Protocol'.

There was some early concern that setting standards would disadvantage or discriminate against small agencies, in favour of the larger more established ones. This concern was articulated on both sides of the Atlantic.

The more significant objections to the ideas being put forward in the Sphere initiative appear to fall into two broad camps. First, there were those who thought that what was being proposed was not achievable (for example, SCF-UK). This debate happened early on, in 1996. It particularly revolved around the implementation of Sphere and regulation. There were also concerns about the potential cost of the initiative – a concern also of the Lutheran World Federation (LWF). However, both these sets of concerns abated – the former as it became clear that regulation would not be incorporated into Sphere, and the latter when it became clear that donors were prepared to fund the initiative.

The second and more fundamental opposition came from those agencies that were opposed ideologically to the way that the Sphere

Project developed. This form of opposition is most closely associated with MSF and with a number of other Francophone NGOs, and has been most evident at headquarters' level.[63] Different individuals have articulated the arguments with different emphases, but a central cause for concern has been the apparent isolation of technical standards from humanitarian principles in what was regarded, uncomfortably by these agencies, as an institutionalization of the Sphere process. When MSF initially perceived Sphere to be a relatively low-key exercise to share technical guidelines and policies between different operational agencies, they were prepared to participate (albeit with reservations about what such an exercise would achieve). However, as the process gathered momentum, and the rather short and minimalist (in MSF's eyes) Humanitarian Charter was added, MSF became increasingly concerned that a highly technical approach to humanitarian action was being promoted, in a high profile way, at the expense of the more difficult and pressing political issues (personal communication, Jean-Marie Kindermans):

In attempting to achieve minimum standards for humanitarian action, there is a risk that humanitarian action may simply become a technical and purely professional pursuit. (Orbinski 1998: 2)

MSF and some of the other agencies also had concerns about how Sphere would be used, for instance by donor governments in evaluations. If donors insisted that their implementing partners adhere to Sphere standards, would their partners be locked into ever-closer relationships with donor governments that may be pursuing political rather than humanitarian objectives, thus compromising the independence of their partner NGOs (Terry 2000)? And by focusing on NGOs, Sphere was in danger of deflecting attention away from where it was really needed – with ruling authorities and the international community who are ultimately, and formally, responsible for providing and protecting humanitarian space (Orbinski 1998). A further criticism levelled at Sphere was its failure to address issues of protection.

This more fundamental opposition did not really surface until 1998, a few months before the Sphere project was launched, when a number of Francophone agencies expressed their disquiet and concerns in what became famously known as the 'French letter'. For a short while it threatened to derail the Sphere process. Should the launch proceed as planned? How could MSF and other significant humanitarian agencies be kept on board? But eventually the decision was taken to go ahead. Although there were attempts to keep these agencies on board, eventually the differences became too great and MSF withdrew from the Sphere Management Committee. Thereafter, positions became polarized and the debate has, at times, been acrimonious.

Although Study 3 of the Rwanda evaluation commended and supported the development of standards, it went further than any NGOs did, at the time or since, in recommending some form of self-managed regulation or accreditation of NGOs to monitor compliance. NGOs have consistently shied away from this, whether on the Sphere Management Committee or outside.[64] There has been an inherent reluctance to go down this route, mainly through fear of the implications. To the frustration of some, the push factors that resulted in Sphere did not seem to have been strong enough for this extra step to be taken. However, during the period of research and writing of this case study, there has been an important development that may signal a shift. The Humanitarian Accountability Project (HAP), which evolved out of the Humanitarian Ombudsman project, has just been established as a self-regulatory body with the specific objective of accrediting its members, particularly in relation to accountability to beneficiaries. The full impact and implications of this development remain to be seen.

Evidence

The researchers and their methodology
The team that carried out Study 3 of the Joint Rwanda Evaluation was generally well respected. A number of the team members had a research background and came from research institutes, and were thus seen as more objective. Others had strong operational experience, or a combination of both. Many of them were well established in their respective fields. This gave the team, and thus their findings, credibility.

As detailed above, in the 'Rwanda evaluation' section, the team adopted a fairly thorough approach to the evaluation, combining an extensive documentation review with many interviews in the field and at agency headquarters. Indeed, the Study 3 team leader observed that:

Study 3 was a veritable Rolls Royce of humanitarian evaluation with unprecedented scope and unprecedented resources available to it, and this made it a privileged and professionally extremely rewarding process ... [It] meant we were able to afford what other evaluation teams would regard as luxuries: a large multi-disciplinary team of very high-calibre individuals; an approach that at times bore a closer resemblance to research than to conventional consultancy ... and a funded follow-up process that enabled some of those involved in the team to 'sell' the report and its key messages within the humanitarian system as well as to monitor and comment upon the reactions to the report and its recommendations by the principal humanitarian agencies. (Borton 2001: 99).

The credibility of the final product was enhanced by the fact that the evaluation was more akin to a research project than to conventional consultancy. The Chair of the Evaluation Steering Committee commended its combination of thoroughness and pragmatism. In his view, the team did a good job in presenting their findings in a practical and accessible form for policy makers, using research methods but without a lot of theorizing (personal communication). This was ascribed to a combination of guidance from the Rwanda Evaluation Management

Group about how best to present the findings, and that many of the evaluators had field experience and therefore a more practical orientation.

However, the team members were mostly European, along with two North Americans. There were no African members – 'the cause of subsequent criticism of the team and the source of some embarrassment to members of the team' (Borton 2001: 85). At short notice, they had difficulty identifying African researchers who were familiar with the Great Lakes region, yet who could also be rigorously objective in that highly polarized context. This was hampered by the fact that neither the Management Group nor the evaluation team leader had an existing network of African emergency evaluators. Evaluation had tended to be somewhat 'Northern'-dominated.

Credibility of the evidence
Generally, the findings of the Study 3 evaluation team were regarded as highly credible, for a number of reasons. First, the report clearly laid out and analysed what most humanitarian agencies already knew to be the case, but it did so in 'a cooler-headed [way] than was happening elsewhere' (personal communication, Nick Stockton). Second, it was regarded as 'categoric, clear and well-documented' (personal communication, Peter Walker), partly related to the research approach that had been adopted. Crucially, at a time of heated debate and public criticism of aid agencies, the evaluation provided an independent and objective analysis.

Nevertheless, there were organizations and agencies who disputed the findings of Study 3 (and other reports) of the evaluation, but they were mostly agencies that were heavily criticized in the report. For example, the French government pulled out of the evaluation's Steering Committee in protest at the criticism of the French government. And UNHCR vociferously disputed criticism of their preparedness for the refugee influx to Goma. This was one occasion where the objectivity of the evaluation team member who had prepared most of the evidence against UNHCR came into question. A lengthy process of dialogue and consultation between the evaluation team leader and UNHCR ensued, not entirely satisfactorily in the view of the team leader (Borton 2001). It was a small minority of agencies who questioned the credibility of the evidence.

Despite this, the structure for managing and directing the evaluation proved critical to safeguarding the independence of the findings of the Study 3 team. This was because of the role of the evaluation's Management Group; most of the agencies being evaluated were represented on the evaluation's Steering Committee and therefore the Management Group was a very important intermediary and buffer, 'in several instances shield[ing] the teams from undue pressure from the agencies and governments' (Borton 2001: 100). For example, some members of the Steering Committee (the UN Secretariat, UNHCR and the Government of France) wanted parts of the reports that were highly critical to be removed or edited. 'The Management Group resisted this pressure by expressing full confidence in the quality of the work and continued to ensure the teams' independence' (Dabelstein 1996: 291). The Management Group also played an important quality-control function, demanding rigorous analysis from the evaluation teams, and supporting evidence. Borton comments that:

> *The fact that the members of the Management Group were all heads of evaluation departments in bilateral donor organisations was helpful in this regard, for they combined the status of being within donor organisations with a strong tradition of objectivity.* (Borton 2001: 100).

Impact
The Joint Rwanda Evaluation had a huge impact on the humanitarian aid sector, immediately and in the following years, for a number of reasons. First, the failure to prevent a crisis of such scale and intensity shocked the many actors involved and prompted major debate. As a result, there was a willingness among most actors to learn the lessons (although also some defensiveness, alluded to above). The scale and process of the Joint Rwanda Evaluation was somehow proportionate to the crisis. In the view of the Study 3 team leader, the evaluators were being encouraged to 'think big' because of the widespread view that things had to change. This was an opportunity to think radically when making recommendations.

The Joint Rwanda Evaluation was also very high-profile – 'it was almost front-page news', in the words of one interviewee. It was taken seriously and read by many, and so agencies had to be seen to be responding.

Second, the process of the Joint Rwanda Evaluation seems to have played a key role in influencing policy makers, partly because they were heavily involved throughout, and also because discussions were on-going – with the evaluators and among themselves – especially once the draft evaluation reports were available. Involving so many different actors in the Steering Committee – UN agencies, donor government agencies, NGOs, etc. – meant that system-wide discussion was going on, probably to a greater extent than ever before. This seems to have increased momentum for the progression of recommendations – for example, some donor representatives threatening to take action if the NGOs did not 'get their act together'.

The findings and recommendations in the evaluation were clearly presented, and were often targeted specifically at particular groups of actors – for example, at donor agencies or NGOs. This was backed up by the JEFF process, whereby members of the evaluation were able to 'sell' the recommendations to different audiences.

However, this does not mean that all the recommendations were taken on board. On the question of improved performance and accountability, one of the proposed options that the UN DHA serve as ombudsman to improve the accountability of humanitarian agencies was 'laughed out of court' because it was regarded as unworkable.

Although Study 3 gave real impetus to the early Sphere initiative, its recommendation of some form of regulation or enforcement to ensure improvement in NGO performance has never yet seen the light of day. The Sphere Project document refers to 'the Humanitarian Charter and the Minimum Standards contributing to an operational framework for accountability in humanitarian assistance efforts' (Sphere 2000: 6). In reality however this has been very limited, partly because of concerns about its achievability, but mainly because of fear of such a radical step. This is also the rock on which the original concept of the ombudsman project foundered.

Links: influence and legitimacy

Key actors and individuals
There are a number of key actors in this story about how the Sphere Project came into being. First, it is worth drawing attention to the way that the Joint Rwanda Evaluation was carried out and to some key features, as these contributed to the status and legitimacy of the final findings and recommendations.

- The fact that the DAC Expert Group on Aid Evaluation was unable to agree, by consensus, to take on the evaluation, fortuitously meant that it became a truly international exercise, with buy-in from a much broader range of agencies. 'Once the critical mass was established no one could stay out – it could be embarrassing for any one agency not to participate' (Dabelstein 1996: 4).
- The evaluation was effectively commissioned by the respective evaluation departments of different donor agencies, represented on the Rwanda Evaluation Management Group, but this was done with the support and input of policy makers who were represented on the evaluation's Steering Committee. Thus, a critical and cooperative link was established right at the outset between those who commissioned the 'research', and the policy-makers at whom the findings were directed.
- Finally, the vision and drive of the Head of Danida's Evaluation Secretariat was pivotal in taking forward such an ambitious project. The lack of a system-wide evaluation since has been remarked upon a number of times in the Active Learning Network for Accountability and Performance in Humanitarian Action (ALNAP). It is partly attributed to the enormous management task that no individual (or donor department) is prepared to shoulder. It may also be due to a wariness of what such a major evaluation entails for individual agencies, in terms of the very public scrutiny to which they are likely to be subjected.

Second, within the NGO community, umbrella organizations played a critical role in translating concerns about NGO performance into action – in particular InterAction in the USA and SCHR in Europe. They provided a forum for inter-agency debate and for inter-agency initiatives, at a time when a system-wide response was clearly required. In some ways, this marked a 'coming of age' of these umbrella organizations. InterAction in the USA was probably more established than equivalent organizations in Europe, and took the first steps towards an inter-agency initiative to identify best practice. By coming together, SCHR and InterAction provided the opportunity (and legitimacy) to launch a global policy initiative, with which other umbrella organizations quickly became associated, for example ICVA and VOICE.

Third, a constructive axis existed between IFRC and Oxfam. Although this depended very much on the work of particular individuals (both in the case of the Code of Conduct in 1994 and in the case of Sphere), the fact that these individuals represented two very different but respected agencies was significant. Whilst Oxfam was a UK-based NGO with a strong record in emergency work, IFRC was more international, with a legitimacy based upon the network of Red Cross and Red Crescent societies around the world.

As far as individuals are concerned, the two key individuals who drove Sphere in its early days were Peter Walker (of IFRC) and Nick Stockton (of Oxfam). They both played a key role in the development and implementation of Sphere, and in promoting ownership and buy-in within the NGO community. According to many interviewees, Sphere would not have happpened without them. What seems especially important was the complementary nature of their skills and approach. Whilst one had a strong vision of what Sphere could be and was able to put a strong intellectual case for the centrality of rights and the Humanitarian Charter, the other, while sharing the vision, was particularly adept at understanding the politics of the international humanitarian system and therefore piloting the idea of Sphere through the rapids of organizational politics. Both were articulate and good presenters: they were able to make a convincing case to colleagues from other agencies. It is also significant that these two individuals were given the 'space' by their respective agencies to develop and run with this idea.

The role of others, such as Jim Bishop of InterAction, was also important in terms of facilitating and encouraging buy-in, in this case among US NGOs. Other key individuals were members of the Study 3 evaluation team, and in particular John Borton, the team leader. They are credited with having done a very thorough job, making clear and in some cases quite radical recommendations for what needed to change in the international humanitarian system.

When the Sphere Project finally did get underway, the role of its first project manager (Susan Purdin) was critical in guiding and managing the process of putting the standards and Charter together. Many of the terms and parameters had still to be defined – for example, what constituted an emergency, and how to differentiate between standards and indicators. Many commentators credit Susan Purdin for holding together this inclusive but challenging and time-pressured process.

Roles and relationships

It is not just the role of the individuals that is important; it is the way in which they interacted that resulted in this system-wide initiative. As previously mentioned, the process of the Joint Rwanda Evaluation was very important in bringing together the evaluators/researchers, policy makers and practitioners. Also, the key individuals mentioned in the previous section were all working to a very similar agenda. Thus, the idea for the Sphere Project (although not the name) was already being discussed before the evaluation report was published. The evaluators were aware of this, and made a point of supporting this initiative as a step towards improving NGO performance; this is reflected in their final text. Meanwhile, both Nick Stockton and Peter Walker, as members of the evaluation's Steering Committee, knew from draft reports how critical the evaluation would be of NGO performance, and were able to use this knowledge to persuade NGOs to sign up to the 'Quality and accountability standards' project. There was similar pressure within InterAction. Thus, there was a clear synergy of interest and of motivation.

It is interesting to note, however, that efforts to build on the positive experience of the Rwanda evaluation, by establishing an 'international standing capacity' to 'provide objective and critical analysis, monitoring, review, reporting and dialogue on the international community's progress in preventing, mitigating and resolving violent conflict'[65] did not come to fruition. Although some of those who had been involved in the evaluation developed the idea, there was not sufficient backing for it to get off the ground.

The experience of the evaluation process had a direct influence on the process that was put in place to manage and take forward the Sphere Project. Achieving agency buy-in was a very specific objective. In the words of Sphere's first project manager: 'we always said the process was as important as the product'. The formation and regular meeting of the Sphere Management Committee, with its observer members, was one part of this, to some extent modelled on the evaluation process. A public relations/advocacy plan for the 'performance standards project' was drafted early on, initially targeted at as many NGOs as possible to encourage their participation and support for the project. Also important was the highly consultative process of putting the Sphere standards together, described above. The sector managers played a key role in raising awareness of Sphere in developing countries by running a series of consultative meetings in Africa, Asia and the Balkans. The funding strategy that was put in place for Sphere was again designed to achieve maximum buy-in. All agencies on the Sphere Management Committee took responsibility for following up with particular donors, thus consolidating the sense of ownership, and also presenting an international image of Sphere. The decision to request funding from many different donors was a strategic one, so that no single donor 'owned' Sphere, but many had bought into it. The NGOs also contributed funds themselves – literally buying in.

Legitimacy
The legitimacy and credibility of the evaluators/researchers is described under 'Evidence: credibility and communication' below. The key architects and advocates of Sphere – Peter Walker and Nick Stockton – established their legitimacy partly as a result of their senior positions within two large and respected agencies. Also, both had field experience and were respected in the policy arena. When it came to putting the Sphere standards together, it was important that each of the sector managers were 'experts' in their field, already tapped into existing sectoral networks,[66] thus reinforcing their legitimacy. However, not all the sector managers saw their role in the same way. Some played more of a facilitator role, some more of an 'expert' role.

Discussion

The context: politics and institutions

In this particular case study, the key policy makers came from the NGO sector, which is not unusual in the humanitarian aid sector. A lot of innovation at the operational end of the spectrum has taken place within NGOs, not within donor organizations (which are rarely operational in humanitarian emergencies), although donor agencies have played a critical funding role. For example, many of the policy initiatives associated with the drive to improve the quality of humanitarian operations have come out of the NGO sector, including Sphere, People in Aid, and the Humanitarian Ombudsman project. Interestingly in the Sphere case, the role of officials within donor agencies was to advocate change, if necessary using implied threats. However, the change they advocated was mainly external to their own agencies/departments. The inertia commonly associated with large bureaucracies is more evident in relation to change **within** those donor organizations (Clay and Schaffer 1984). For instance, the concept of 'good donorship' has taken another six years to come onto the agenda since discussions began in the NGO sector.

In the immediate aftermath of the Rwanda crisis there was a lot of room for manoeuvre within the humanitarian aid system. Discomfort and disaffection with NGO performance had been around for a few years beforehand, but became much more urgent and widespread as a consequence of the crisis. This seems to be quite typical of the humanitarian system, which is most responsive to change under pressure when the push factors are strong. This was never more so than after the Rwanda crisis, with its high-profile media coverage and criticism. There were simultaneous initiatives for change on both sides of the Atlantic. At this stage, the discussions and initiatives were mainly Northern-driven, which is again typical of how the humanitarian aid system is structured. Most international humanitarian NGOs have their roots and headquarters in the North – in Europe or North America – and this is where most policy discussion takes place. Southern-based

NGOs are represented by umbrella organizations such as ICVA, LWF, Caritas Internationalis or IFRC. Southern-based international humanitarian agencies, such as African Humanitarian Action (AHA), argue that they do not have the luxury of engaging in this kind of policy discourse because of lack of resources and therefore being tightly locked into a contract culture with donors and others.[67]

The strength of the push factors meant that the Sphere policy decision was of the 'fundamental and emergent' type (Lindquist 2001). It goes beyond a questioning of underlying assumptions, to propose a broad new vision based on rights and professionalism. A number of the NGO policy initiatives to improve quality and accountability fall into this category. This appears to be in contrast with the predominant nature of humanitarian policy change within donor organizations, which is more 'incremental' in nature (Lindquist 2001),[68] but this requires further research to be conclusive. However, the story of how Sphere came into being does seem to follow Kuhn's thesis of a paradigm 'bumbl[ing] along quite happily making sense of the world until the puzzles it cannot solve become so numerous that it causes a crisis' (Crewe and Young 2002: 9). Crudely, in this case study the paradigm that caused the crisis was of unregulated humanitarian agencies 'doing good' and meeting the needs of those affected. In the goldfish bowl of Goma in 1994–5, it became starkly apparent that this was not the case. Three new paradigms emerged. The first has developed into the rights-based approach, where the starting point is the right of the affected person rather than an agency's assessment of that person's need. This is at the heart of the *Humanitarian Charter*. The second paradigm is to do with professionalizing and improving the quality of performance of NGOs – represented in Sphere as the minimum standards. The third paradigm involves strengthening the accountability of humanitarian agencies, specifically NGOs. In the Rwanda evaluation, this was captured in the recommendation that there be some form of accreditation or regulation of NGOs. Although it has been discussed many times, this is the paradigm that has resulted in least action. This is evidence of the 'street bureaucrats' (the operational NGOs) ultimately making the decision about which of the researchers' recommendations for policy change they were prepared to accept: designing aspirational standards to improve quality, but not going as far as regulation or accreditation (although there may be some shift in this direction through HAP).

Evidence: credibility and communication

The Rwanda evaluation fulfilled two criteria regarded as important if research is to influence policy. It was good-quality research and widely regarded as such, and it was effectively disseminated through the JEFF process. Many of the reasons why it was good-quality research have been described previously in this chapter, including the fact that it was a 'Rolls Royce' of an evaluation. The researchers/evaluators in this case study defy the ivory-tower image. Most of them also had operational experience, and this seems to have been important in terms of their credibility with NGO policy makers, and in terms of their ability to communicate with these operationally oriented policy makers. Also important was the role of the evaluation's Management Group as a kind of peer review/quality-control mechanism.

Another notable feature of Study 3 was its ability to make the connections from the detailed evidence of what did and did not work to system-wide analysis and recommendations. Much has been written about the temptation for researchers to simplify their messages in order to have maximum impact. Study 3 put across its recommendations in a concise and simplified way, but they were backed up by a great deal of detail.

Nevertheless, it is worth mentioning how one of the evaluation's key messages has been distorted and misinterpreted by policy makers, in particular donor policy makers. The message was '... that humanitarian aid cannot be a substitute for political action', making the case for increased coherence between political and humanitarian efforts, so that the mistakes of the response to the Rwanda crisis would not be repeated. It was the absence and ineffectiveness of the political response that had compromised protection of and assistance to the victims in Rwanda. Macrae and Leader (2000) have demonstrated how this evolved into the 'new humanitarianism', where humanitarian and political objectives became integrated, and relief was not only a substitute for political action but also the primary form of political engagement at the geopolitical periphery, in countries such as Afghanistan before 11 September, 2001. This is an important reminder of how research results can be used and distorted to support a particular policy position.

The way that the evaluation influenced policy can partly be explained using marketing theory. As described above, in the analysis and in particular in the recommendations there was an effective segmentation of the audience (for example, by UN agencies, NGOs and donors) within this piece of work about the whole system. Particular messages were directed at particular types of agencies. And the 'stickiness' factor (in other words, the findings having an impact) is partly due to Study 3 saying what everyone knew already, but in a much clearer, and cooler headed way (Kotler at al. 1999).

The process that led to the Sphere Project was more of a cumulative 'snowball' effect than the 'whisper' effect identified by Stephens (cited by Berkout and Scoones 1999). However the snowball effect was less to do with research, and more to do with increasing concern in the NGO sector, at an operational level, about the discrepancy of standards, performance and expertise between agencies. This started as snowflakes in the mid-1980s, snowballing in the early 1990s, and becoming a veritable avalanche as a result of the Rwanda crisis. The Rwanda evaluation gave clear direction about how these concerns could be addressed, supporting and giving impetus to the embryonic Sphere initiative.

As described above, in the section on 'Roles and relationships', the way in which the Rwanda evaluation influenced NGO policy makers seems to be more to do with the 'insider model' described by Saywell and Cotton (1999), due to the close links between evaluators and policy makers throughout the evaluation process. The fact that the 'research' was commissioned and the researchers chosen by the policy makers contributed to some degree to their credibility and the trust bestowed upon them. This is different from the way most research is conducted.

Links: influence and legitimacy

This case study of how Sphere was born, and in particular of the relative influence of the Rwanda evaluation, supports the hypothesis that close links (whether institutional, in terms of regular contact, or common interest) between researchers and policy makers greatly increases the likelihood of research influencing policy. Those links were institutionalized in the structure put in place for the Joint Rwanda Evaluation. Although it may not always be possible to replicate this inclusive structure involving so many stakeholders, there may be elements of it that can be replicated. The buffer role of the evaluation's Management Group, to protect the objectivity and independence of the researchers, is an important one to bear in mind when research, which may be controversial, is commissioned.

The researchers/evaluators were really part of the same policy network as the policy makers, not least because some of the evaluators had actually worked for the same agencies. So what kind of network was this? Using Stone's typology (2001), it has elements of a number of different networks. To some extent it was a 'policy community' and, at least temporarily, this was created through the structure of the Rwanda evaluation, especially through the Steering Committee. To some extent it was a 'discourse coalition', whereby both evaluators and key NGO staff shared the same beliefs about how the system – and in particular, NGOs – needed to change. This is part of what has been called the 'accountability revolution' in the humanitarian aid sector, spearheaded by NGOs. To some extent it has elements of an 'advocacy coalition', whereby different people in different parts of the sector shared a similar vision and were prepared to support each other to bring about the change they thought necessary. However, as described previously, it was also a network dominated by expatriates – a source of some embarrassment to the evaluation team, but not untypical of policy discussion within the humanitarian sector, and as Nindi asserts, within the development sector more generally.[69]

There was another, smaller policy network that came together in the Sphere Management Committee that was responsible for getting the project off the ground. Again, this had elements of a number of different types of policy network. To some extent it was an issue network, bringing together members concerned about improving NGO performance, but differing in their views about how to do so. (These differences really came to the fore towards the end of Phase 1 of Sphere.) To some extent the Management Committee was a discourse coalition, but there were also elements of an advocacy coalition.

Particularly noteworthy is the role of the 'policy entrepreneurs', especially Peter Walker and Nick Stockton. In Gladwell's (2000) terms they were both connectors (i.e. networkers) and salesmen (i.e. persuasive, listened to and trusted). They were also innovators and they spotted the policy window to take forward their ideas. Other individuals, such as Jim Bishop of InterAction and Susan Purdin, Sphere's first project manager, also played critical connector roles.

Conclusions

This case study shows that the policy impact of Study 3 of the Rwanda evaluation, on finding ways of improving NGO performance, was more or less immediate in terms of the impetus it gave to the embryonic Sphere Project. But, the impact was also partial. The more challenging and radical recommendations around accreditation and regulation of NGOs were ducked and have been consistently evaded.

This study of how Sphere was born supports all three hypotheses set out in the research framework in Chapter 2, namely that research is more likely to contribute to evidence-based and pro-poor policy making if:

1. It recognizes and acknowledges the political and institutional limits and pressures of policy makers, and resonates with their ideological assumptions, or sufficient pressure is exerted to challenge those limits.
As clearly demonstrated, the high-profile failure to respond adequately to the Rwanda crisis (in particular, to the refugee crisis) expanded the boundaries of what policy makers would accept as necessary change. An unprecedented policy window of opportunity was created which the evaluation exploited, and which certain policy makers within the NGO sector seized upon.

2. Researchers and policy makers share particular types of networks and develop chains of legitimacy for particular policy areas.
Shared networks were formalized in the structure of the Rwanda evaluation, although the networks also went beyond this temporary structure. In this case study, research was not of the conventional type. Instead, it was conceived of as an evaluation, and was commissioned by the policy makers, which all contributed to the results being taken seriously and having a major impact.

3. Outputs are based on local involvement and credible evidence, and are communicated via the most appropriate communicators, channels, style, format and timing.
In the Sphere case study, the credibility of the evidence was high, which was a very important factor for it to have influence. Local involvement is harder to comment upon because it was limited, but effective communication of the findings through a deliberate strategy of dissemination does seem to have been important.

Chapter Five
Animal healthcare in Kenya: the road to community-based animal health service delivery

JOHN YOUNG, JULIUS KAJUME and JACOB WANYAMA

Introduction

Livestock services, and in particular clinical veterinary services, were among the first rural services targeted for privatization under structural adjustment programmes (SAPs), particularly in sub-Saharan Africa. As clear 'private goods', and as most livestock keepers seemed to be prepared to pay for them, finance departments and experts regarded them as an easy target. However, veterinarians in most sub-Saharan countries, who were mostly employed by the government, proved very reluctant to move into private practice. Around the same time many NGOs and some government departments established very successful small-scale decentralized animal healthcare (DAH) programmes, where trained livestock keepers provided clinical veterinary services, for a fee, to their neighbours (de Haan and Bekure 1991). The veterinary profession was however very suspicious of these programmes and, despite good evidence that decentralized animal programmes provide an effective, cost-efficient and safe service, few livestock departments were prepared to change policies to promote the expansion of these approaches. More recently, some governments in Eastern Africa and the Horn of Africa are reconsidering the policy framework as part of re-orientating agricultural services under poverty reduction strategies, and legislation is under review with a view to legalizing decentralized animal health services in Kenya (KVB 2002b).

This chapter presents the results of a case study on livestock service reform in Kenya,[70] where during the 1980s and 1990s non-governmental organizations introduced a new model of community-based livestock services. Intermediate Technology Development Group (ITDG) was one of the early pioneers in the mid-1980s, and adopted an action research approach with a clear objective to use the results, if positive, to influence the policy environment to allow the approaches to be widely replicated. This case study explores the reasons why, despite the outstanding success of the new community-based decentralized animal healthcare approaches, it took more than 15 years to convince policy makers to develop policies and legislation to allow this to happen – which still have not been formally adopted, despite the proliferation of community-based livestock services throughout the arid and semi-arid lands (ASAL) of Kenya.

The evolution of animal healthcare in Kenya

The colonial era: private veterinary practice

During the colonial and immediately post-independence era most clinical vet services in Kenya were provided by private practitioners and 'vet scouts'. The private practitioners were confined to high-potential areas, mainly in the so-called white settler areas. Vet scouts were local livestock-keepers who received informal training from local vet staff, were employed by the county council and seconded to the government, and lived and provided clinical and other services in the villages. The provision of private animal health services was, and still is, mainly governed by the Veterinary Surgeons Act (Cap 366) and the Pharmacy and Poisons Act (Cap 244). The Veterinary Surgeons Act was borrowed mostly unchanged from the British Veterinary Surgeons Act. This Act broadly limits the practice of veterinary medicine and surgery to registered veterinary surgeons and staff under their direct supervision. However there are two clauses at the end of the Act added in recognition of the fact that many of the larger commercial farmers of the time provided their own veterinary services. These clauses allow anyone to treat their own animals, or those belonging to a neighbour, provided it is not done for profit. The Pharmacy and Poisons Act limits the sale of pharmaceuticals (including veterinary pharmaceuticals) to registered pharmacists. Veterinarians are allowed to keep limited stocks of drugs for their own use while treating animals, but they are not allowed to sell them.

The 1960s and 1970s: free services for all

Sessional Paper No. 1 of 1965 (Government of Kenya 1965), 'African socialism', set the scene for a massive increase in government livestock services, to be provided for free throughout the country, and massive investment in the professionalization of the veterinary service. Vet scouts at village level were gradually phased out and replaced by vets and animal health technicians (AHTs), based at divisional and locational level respectively. The private practitioners went out of business; many were expatriates and left the country. Although clinical services became more accessible in the high-potential areas, they did not improve much in the arid and semi-arid areas (ASAL) because relatively fewer vets and AHTs were posted there and, without enough vet scouts or any other intermediaries, they could hardly reach the ASAL nomadic herds because of the vast distances, poor terrain and inadequate road network.

1980 to 1992: structural adjustment and covert operations

In 1980 an NGO in Turkana District, an ASAL area in northern Kenya, quietly established the first DAH scheme. Dr Darlington Akabwai, a Ugandan vet, trained some of the catechists of the Catholic Diocese of Lodwar to treat common livestock diseases as they travelled around doing their other duties. This model of animal healthcare delivery gradually evolved into the Adakari Vet Scout programme promoted by the EEC-funded Turkana Rehabilitation Programme in the late 1980s and the Norwegian Agency for Development Cooperation (NORAD) programme in Turkana in the early 1990s.

The first inklings of change in the livestock subsector emerged through a series of research papers produced by the Ministry of Livestock Development in 1982 and 1983, leading to a policy paper on the privatization of veterinary services. The Minister for Livestock Development warmly received the paper, and he was perceived to be ahead of the game within government. But these plans were never implemented.

The second DAH scheme got underway in 1984, again under the auspices of the Catholic Church, this time in Narok District, another ASAL area in south-western Kenya, but collapsed when Kit Flowers, the expatriate vet who set it up, left the country.

Sessional Paper No. 1 of 1986 (Government of Kenya 1986), 'Economic management for renewed growth', set the stage for structural adjustment within government and the gradual privatization of public services. Serious planning for reform in the Ministry of Agriculture (which had by that time subsumed the Ministry of Livestock Development) began with the donor-funded Agriculture Sector Investment Project in the mid-1990s. But an interdepartmental committee set up to look at the implications for the Department of Veterinary Services (DVS) failed to reach any concrete conclusions before quietly collapsing following the transfer of the committee chairman.

In 1986, ITDG, a UK-based NGO, arrived in Kenya to work with the Catholic Diocese of Meru at Kamujini Farmers' Centre (KFC) in the lower-potential areas of Meru District, central Kenya. ITDG had become interested in the dramatic improvements in rural healthcare provision in China during the 1970s (White 1998), and in whether the 'barefoot doctor' approach could be applied in the livestock sector (Darroch et al. 1982). They were also influenced by World Bank proposals for new privatized livestock services in sub-Saharan Africa (de Haan and Nissen 1985). In early 1987, based on the results of some preliminary studies (ITDG 1987), ITDG trained 17 community animal-health workers (CAHWs) at Kamujini. From the beginning, ITDG intended to test the approach and, if successful, to seek to influence the policy environment so that the approach could be replicated more widely. ITDG established several other CAHW schemes over the next few years with different partners in many different parts of the country including East Pokot (also in 1987), Machakos (1988), Makueni, Samburu (1989), and Turkana (1990) (ITDG 2000b,c).

Budget restrictions began to bite in the late 1980s, and the government stopped automatically employing all vets and AHTs on graduation in 1988, and froze recruitment into vacant posts. This had a disproportionate impact in the ASAL areas (commonly referred to as hardship areas), as vets and AHTs in those areas frequently requested transfers to less remote areas. The university and technical training institutes carried on training veterinary staff, turning out about 50 veterinary graduates and approximately 300 AHTs each year. Although some of the vets and AHTs started working privately, and others were employed by private sector companies, NGOs and cooperatives or moved into different professions, the gradually increasing number of unemployed vets and AHTs became a significant pressure group for change over the next few years.

Dr Julius Kajume, later to become one of the leading supporters of the CAHW approach within government, moved from a veterinary public health post in Nairobi to become Provincial Director of Veterinary Services in Eastern Province in 1989. This brought him face-to-face with the difficulties of trying to provide adequate animal health services in the ASAL areas with ever-dwindling resources.

In 1988 ITDG organized the first of what was to become a series of annual workshops for vets involved in DAH projects (ITDG 1991, 1993, 1994, 1999, 2000a). The workshop, held at KFC in Meru District, was attended mainly by ITDG and their partners' staff, and included three government vets who had been involved in setting up the programmes. Gradually over the following few years, the proportion of government veterinary staff among the participants increased to nearly 50 per cent, including some provincial-level veterinarians and senior researchers. Towards the end of 1989, there were signs that the Director of Veterinary Services was aware of, and interested in, the CAHW approach.

In a move that caught many by surprise, Dr Wamukoya, the head of the Clinical Studies Department of the Veterinary Faculty, University of Nairobi, was appointed as Director of Veterinary Services in 1990. He brought with him an emphasis on standards of professionalism and professional ethics that were very difficult to realize in the harsh reality of declining veterinary budgets and collapsing services, especially in the ASAL areas. He was disinclined to consider options that he thought would compromise the high standards of the veterinary service, especially if they contravened the Veterinary Surgeons Act. When Jeff Mariner, an expatriate vet working with the Organisation of African Unity/International Bureau for Animal Resources Pan Africa Rinderpest Campaign (OAU/IBAR PARC), called him about a proposal he had written about training CAHWs to vaccinate cattle against rinderpest in northern Kenya, Dr Wamukoya said: 'If I had known the proposal was about training CAHWs, I could have saved you the trouble of writing it' (Mariner, personal communication). Later, in 1993, while visiting a German Technical Cooperation (GTZ) project working with government departments including the Department of Veterinary Services in Marsabit District (an ASAL area), with the Permanent Secretary of the Ministry of Agriculture and Livestock Development, Dr Wamukoya strongly opposed the project's plans to train contact herders (a form of CAHWs). Fortunately for the project, and for the CAHW policy story, the Permanent Secretary, who was from an ASAL area himself and was impressed by the approach, overruled Dr Wamukoya.

More CAHW schemes were quietly established by bilaterals and NGOs during the early 1990s, usually working with district veterinary staff, but these schemes were largely invisible to the DVS and to the Kenya Veterinary Board (KVB) and Kenya Veterinary Association (KVA).

Jeff Mariner started the Thermostable Rinderpest Vaccine Technology Transfer (TRVTT) Project with OAU/IBAR in 1990. The project aimed to transfer the production of a thermostable rinderpest vaccine, developed in the USA, to laboratories in Africa. This vaccine has a long shelf-life without refrigeration, and can be distributed and used much more easily than earlier vaccines which required an efficient cold chain. The project successfully established vaccine production facilities in Cameroon and Ethiopia (though not in Kenya), but the national veterinary departments supported by the OAU/IBAR PARC continued to use the same inefficient cold-chain routes and systems.

In 1992, despite the DVS's opposition (see above), the GTZ-funded Marsabit Integrated Development Programme started to train contact herders with local department of veterinary services staff. Over the next few years, the approach they developed was gradually taken up by a number of other GTZ-funded projects in other parts of Kenya.

Also in 1992, after three national vets' workshops, ITDG organized an international workshop in Kenya, with participants from 18 countries worldwide. Several Kenyan vets were also invited to the workshop, which included field visits to DAH projects in various parts of the country. The degree of international interest encouraged the Kenyan participants, and the workshop allowed Jeff Mariner to get to know Darlington Akabwai and Tim Leyland, who later joined the TRVTT and subsequent participatory and community-based vaccination (PARC-VAC) project and became key players in the DAH policy story in Kenya.

Still unaware of the growing number of DAH projects in his province, in 1993 Dr Kajume received letters from several of his district veterinary officers (DVOs) requesting permission to attend ITDG's fourth annual Vets' Workshop at Hunters Lodge (ITDG 1993). Annoyed that he had not been informed himself, he asked the Director of Veterinary Services if he knew anything about it. The Director did not, and asked Dr Kajume to find out more. Dr Kajume decided to attend the workshop personally and was surprised to discover so many government staff in attendance and to hear about so many apparently successful schemes to improve animal health services in ASAL areas. Knowing from personal experience how difficult it was to provide adequate services in these areas, he became convinced that the CAHW approach should be replicated more widely – albeit under better control from the veterinary department. By this time however, the emphasis of the early vets' workshops as a vehicle to exert policy influence had waned, and workshops between 1994 and 1997 became more concerned with sharing experiences between DAH schemes – a sort of DAH project club – with the same participants turning up year after year (see, for example, ITDG 1994). Those in the club valued the workshops as opportunities to discover about each other's experiences, while those outside the club knew very little about them.

1994 to 1997: the conspiracy of silence

Dr Wamukoya's secondment to the department came to an end in 1994, and Dr Kimanzi succeeded him. Dr Kimanzi, like Dr Kajume, had worked both in the Veterinary Public Health Division and as Provincial Director of Veterinary Services in Nyanza and Eastern Provinces. Dr Kajume had worked for Dr Kimanzi while both were in the Veterinary Public Health Division in the late 1980s, and Dr Kimanzi brought Dr Kajume back to Nairobi towards the end of the year.

Dr Kajume became increasingly involved in CAHW schemes over the next two years, and from this time national animal-health policy makers were fully aware of the gradually expanding number of CAHW projects. However they deliberately chose to do nothing about it, despite an increasing number of requests for clarification from field-based veterinary officers who were involved in CAHW schemes. As registrar for the KVB, the Director of Veterinary Services was in a difficult position. He could not confirm that CAHW schemes were legal, and he knew that seeking to change the prevailing policies and law to make them so would encounter strong opposition from the entire veterinary profession, yet closing them down would dramatically reduce the availability of animal health services in the ASAL areas.

After many years in preparation, the KVA Privatization Scheme was finally launched in 1994. This EC-funded scheme provided soft loans to veterinarians wishing to set up in private practice. Originally conceived in 1989, it had taken nearly five years to develop because the KVA, dominated at that time by government vets, could not find an affordable loan package attractive enough to encourage any government vets to leave the security of a government job. Meanwhile, many of the unemployed vets had quietly established private practices without any loan at all.

The unemployed AHTs had a harder time however. Although they were all secondary-school leavers with two or three years' tertiary training in animal healthcare at technical institutes, the Veterinary Surgeons Act forbade them to provide veterinary services except 'under the supervision of a veterinary surgeon'. Private vets or drug companies had employed some of them, and some had started to practise illegally, but many were still unemployed and increasingly unhappy. In the early 1990s, they decided to establish an association to represent their interests, but encountered strong opposition in the DVS. The Kenya Association of Livestock Technicians (KALT) was finally registered in 1995, only after they had threatened to march to State House to express their grievance to the head of state. The Minister also promised to change the law to allow them to establish private animal health services in their own right (Kimanzi 1997).

Shortly after ITDG's international DAH workshop (in 1992), Darlington Akabwai joined the Tufts/TRVTT project and started testing CAHW schemes to deliver rinderpest vaccination programmes in Uganda and Ethiopia. In 1995, Tim Leyland also joined Tufts and the

TRVTT project and working through Operation Lifeline Sudan tested the approach in southern Sudan. The approach was very successful, achieving much higher coverage rates for a fraction of the cost of the other more traditional government vaccination programmes, convincing OAU/IBAR to adopt it as the key principle for the PARC-VAC project.

During 1996, in an attempt to convince the Kenyan government to adopt the CAHW approach to rinderpest vaccination, the TRVTT project organized a visit for Kenyan vets to south Sudan to see the CAHW programme. The Kenyans were impressed by the results, but were reluctant to accept that an approach that seemed to work in neighbouring but war-torn Sudan could be appropriate in Kenya. So TRVTT then took them to Afar in Ethiopia to see a similar approach but in a country with an effective veterinary department, and indeed they became more interested.

By this time there were a large number of CAHW schemes throughout the ASAL areas of Kenya, meeting annually at the ITDG vets' workshops, and some donors were also training CAHWs in medium-potential areas. The FARM Africa Goat Project, a collaborative project established at the request of the Kenya government, had started to develop a programme with the Department of Veterinary Services in Meru District, incorporating both private veterinarians and CAHWs. In 1996 Dr Kajume became the main contact point for DAH programmes within the DVS and was frequently consulted on policy issues.

The number of CAHW schemes continued to increase during 1997, but the Director of Veterinary Services chose to turn a blind eye. OAU/IBAR started negotiating with the DVS to start vaccination programmes using CAHWs in northern Kenya, meanwhile running training of trainers' workshops for NGO staff involved in training CAHWs in south Sudan and northern Kenya. The NGOs started talking once more about lobbying for policy change and legal reform to promote DAH schemes, and were joined by KALT, who were becoming increasingly militant since there was still no sign of the necessary reforms to allow them to practise. Then, ironically, just when there seemed to be a real opportunity to promote change, ITDG's animal health programme ran out of funds after the seventh annual Vets' Workshop in Marsabit. The KVB and KVA had only gradually become aware of the CAHW movement, but became increasingly alarmed as they learned more about it. They generally regarded CAHWs as a threat to veterinary professionalism, but were particularly concerned to discover that some schemes were operating in medium-potential parts of the country where some private vets were trying to establish private practices, and that many of the schemes had been established by expatriate vets working in Kenya without registering with the Board. Their concern finally boiled over at a FARM Africa workshop in Embu in December 1997.

1998 to 2000: the tipping point

After more than a year's work with local veterinary staff, FARM Africa had finally found a workable model for the animal-health component of their goat project. Their plan involved establishing private vets with loans from the Kenya Veterinary Association Privatisation Scheme (KVAPS), working with animal health assistants, who would support self-employed CAHWs at village level, to provide the necessary service to farmers. This proved too much for a representative of the KVB who had been invited to the inaugural workshop in Embu, who angrily warned the Kenyan project vet that what he was proposing was illegal and that he would be struck off the veterinary register if he proceeded.

Shortly afterwards, in January 1998, the KVB placed a full-page advertisement in the national newspapers pointing out that it was illegal to train CAHWs and that any vets doing so risked being struck off the veterinary register. This alarmed everybody working on DAH schemes. ITDG and others decided that the best defence would be to try to get all parties together to discuss the issues and find a solution. But ITDG had no money and had to look for resources from other organizations. OAU/IBAR, still waiting for approval for their proposed CAHW programme in northern Kenya, was also keen to find a solution. They and the Netherlands Development Agency (SNV) offered to fund the workshop, provided all stakeholders supported it. ITDG then formed a committee of a few individuals, including Dr Kajume, to develop the workshop. In view of the sensitivity of the workshop theme ('Practice, policy and the law in the delivery of animal-health services particularly in arid and semi arid lands (ASALs)'), Dr Kajume advised ITDG to include representatives of all key parties in the planning committee.

The Vet Board letter also unblocked a study of livestock services in ASAL areas that had been proposed some months earlier by the European Union Rural Development Adviser. Dr Kimanzi, initially hesitant to give clearance, was eventually convinced of the value of the proposed study, and on his part Dr Kajume, seeing an opportunity to broaden the debate, recommended that the study should go ahead but with two Kenyan team members rather then the one originally proposed. Dr Kajume, Professor Gathuma from the Faculty of Veterinary Medicine and Dr Hübl, an expatriate consultant, undertook the study between February and May (Hübl et al. 1998). The study included stakeholder workshops in each region, and culminated in a major workshop to discuss the findings at Nairobi in May 1998. The workshop was well attended by all livestock service stakeholders, and highly influential in changing official attitudes towards CAHWs. The issue was out of the closet and open for debate.

At around the same time, the DVS finally signed a memorandum of understanding allowing PARC-VAC to establish a pilot scheme using CAHWs in Turkana and West Pokot. An international workshop on DAH held at Arusha in December, focusing on delivery of animal health services in Eastern Africa, added further impetus. In planning for this workshop, each of the three East African countries (Uganda, Tanzania and Kenya) had a coordinator – Dr Kajume was the country coordinator for Kenya. It was well attended by participants from Kenya, who were impressed by the degree of interest being shown by other countries, by the evidence of the effectiveness of CAHW schemes presented by delegates, and the endorsement of the approach by OAU/IBAR – an increasingly important donor for livestock services in Kenya.

In May 1999, the 8th ITDG Vets' Workshop, renamed a DAH Workshop, was held at Meru, following several months of planning by a committee including representatives of all the main stakeholders (ITDG 1999). The programme included key presentations from all of the stakeholders, and covered the right spectrum of participants. The workshop endorsed the CAHW approach, established multi-stakeholder working groups to develop guidelines and standards for CAHWs in Kenya, and recommended a review of the legislation and policy. After much negotiation, ITDG obtained funding for a further three years of work, with explicit outputs relating to policy reform. The memorandum of understanding between DVS and PARC-VAC was expanded to include SNV and Veterinaires Sans Frontières (VSF, Belgium) as implementing agencies and to cover more divisions in Turkana and West Pokot (DVS 2000). Dr Kimanzi retired in September, and Dr Kajume took over as Acting Director of Veterinary Services for six months until April 2000, during which period he initiated the policy and legal review processes.

2000 to 2002: rocks ahead

Unfortunately for the DAH policy story, Dr Kajume did not get the Director of Veterinary Services post. Instead it went to Dr Chong, a more traditional veterinarian who spent most of his veterinary career in the veterinary laboratory services division. Nevertheless, he supported the process of policy and legal review, focusing on the entire scope of veterinary services and culminating in a series of five multi-stakeholder workshops to gather views and recommendations, held between September and November 1999. During this time, many new NGOs became involved in training CAHWs as part of short-term relief programmes in ASAL areas following the 1999–2000 drought. With only short-term funding, some of these programmes were implemented too quickly, neglecting the essential and time-consuming community awareness and education elements of successful programmes. Many collapsed as soon as the agency withdrew, attracting criticism from veterinary professionals and providing evidence of the dangers of the approach for its opponents.

Changes in the executive committee further undermined support in the KVA, and in April 2000 the annual KVA Conference at Mombasa narrowly sidestepped a motion proposing to lobby to ban CAHWs (KVA 2000). The motion did not go through but gave a clear signal that there was significant resistance to the DAH approach within KVA. Surprisingly, there was no discussion at all about CAHWs at the next KVA annual general meeting in April 2001. The KVB and DVS finally approved the minimum standards and guidelines for CAHWs in early 2001 (KVB 2002a), and since then these guidelines have been tested in the field. In the meantime, the animal-health policy review process was being carried out, and at the OAU/IBAR 50th anniversary party in November 2001, the Minister of Agriculture promised to push the new policy through Cabinet if it could be completed by February 2002.

The new animal-health policy document was duly completed in early 2002 (Ministry of Agriculture and Rural Development 2002), and a draft submitted to the Permanent Secretary, Ministry of Agriculture and Rural Development for further scrutiny. Some unfortunate drafting in the new Veterinary Practitioners Bill, which defined CAHWs as 'veterinary surgeons', provoked a very strong reaction at the annual KVA meeting in Kakamega, where delegates strongly opposed any further moves to legalize CAHWs and proposed to petition for an injunction (KVA 2002a,b). Recent information indicates that KVA has already petitioned DVS to withdraw the document to allow inclusion of their input. It seems that it may be a while yet before CAHWs are finally legalized in Kenya.

The critical factors

The policy context: politics and institutions

Political, social and economic structures and interests
A key contextual factor in this case study has been the fact that government investment policy in Kenya favours the high-potential areas. The result has been that while more than 75 per cent of Kenya's livestock is in the ASAL areas, these areas are served by fewer than 10 per cent of livestock service staff. The ASAL areas are considered a hardship post and few vet staff want to work there. There has always been reluctance in Kenya to address the complexity of different policies for different parts of the country, despite the enormous social, economic and political difference between the high-potential areas and the ASAL areas. Whereas the Veterinary Surgeons Act and Pharmacy and Poisons Act may be sensible in high-potential areas, they make little sense in the ASAL areas where there are few vets, few roads, few shops and vast distances between settlements and the nomadic herds.

A second, key set of factors centres on the Department of Veterinary Services and its directors. Traditionally, the DVS has been the source of policy directions. The DVS gives policy directions in the form of circulars to the veterinary field staff, who disseminate them to livestock farmers and the public in general. There have been various attempts to develop livestock development and animal health policies and strategies in the past, but with little success. In addition, the DVS and its Director have gradually been demoted following transfer of livestock-production functions from the department mandate. In the 1960s, the Director of Veterinary Services, although only head of the Veterinary Department, held the same rank as the Permanent Secretary. The department enjoyed a high profile in terms of budgetary provisions and good performance but this has changed over the years and is no longer the case. The Director of Veterinary Services is currently at a lower grade than his counterparts in the Ministry of Health and Department of Agriculture and Livestock Production. The Director of Veterinary Services used to manage all government livestock services, which included both Veterinary Services and Livestock Production. Livestock Production has been absorbed into the Department of Agriculture and Livestock Production, leaving the Department of Veterinary Services as a separate department in the Ministry of Agriculture and Rural Development. The Director of Veterinary Services now has no control over Livestock Production or Livestock Extension activities.

There is a very strong focus on professionalism in the Veterinary Department and the veterinary profession as a whole in Kenya. This is thought to date from the colonial era, and the adoption of both the Veterinary Surgeons Act and attitudes towards the veterinary profession from the UK. Veterinary departments in other East African countries have envied Kenya's Veterinary Department because it has always been relatively well resourced. Dr Wamukoya (Director of Veterinary Services from 1990 to 1994) was particularly pro-professionalism and professional ethics. He came to the department from the Department of Clinical Studies in the Veterinary Faculty of the University of Nairobi, and his field experience in government veterinary services was limited.

Between the mid-1980s and mid-1990s, the inexorable reduction of Veterinary Department budgets left very little room for manoeuvre. The inability of the Department to implement an orderly organizational reform programme meant the Director had to try to share ever-dwindling resources across a largely unchanged organization. Most of the cuts were made in the operational budgets, so by the late 1980s vets in the field had virtually no resources for travel or equipment and, unless they could find some running costs from elsewhere, they could do little work in the field. This factor made them more willing than they might otherwise have been to collaborate with NGOs and bilateral projects wanting to implement CAHW programmes, even though everyone knew that they were, strictly speaking, illegal.

The personal attitudes of successive Directors of Veterinary Services had a major influence on their willingness to consider new options. Dr Wellington Ngulo (1987–90) was relatively open minded, but the CAHW 'experiment' in Kenya had not developed a critical mass of evidence and experience, nor contacts at a sufficiently senior level in government to seek to influence him before he left the department. Dr Wamukoya (1990–94) was openly opposed to any innovation that he felt threatened the professionalism of veterinary services (see above and the Jeff Mariner and 'Marsabit visit' stories). Dr Kimanzi (1994–99) had worked in veterinary public health and in the field, and was much more open to new ideas. He was acutely aware that addressing the CAHW issue would not be well received by a large section of the profession, and quite deliberately chose to ignore requests for clarification from district veterinary officers involved in CAHW programmes in the early 1990s.

However he was quick to seize the opportunity provided by the Vet Board advertisement in the newspaper in early 1998, to allow policy debate without interfering or committing himself. Julius Kajume (District Veterinary Officer from October 1999 to March 2000) was extremely supportive of the CAHW approach, and there may have been an opportunity to approve new policy and legislation at that time had it been ready then. Unfortunately, in April 2002, he had to hand over to the new permanent Director of Veterinary Services, Dr Chong, who had spent most of his career in the veterinary laboratory service, and had limited field experience.

Sessional Paper No. 1 of 1986 (Government of Kenya 1986), 'Economic management for renewed growth', set the scene in Kenya for structural adjustment, streamlining of government and privatization. Although the Livestock Ministry had considered some of these issues in a series of research and policy papers in the early 1980s (initiated by David Leonard, an expatriate adviser), they were never implemented. However, attempts at structural reforms were pursued later in the 1990s under the agricultural investment sector programme (ASMP II) but with limited success.

There was pressure for the privatization of veterinary services from the World Bank and the EC in the mid-1980s (de Haan and Nissen 1985), which finally resulted in a project – the Kenya Veterinary Association Privatisation Scheme (KVAPS) – which started in 1994. The scheme provided soft loans to vets to help them set up in practice. Originally conceived as a mechanism to encourage vets to leave government service, the planning was left to the KVA, which was, at that time, dominated by government vets. The packages they came up with, which included money to purchase vehicles, rent premises and provide income guarantees, were unaffordable. The much more modest package which was finally agreed, although on the best credit terms available anywhere in Kenya and with an interest discount for vets who paid on time, was not good enough to encourage many vets to leave government service. It did however attract many vets who had not been employed by the government since the cessation of automatic recruitment in 1988. The scheme has become one of the most important functions of the KVA and has done much to raise awareness of the need to establish private practices, especially in the high-potential areas.

Institutional and professional tensions also played an influential role in the political context. Unemployed vets and animal-health technicians were very reluctant to see CAHWs licensed to practice, and applied pressure on the Department of Veterinary Services through personal contacts and through the KVA to block their acceptance. Animal health technicians formed KALT. The government trained (and are still training) these technicians, who they stopped automatically employing on graduation in 1988. Many technicians remain unemployed and the Veterinary Surgeons Act prohibits them from practising except 'under the direct supervision of a veterinary surgeon', so they cannot set up their own businesses legally.

Despite promises from the Director of Veterinary Services and the Minister of Agriculture and Livestock Development at successive graduation ceremonies that this problem would be resolved, nothing had happened by the early 1990s, and the animal health technicians decided to register an association to help them lobby for change. This move was resisted by the Department of Veterinary Services for several years, until in 1995 an increasingly militant KALT threatened to march to State House to take their grievance to the head of state. The Minister then finally allowed them to register the association and promised, again, to resolve the problem. When the problem still had not been resolved by 1997, KALT decided to join the growing NGO-lobby for reform, even though they were quite aware that the NGO-lobby about CAHWs would not, in the long run, be in their interest. Successive Directors of Veterinary Services have faced a dilemma since the mid-1980s because of two conflicting forces within the department. On the one hand, a large number of Nairobi-based staff and those working in high-potential areas have opposed the CAHW approach, since they feel it undermines the veterinary profession, but on the other hand field-based staff in the ASAL areas support it, and are often actually working with NGOs and other agencies to establish and support CAHW schemes.

The KVA has been vocal in opposition to legalizing CAHWs. Initially dominated by Nairobi-based government vets, the association has expanded rapidly and has set up branches, especially in high-potential areas where many vets are establishing private practices. The Central Region Branch, dominated by both private practitioners and government vets, is especially vocal.

NGOs have been seeking to influence the government in favour of CAHW schemes since the mid-1980s. The focus initially was on convincing field staff to help establish pilot projects, and later on identifying and developing individual supporters at provincial and national levels and in research institutes. Only in late 1997 was serious thought given to ways of lobbying the Department more effectively. Then, in early 1998, matters were brought to a head by the KVB letter in the national press.

In the mid-1990s DFID, the EU and OAU/IBAR started to put pressure on the Kenyan government to support CAHW schemes. The EU and DFID supported some of the early CAHW schemes being developed by ITDG in Kenya from the late 1980s, and the EU, as the major donor in the KVAPS, became more directly involved in veterinary-service policy issues in the early 1990s. OAU/IBAR had achieved great success with CAHW schemes eradicating rinderpest in south Sudan and Ethiopia in the early 1990s, and wanted to use the same techniques to eradicate the remaining endemic areas in northern Kenya. Following a failed attempt to interest the DVS in a CAHW scheme in 1992, they started trying again in 1996.

Assumptions and attitudes
Vets everywhere object to the idea of non-vets providing even relatively simple veterinary services. Most believe that they are the only people

sufficiently well qualified to treat animals. Most countries have legislation preventing non-vets treating animals (usually in something similar to the Veterinary Surgeons Act) and possessing ethical drugs (in something like a Pharmacy and Poisons Act). Kenyan vets seem to hold this view particularly strongly.

In addition, vets attempting to establish private practices in Kenya perceive CAHWs (and AHTs) as competitors who, through lower prices, might take some of their business. There is a remarkable blindness to the possibility that a private vet working with AHTs and CAHWs could cover a much larger area, make a lot of money from medicine sales, and to the fact that CAHWs at village level could provide an extremely effective disease early-warning system. These concepts are now being discussed, but few vets are convinced. Supporting CAHW schemes would be a fundamental policy shift in Kenya and would require the complete overhaul of animal health policy and changes to relevant laws.

Most of the early CAHW schemes were established by NGOs, sometimes working with local government veterinary officers and sometimes not. Most government vets at field level were keen to work with NGO programmes because they provided some additional much-needed resources at a time when they had very limited operational budgets from the government. Some projects managed to persuade the government to second veterinary staff to help establish CAHW schemes, but the exact nature of the project was usually not explicit. By 1992, the Director of Veterinary Services was aware of and completely opposed to the CAHW concept (see the Jeff Mariner story), but was probably not aware of how many schemes were already operating in Kenya. Gradually, with the increasing involvement of bilateral and multilateral agencies, the government became more aware of them. Julius Kajume, then Provincial Director of Veterinary Services for Eastern Province, first heard about CAHWs when he attended ITDG's fourth annual Vets' Workshop in 1993. He quickly became convinced of their value, and maintained close contact with two former government vets who had joined ITDG's CAHW programme. When he returned to the headquarters in Nairobi as Deputy Director of Veterinary Service (Administration and Management Support) in early 1995, he became the key contact point for CAHW schemes in the Veterinary Department, as well as one of the approach's strongest advocates.

While support for the CAHW concept grew slowly in the Department of Veterinary Services, the Kenya Veterinary Board, driven mainly by the professional and ethical concerns described above, became increasingly concerned, until they published an advertisement in the national press in January 1998 threatening to de-register any vets who trained CAHWs. Later on however, after the Hübl study report meeting at Nairobi in May 1998, the KVB joined a multidisciplinary committee to prepare for ITDG's 1999 DAH workshop, and following the workshop took a lead role in the working group to review the policy and legislation relevant to animal health services.

The KVA, on the other hand, still opposes the CAHW concept. Initially strong supporters of the KVB position and their 1998 advertisement, KVA representatives were subsequently persuaded to join a multidisciplinary planning committee for the 1999 DAH workshop. They attended the meeting and subsequently joined a working group to develop new policies and legislation. In 1999 the entire KVA executive committee changed (the KVA elects its leadership annually), but for the sake of continuity they decided to keep the same representative (a member of the previous executive committee) on the working group. Gradually however the new committee, strongly influenced by vets in the Central Region Branch of KVA who opposed the CAHW concept, became annoyed that an ex-committee member represented them in the working group, and the annual KVA meeting in late 2000 came close to passing a motion banning CAHWs from practising (KVA 2000). Their opposition hardened still further at the 2002 annual conference in Kakamega, where they unanimously demanded that the government withdraw the proposed Veterinary Practitioners Bill (and instead strengthen the existing Veterinary Surgeons Act) and that the KVB should withdraw its support for the new curriculum on training CAHWs (KVA 2002a,b). Understandably, the KVA's argument is that KVB has no mandate to produce any such curriculum under the provisions of the Veterinary Surgeons Act, under which the KVB was established.

Evidence: credibility and communication

The researchers
ITDG and other early promoters of the CAHW approach in Kenya were informed and motivated by a range of new ideas about rural development from different disciplines. The development discourse in the early 1980s was influenced by an increasing recognition of the value of indigenous knowledge and indigenous systems, especially in pastoral areas (Toulmin 1986). The rural health revolution in China, based on barefoot doctors (as described in White 1998), stimulated much debate about the potential value of para-professional services in other sectors. World Bank studies describing the collapse of livestock service provision in sub-Saharan Africa (de Haan and Nissen 1985) spawned a number of experiments in more decentralized services based on privatized service providers, which showed promise (de Haan and Bekure 1991).

On the ground however, most NGO projects only collected the information they needed to establish and manage their projects, although most also incorporated simple monitoring and evaluation systems, allowing them to monitor how many animals had been vaccinated or treated and for what diseases. Most of this research was done with project beneficiaries using participatory methods.

Working with its partners, and using participatory techniques, ITDG collected socio-economic data (disaggregated by wealth and agro-ecological zone), information about livestock production and pre-existing animal health services, and information about traditional healers and ethno-veterinary knowledge. ITDG also monitored their programmes closely, both for internal project management and to gather evidence with which to convince others of the effectiveness of the approach. ITDG specifically collected information that might allay the usual veterinary fears over such schemes: the danger of misdiagnosis; incorrect and/or over-prescribing of drugs; and overcharging. Much of this information was made available to other organizations implementing CAHW projects in Kenya and elsewhere through publications, seminars, workshops and conferences, but little was directed specifically at the Department of Veterinary Services at policy level in Nairobi. However, there were continuous attempts at inviting the Director of Veterinary Services to attend the ITDG-EA annual vets' workshops. In addition it must be mentioned that over the past 10 years, ITDG, OAU/IBAR and others have organized field visits and study tours to project sites around Kenya and elsewhere to allow people to learn about CAHW projects at first hand.

Bilateral and multilateral donor-funded projects also undertook research for project planning and had substantial monitoring and evaluation systems. Some employed consultants to undertake traditional studies; others used participatory approaches with local communities. GTZ commissioned the Kabete Vet School to undertake a serological survey in its project areas to assess the effectiveness of the contact herders' programme.

The OAU/IBAR TRVTT project undertook traditional (serological) and participatory epidemiological research on rinderpest and other diseases before, during and after implementing CAHW vaccination programmes, as well as collecting data about the delivery of the vaccination programme itself. This information influenced OAU/IBAR, which until that time had been using more traditional approaches to support and develop the CAHW approach. This subsequently became the PARC-VAC project. The PARC-VAC project also collected substantial amounts of data to measure the effectiveness of the approach and to influence governments in the region to adopt the CAHW approach.

Various research studies were undertaken during the 1980s and 1990s by researchers from the University of Nairobi and elsewhere, but the academic community largely managed these projects, and the results rarely percolated widely outside. The first study of livestock services in the ASAL areas with substantial government ownership was commissioned in 1998 and became widely known as the Hübl study. In 1997 the EC Rural Development Adviser developed the initial proposal for the study, which proposed a two-person team of one expatriate and one Kenyan. The Department of Veterinary Services initially showed little interest in the study but eventually gave clearance and also agreed to participate. The Department however proposed that government involvement should be increased to two team members, one from the DVS (Dr Kajume) and one from the university (Professor Gathuma). The proposal from the DVS was accepted and the study got underway in February 1998. As well as field visits to investigate the situation on the ground in the ASAL areas, it included a series of stakeholder workshops in different parts of Kenya to gather as many views as possible (Hübl et al. 1998).

Credibility
Practical field experience in ASAL areas is often cited as a precondition for understanding the CAHW approach. People who have worked there and know how difficult it is to provide services in such environments usually support the approach the first time they hear about it. Others who have visited CAHW schemes claim that they were convinced by the evidence of their own eyes, the evidence presented by veterinary staff involved in the schemes, and the enthusiastic support of the schemes by livestock owners. Throughout the evolution of the approach, all players emphasized the effectiveness of taking people to see CAHW schemes in action, regardless of their position and role.

It is clear that specific evidence works for specific audiences. Reports from government vets in the field were highly valued by government staff, but few field-based vets submitted reports that explicitly described CAHW programmes until the mid-1990s. On the other hand, NGO/donor studies were valued by NGOs and donors but considered suspect by government staff, who perceived them to be biased. The evidence and recommendations of the Hübl study were highly regarded by everyone. The Department of Veterinary Services trusted it because there were two well-regarded Kenyans on the team, and the donors respected the expatriate team leader Dr Hübl. The approach they used, including discussions with a very wide range of stakeholders at workshops throughout Kenya, also contributed to a high degree of credibility.

ITDG's emphasis for information dissemination in the 1980s, including project reports, training materials and booklets based on project experience, focused on providing the information needed by others to implement the approach. Once there were several projects up and running, ITDG organized annual vets' workshops as a forum to share experiences. Workshop reports from the early 1990s, however, already emphasize the need to attract a wider range of participants, including policy makers (ITDG 1991). Despite this concern, ITDG continued to produce substantial 'how-to-do-it books' rather than materials designed for policy makers (e.g. ITDG 2000b,c).

Impact of the evidence
Until 1998, policy makers in Kenya largely ignored evidence of the value of CAHW schemes. Initially this was because they were invisible, but from 1994 the Director of Veterinary Services, although aware of the approach, deliberately chose not to engage in what he knew would involve enormous policy reforms which would not be popular with many of his colleagues and peers. OAU/IBAR raised the policy stakes considerably when they tried to obtain permission to train CAHWs for the PARC-VAC project in northern Kenya. As an intergovernmental organization they could not work without a clear agreement with the

government at national level. Their attempts to get a memorandum of understanding in 1997 helped to bring the policy issues into the open.

The lack of institutional memory and continuity in the KVA, caused by their annual replacement of the executive committee, and lack of clear policies, has been a major problem. While apparently supporting the process of policy and legal review during 1999 and 2000, there are a few KVA members in the Central Region Branch who have spent many years building up their private practice and who have always opposed it, fearing that the CAHWs might take away some of their business. They, and a small clique who are also strongly opposed but for hidden reasons, managed to turn the KVA against the process at the annual general meetings in 2002 (KVA 2002a,b). However in late 2002, the current chairperson moderated his position because he looked back through the files and discovered that the KVA has in fact been substantially involved in the discussions over the past few years. But he is facing stiff opposition from some executive committee members.

Links: influence and legitimacy

Roles and relationships
NGOs and especially the Catholic Diocese provided the first entry point for the international NGOs who established many of the first CAHW projects in Kenya. International NGOs and bilateral donors developed close working relationships with local veterinary staff to obtain the local approval to set up the projects. Later, many NGOs, bilateral and multilateral projects employed vets and other animal health staff directly.

Although ITDG had attracted some individual supporters and collaborators from national-level veterinary and research departments by the late 1980s, it was not until Dr Kajume attended the fourth annual Vets' Workshop in 1993 that there was significant contact between the action research community (those involved in establishing DAH projects) and the policy community (the Department of Veterinary Services). Between 1989 and 1997 ITDG's annual vets' workshops grew into a 'club' of organizations involved in CAHW work. Those in the club came to the workshops and shared much useful experience, whereas those outside knew very little about them. Although early workshop reports stress the need to expand membership to include national-level policy makers, this did not happen to a significant degree until the eighth workshop in 1999, after the KVB letter was published.

The CAHW idea itself served to connect various actors. KALT was registered in 1995, and became aware of the CAHW concept soon after. When the promised legal reform that would allow them to practise more freely failed to materialize, they joined forces with the NGOs to lobby for policy and legal reform – even though they knew that the different interests of CAHWs and AHTs might become a problem later on. SNV and GTZ both became involved in CAHW projects with the government in the mid-1990s. Their involvement helped to bring the

CAHW concept into the open and the government started to address the policy issues. DFID and EC advisers played a significant role in raising the policy debate in the mid- and late 1990s. The EC proposed and funded the influential Hübl study in early 1998.

In early 1992, OAU/IBAR first engaged with the policy debate, with a proposal under the TRVTT project to test a new CAHW approach to rinderpest vaccination in northern Kenya. The Director of Veterinary Services was not interested, and TRVTT developed the approach in Ethiopia, Uganda and south Sudan instead. In 1996, OAU/IBAR again tried to convince the Kenyans under the PARC-VAC project, and took Kenyan vets to see the field projects in south Sudan and Ethiopia. Eventually, in 1997, they obtained a memorandum of understanding to implement a pilot scheme in northern Kenya. The TRVTT and PARC-VAC projects taught OAU/IBAR that changing attitudes among government staff was key to the success of CAHW approaches, and that if they were to be sustainable in the longer term, animal health policies and legislation would need to be changed in many countries. OAU/IBAR seized the opportunity presented by the KVB letter in the national press in early 1998 to push for policy and legislative review in Kenya – and saw the ITDG vets' workshops as a suitable forum.

Key individuals and organizations
ITDG started some of the earliest CAHW projects in Kenya, and unlike others, had an explicit focus on developing the approach, 'proving the case', then influencing the policy environment and other actors to promote its wider replication. ITDG's annual vets' workshops became the main forum for government and non-government agency dialogue about the approach in the late 1980s and early 1990s. In 1992 an international workshop organized by ITDG both raised the profile of the approach in Kenya and brought together several individuals who would become influential in the process later on through OAU/IBAR. In the mid-1990s, ITDG put more effort into scaling-up the CAHWs approach in Kenya and the Eastern African region, through helping other organizations to establish CAHWs projects and sharing experiences in the vets' workshops. This helped to build up the critical mass of organizational and individual support to the approach. In 1995, ITDG established a decentralized animal health support unit, which was headed by one of the two ITDG vets.

The KVB letter in the national press galvanized ITDG into organizing another vets' workshop to bring together the main actors and decide what to do. However, at that time ITDG had no budget to run further workshops and had to look for resources elsewhere. OAU/IBAR offered to fund the workshop (along with SNV) but insisted that it should include all the stakeholders, including the Department of Veterinary Services, the KVA, the KVB, the Vet School and the donors. By that time, ITDG had also developed a close relationship with Dr Kajume, Deputy Director of Veterinary Services in Nairobi through the vets' workshops, and because he had contacts with the two ITDG vets (one of whom had worked with him while he was Eastern Provincial Director of Veterinary Services). Dr Kajume advised ITDG to establish a committee including representatives of all stakeholders to develop the workshop 'so that they could fight their battles before the workshop' (Kajume, personal communication). The workshop finally took place in May 1999 and was a great success. All parties agreed that CAHW schemes offered great potential to improve livestock services in ASAL areas, and established a multi-stakeholder working group to develop guidelines and standards for training of CAHWs in Kenya, and follow-up recommendations for the legislative and policy framework.

Dr Julius Kajume graduated as a vet in 1976 and has worked in the Department of Veterinary Services ever since, initially in the veterinary public health division at the Athi River Slaughter House, southern Kenya, then in Mombasa, then at the Uplands meat factory. He completed an MSc in veterinary public health at Edinburgh University in 1980, then returned to various posts in veterinary public health in and outside Nairobi, working closely with Dr Kimanzi (later to become Director of Veterinary Services) before being posted as Provincial Director of Veterinary Services in Eastern Province in 1989. While there he became involved in various CAHW initiatives including the early ITDG vets' workshops in Hunters Lodge, eastern Kenya, and Isiolo, central Kenya. In early 1995 he returned to headquarters at Kabete, central Kenya, as the Deputy Director of Veterinary Services under Dr Kimanzi, who trusted him and gave him a relatively free hand to handle policy responsibilities, including CAHW issues. Dr Kajume was highly influential in events following the publication of the KVB letter in January 1998, including the Hübl study. He also made relevant presentations at various forums, including workshops and seminars. After Dr Kimanzi retired in September 1999, Julius was acting Director of Veterinary Services until April 2000.

The EU first proposed what became known as the Hübl study in 1997, but the Department of Veterinary Services saw this as yet another expatriate donor initiative and was not very interested. After the publication of the KVB letter however, Dr Kajume saw the study as an opportunity for the Department of Veterinary Services to be seen as responding to the issues, and taking some control. He suggested to Dr Kimanzi that the study should go ahead, but with two Kenyans on the team: one from the Department, the other from the University. The study took place between March and May 1998, and largely because it was seen as a Department-led study, it convinced others in the Department, the KVB and the KVA of the need to look seriously at the CAHW approach (Hübl et al. 1998).

The OAU/IBAR Pan African Rinderpest Project has been supporting the Department of Veterinary Services' rinderpest vaccination programme since 1990s. Until the mid-1990s, the programme used a vaccine that required refrigeration and a traditional approach to vaccination campaigns. OAU/IBAR's TRVTT project developed a new approach using a thermostable vaccine delivered by CAHWs during the early 1990s. The project had tried unsuccessfully to interest the Department of Veterinary Services in a pilot project using the approach in northern Kenya in 1992, but had achieved very good results in neighbouring Ethiopia, Uganda and south Sudan, leading to the development of the PARC-VAC project in 1996. It took OAU/IBAR one year to convince the DVS in Kenya to try the approach in Kenya – during which time the CAHW issue came to a head, culminating in the KVB letter in January 1998. Since then, OAU/IBAR has been a major player in the policy and legal reform process by funding and encouraging many of the multi-stakeholder preparatory and drafting processes.

Legitimacy
Legitimacy was established at several levels throughout the livestock services process in Kenya. Some of the most influential evidence seems to have been the enthusiasm of the communities themselves for the CAHW approach, both to participate in them and to talk about them with visitors. ITDG and other NGOs organized many field visits for vets and others to visit project sites and meet the vets and livestock owners involved in them. The Hübl study was highly regarded by everyone because it was perceived as a Department of Veterinary Services study; it included highly regarded researchers from the Department, the University and an internationally respected expatriate consultant; it gathered evidence from a very wide range of stakeholders; and it discussed the results and recommendations in a open forum to which all stakeholders were invited. Subsequent workshops and working groups have been influential because great care was taken to ensure that all the key stakeholders were involved at all stages: developing the approach, undertaking the work, discussing the results and agreeing the final recommendations.

Discussion

Chapter 2 of this volume presents the integrated three-dimensional framework and some of the theory behind it. The Kenya case study seems to fit both well.

Politics and institutions

Political systems in Kenya are intrinsically conservative and slow to change. Animal health policy in Kenya in the 1980s was largely controlled by the Director of Veterinary Services and a small group of close advisers, whose attitudes towards animal health services were based largely on European models that they had tried to emulate throughout the country. Field veterinarians very quickly discovered that this was not possible under the financial constraints of the early 1990s, and many started working with NGOs and bilateral agencies to implement community-based animal healthcare programmes. But it took many years for policy makers in Nairobi to accept the need for change, possibly because the Director of Veterinary Services between 1990 and 1994, who had been seconded into the position from the University, brought with him very traditional views and was strongly opposed to anything that appeared to undermine professional standards and ethics. Williams (1973) would explain the prevalent, rather traditional, attitudes towards animal health services among veterinarians in Kenya as the 'dominant' view; the new Director's emphasis on professional standards and ethics as 'residual'; and the new ideas among NGOs, bilateral donors and some government staff in the field supporting the new DAH approaches as the 'emergent' view. Since the emergent view presents itself as an alternative to the prevailing dominant view, it poses a threat to several powerful people and institutions, and is likely to face considerable opposition before it eventually (if ever) replaces the dominant view. Chambers (1993) provides a similar perspective when he describes the professions as inherently stable and conservative, with strong in-built barriers to change.

Meanwhile, vets in the field or 'street-level bureaucrats' (Lipsky, 1980), finding themselves with virtually no operational budgets, adopted the community animal healthcare approaches being promoted by NGOs and bilateral agencies as the only way they could continue to provide any services at all.

The interplay between external pressures for change, financial reality at field level, and structural adjustment policies at central level, and professional attitudes, pragmatic at field level and idealistic at central level, created a climate in which, although the new approaches could develop in the field, they were unlikely to be accepted in the centre, at least until a more open-minded Director of Veterinary Services took over in 1994.

By that time, the policy context was much more complex. There were more players involved – NGOs, bilateral and multilateral agencies were promoting community-based animal healthcare services; many field veterinarians were already involved in them; and the KVB and KVA being distinct bodies, independent of government, were increasingly representing the views of private veterinarians. The policy process had become the sort of complex, highly politicized process described by Sutton (1999) and Keeley and Scoones (1999), with increasingly polarized views developing in the different camps, and no mechanism for dialogue and resolution.

In early 1998 the publication of a letter in the national press by the KVB, threatening to de-register any vets involved in community animal healthcare programmes, brought matters to a crisis, forcing the NGO community, bilateral donors and government to get together to find a solution. It is very difficult now to find out exactly what provoked the KVB to publish the letter: there are several competing narratives that are described earlier.

Whatever the cause, the KVB letter brought about the kind of crisis necessary to allow a new problem-solving paradigm to emerge. Kuhn (1970) explains that new paradigms often run in parallel with existing paradigms until the old paradigm is no longer able to provide solutions to the continuous stream of problems. When enough 'insoluble' problems stack up, a sense of crisis sets in, and people are then willing to turn to alternative or new paradigms that offer to provide new solutions. If the new paradigm is able to deal with the problems, it will gradually come to be accepted.

The case in Kenya shows that this sense of crisis can set in at different times for different groups in the policy and implementation process. Street-level bureaucrats are often forced to deal with new problems before high-level policy makers, and therefore go through the process of crisis and adoption of a new paradigm earlier. The coexistence of different problem-solving paradigms that can be seen in the different levels of policy making and implementation in Kenya seems to have contributed to the delayed official policy change and also to the sense of confusion.

Evidence and legitimacy

Most of the NGOs involved in community-based animal healthcare programmes in Kenya did not set out to research how to improve animal healthcare; they simply applied a generic and relatively well-known international model (based on the Chinese barefoot doctor model) using highly participatory approaches. They were very successful, and farmers and local veterinarians very quickly became enthusiastic supporters. The visible evidence, on the ground and as described by farmers and local veterinary personnel, had high legitimacy and was extremely convincing for visitors. Watzlawick (1978) contends that some of the most effective communication is unintentional, tacit communication between two individuals who happen to be in the same place at the same time, and can have an enormous impact.

ITDG generated more technical information, specifically to engage with policy makers, circulated it through workshops and seminars which few policy makers attended, and packaged it in handbooks and guidelines for practitioners rather than policy briefs for policy makers. The choice of the term 'community animal-health worker' may have made the task of explaining the approach more difficult than it need have been. Using the term 'community-based vet scout' might have been easier for veterinary professionals to accept, since vet scouts had been an essential component of early veterinary services in Kenya.

Bilateral and multilateral donor-funded projects generated yet more scientific data, partly to provide evidence to protect government vets working with them, which they presented in scientific meetings in Kenya and in neighbouring countries. All of these contributed to the general debate, but mainly among practitioners already engaged in community-based animal healthcare projects. Although different information materials were developed for different audiences, there is little sign of the sort of coordinated policy-advocacy campaign increasingly recognized as essential to influence policy makers (for example,

Chapman and Fisher, 1999), and much of the early NGO-based evidence was discounted by the veterinary profession in Kenya as biased.

The Hübl study in 1998 was the first research to be taken seriously, and was frequently quoted as being highly influential by informants from all sides. The study was launched in early 1998, immediately after the KVB letter, and was implemented by a team of three – one expatriate and two national veterinarians. The process was highly participatory, with multi-stakeholder workshops at regional and national level.

Although not really research, the ITDG vets' workshops, and regional and international workshops on community animal healthcare, mainly organized by NGOs, were also regarded as influential, particularly the 1992 ITDG workshop which brought participants from many other countries to Kenya, and the VetAid 1997 workshop in Tanzania which was attended by many Kenyan vets.

Various forms of information were clearly important in the animal healthcare story in Kenya, but it is difficult to estimate what was the most effective and for whom. McPherson (1994) stresses the need to find mechanisms to quantify the value of information as an asset that can reduce uncertainty and risk, and improve coordination and efficiency.

Links: influence and legitimacy

Policy networks are widely recognized as important instruments for establishing and promoting discourses and policy reform (Keeley and Scoones 1999). Various forms of policy networks have been described in the literature and the key distinguishing feature seems to be the position of their members in relation to the policy making process (Crewe and Young 2002).

Networks clearly played a crucial role in the decentralized animal healthcare story. The ITDG annual vets' workshops, which started in 1988 as a mechanism to share ideas between the emerging DAH projects and government staff, became a well-established network during the early 1990s. Although there was a clear objective early on to engage with government policy makers, by the mid-1990s it seems to have become a 'club' of like-minded practitioners sharing expertise about project implementation, sometimes called an 'issue network', rather than a policy community or advocacy coalition, engaging with and seeking to influence government policy. By 1997, it had more or less run out of funds and steam. A campaign by the NGOs to stimulate discussion of the principles and practice within the DVS at that time could have generated support within the Department much earlier.

By that time, some other major players including OAU/IBAR and SNV had started implementing community animal healthcare programmes in Kenya, and had already negotiated official agreements with the Kenyan government. In 1999 they helped to fund and organize the influential vets workshop (renamed DAH workshop) at Meru, which established the more inclusive, policy-orientated network, the DAH working group.

Chapman and Fisher (1999) stress that legitimacy is a vital component of advocacy campaigns, and this can often only be achieved through a long involvement with grassroots organizations. The recently defunct ITDG vets' workshops therefore provided a useful vehicle for the 1999 workshop at Meru because it was well established and well regarded. The workshops were often held in the field so that participants could visit DAH projects and learn about them directly from the communities and animal health staff involved in them.

Opportunities for change

The section above titled 'The evolution of animal healthcare in Kenya' provides a detailed narrative of events leading to the development of new policies for decentralized animal healthcare in Kenya. Although all were important, some events indicate clear changes in the political context, quality of evidence or relationship between policy makers and DAH researchers/practitioners:

a) The arrival of ITDG in 1986 with an explicit focus on developing and testing new approaches, then seeking to influence the policy environment so they can be implemented more widely. A major part of ITDG's work was to gather the evidence to make the case for DAH approaches. Sessional Paper No. 1 of 1986 (Government of Kenya 1986), 'Economic management for renewed growth,' set the stage for structural adjustment within government and the privatization of public services created a favourable macro-policy context for the reform of livestock services.

b) The first ITDG vets' workshop in 1988 marked a vital increase of interaction between researchers/practitioners and policy makers.

c) Dr Wamukoya's appointment in 1990, and his emphasis on veterinary professionalism and ethics, reversed an emerging interest in policy reform driven by falling government budgets, and emerging evidence of the value of the alternative decentralized animal healthcare model.

d) The establishment of bilateral DAH projects in 1992 added weight to the evidence in favour of DAH approaches, and ITDG's international DAH workshop strengthened the emerging network of practitioners and links between policy makers and practitioners.

e) Dr Kajume's attendance at the vets' workshop in 1993 marked further improvement in linkages between researchers/practitioners and policy makers.

f) Dr Kimanzi's appointment as Director of Veterinary Services in 1994 and the return of Dr Kajume to Nairobi dramatically improved the policy context for DAH approaches.

g) The gradual increase in the number of agencies training CAHWs between 1994 and 1997 further strengthened the evidence in favour of DAH approaches, and also contributed to the publication of the letter by the KVB in 1998.

h) The publication of the letter by the KVB in 1998 brought all stakeholders together into a policy network to try to find a solution to the problem, and the Hübl study increased the weight of evidence still further.

i) The Meru workshop in 1999, which provided a clear signal from policy makers that they were interested in finding a solution, improved the policy context still further.

j) The policy context could not have been better while Julius Kajume was acting Director of Veterinary Services in late 1999 and early 2000, but decreased significantly with the appointment of the more conservative Dr Chong.

k) Increasing opposition to the new policies from the KVA both undermined the policy coalition reducing the link between researchers/practitioners and policy makers, and complicated and worsened the policy context.

These changes can be plotted cumulatively on a graph to show visually how the overall context for policy change varied over time (Figure 5.1).

Figure 5.1 *Opportunity for Policy Change*

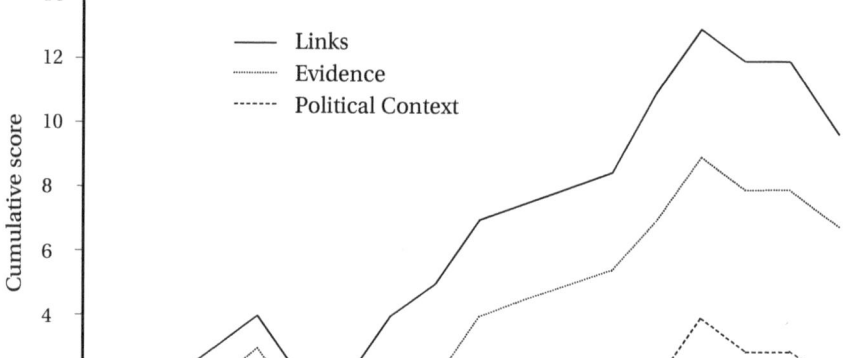

The figure shows a gradual improvement in the overall context for policy change up to the end of 1989, shortly after the launch of the ITDG vets' workshops, but this worsened dramatically in 1990 with Dr Wamukoya's emphasis on professionalism. Although the weight of evidence and links between researchers/practitioners and policy makers improved gradually over the following few years, the political context did not improve until Dr Kimanzi took over in 1994. Thereafter, his turning of a blind eye to the development of DAH services in the field allowed a gradual increase in evidence and links, but the political context did not really improve until after the KVB letter in 1998. The opportunity for policy change peaked in late 1999, when the multi-stakeholder working group had developed new policy papers and while Dr Kajume was acting Director of Veterinary Services. Since then, the appointment of Dr Chong and opposition by the KVA has once again reduced the opportunity for policy change.

As of October 2002, new draft policy documents and legislation for veterinary services and pharmacies which would legalize community-based animal health workers had been prepared and were 'in the system,' but nobody quite knew where, or what would happen next.

Conclusion

This case study reaffirms much of the current theory of research–policy linkages. The policy process was influenced far more by the political context than by anything else, and personalities and personal relationships, both in the research/practitioner and policy communities, were at least as important as any formal relationships and structures.

The crisis caused by the KVB letter in 1998 was clearly the tipping point. Beforehand there was a long period where CAHW schemes gradually proliferated, generating powerful evidence of their value, and providing an issue around which different groups of stakeholders, supporters and antagonists could form formal and informal networks. Afterwards, there was a surprisingly long process where all stakeholders came together to develop a new policy framework.

Over the last year or so, the process has reached a stalemate. The documents are somewhere in the system, but nobody knows quite where, or even what the process is now to get them adopted and the necessary legislation changed. It seems that many senior officers in the Kenyan government system do not have a clear understanding of how policies and legislation are developed and enacted.

Although ITDG and other early promoters in Kenya were clearly influenced by new ideas about the value of indigenous systems, para-professional services and the need to privatize some government services, emerging in the development discourse, formal research seems to have contributed relatively little to the policy process in Kenya, and research reports even less so (with the exception of the Hübl study). Evidence generated by operational CAHW schemes, communicated directly to visitors by livestock owners and the animal health staff directly involved in them, seems to have been much more important. Early on, this evidence contributed to the rising popularity of DAH programmes with donors and field veterinarians, and in the mid-1990s, albeit second hand, to the alarm of the KVB resulting in their open letter to the national press, which brought everybody together and resulted in the new policy framework legitimizing the approach – the exact opposite of what the KVB had hoped.

Although it is relatively easy to understand how the process evolved and why it took so long, it is difficult to see how it could have happened much faster. A carefully managed process to try to influence Dr Wamukoya's attitudes might have helped him to see the benefits of the approach, but nobody in the research/practitioner camp had the necessary connections to do that at the time. By the time Dr Kimanzi took over, there was more evidence and Dr Kajume was already onboard and supporting the idea. At this time, it may have been possible to develop a campaign to increase contact with the veterinary department in order to accelerate enthusiasm for a new policy framework. The fact that this did not happen may be because the most prominent network, based around ITDG's vets' workshops, had lost their policy edge, and ITDG's publications were aimed at practitioners rather than policy makers. Ensuring the vets' workshops continued to include senior policy makers, rather then government vet practitioners, and a communication strategy to target tailor-made communication materials at policy makers may have accelerated the process considerably in the mid-1990s. It may have been possible to promote more widespread reform within the Veterinary Department, with DAH as one component, by working with the ASMP in the mid-1990s. Since the KVB letter provoked the crisis that brought all the stakeholders together, another option might have been to deliberately provoke a crisis earlier. This however would have been very risky for an NGO in Kenya.

With the benefit of hindsight, distance and the results of this study, it is possible to suggest some changes in what was done, that might have accelerated the process.

- More effort by ITDG to understand the policy context for DAH programmes – the legal and policy framework, the key actors, their attitudes and influences, and the reform processes and programmes (for example, the ASMP).
- More effort earlier on to get government staff, especially those opposed to the idea, to visit operational CAHW schemes and learn first hand about the conditions in pastoral areas, how effective the schemes were, and how they could compliment the government system.
- More effort early on to generate interest among non-veterinary government staff and Members of Parliament at local level, convincing them of the value of the approach for poverty alleviation in their district.
- Once there were a number of schemes up and running, a clearer communication strategy to influence government vets and government policy could have been put in place. This could have included ensuring that policy makers attended the vets' workshops, helping the government vets that were already involved in working schemes to communicate with policy makers, and producing information materials designed for policy makers rather than practitioners.

- A deliberate strategy to get to know the key players – the Director and Deputy Directors of Veterinary Services in Nairobi – and work out how best to influence them. This might have included overseas visits, collaborative work (helping government vets to prepare and present papers at international conferences proved very successful in the DFID DELIVERI project), and mobilizing non-veterinary civil servants (those convinced of the approach through the third point above) to apply pressure on the Veterinary Department.
- More effort to understand the policy process – how new ideas become incorporated into policy, and new legislation enacted.
- Accelerating the process of preparing the new policy papers so that they could have been approved while Dr Kimanzi was the Director and Dr Kajume his deputy, or while the latter was acting Director of Veterinary Services.

However, it is also clear from this case study that taking the time to develop strong relationships with local communities, and working with them to develop effective and sustainable community-based services, is essential to prove the effectiveness of an approach, and acquire the fundamental legitimacy to advocate for change. That takes time, and the early pioneers of the approach in Kenya, the Catholic Diocese of Lodwar (northern Kenya), ITDG and its partners, and early members of the vets' workshop network deserve recognition for the enormous effort they have made over the past 17 years.

Chapter Six
Sustainable livelihoods: a case study of the evolution of DFID policy

WILLIAM SOLESBURY

Introduction

This case study examines the influence of research on a particular shift in policy of the UK Department for International Development (DFID).[71] The policy in question is known as the sustainable livelihoods approach (SLA).[72] A sustainable livelihood is commonly accepted as comprising:

... the capabilities, assets (including both material and social resources) for a means of living. A livelihood is sustainable when it can cope with and recover from stresses and shocks and maintain or enhance its capabilities and assets both now and in the future, while not undermining the natural resource base. (DFID 1999d)

The concept of sustainable livelihoods was an important element in the new Labour administration's 1997 White Paper on international development. Its core commitment was to:

... refocus our international development efforts on the elimination of poverty and encouragement of economic growth which benefits the poor. We will do this through support for international sustainable development targets and policies that create sustainable livelihoods for poor people, *promote human development and conserve the environment*. (DFID 1997: summary, emphasis added)

The concept, which first appeared in research literature in the 1980s,[73] by the late 1990s had become one of a trio of principles underpinning UK development policy and the basis for a number of DFID programmes and practices.[74] How did this happen? This chapter first provides a roughly chronological account of the evolution and adoption of the SLA concept; then identifies some key stages in the narrative at which important interactions between research, policy and/or practice occurred; finally it analyses the case study in terms of context, evidence and links.

The development of the sustainable livelihoods approach

The Brundtland Commission and the first UNDP Human Development Report

The Brundtland Commission Report of 1987 saw the first appearance in policy debate of what was conceptualized later as SLA. The report put the concept of sustainable development firmly on the global political agenda. It defined sustainable development as:

> ... *development that meets the needs of the present without compromising the ability of future generations to meet their own needs. It contains within it two key concepts: the concept of 'needs,' in particular the essential needs of the world's poor, to which overriding priority should be given; and the idea of limitations imposed by the state of technology and social organisation on the environment's ability to meet present and future needs.* (World Commission on Environment and Development 1987a: 43)

It went on to argue that the pursuit of sustainable development requires:

- a political system that secures for citizens the opportunity to participate effectively in decision making;
- an economic system that is able to generate surpluses and technical knowledge on a self-reliant and sustained basis;
- a social system that provides for solutions for the tensions arising from disharmonious development;
- a production system that respects the obligation to preserve the ecological basis for development;
- a technological system that searches continuously for new solutions;
- an international system that fosters sustainable patterns of trade and finance;
- a flexible administrative system that has the capacity for self-correction (World Commission in Environment and Development 1987a: 65).

The first Human Development Report from the United Nations Development Programme (UNDP) shared much of this analysis (UNDP 1990). This and subsequent reports addressed development in terms of individual and household health, education and well-being, thus shifting the focus away from the (macro)economic bias of development thinking through the 1980s.

Many of the ingredients that subsequently characterized the SLA were evident in the Brundtland and the Human Development reports: the focus on poor people and their needs; the importance of citizen participation; the emphasis on self-reliance and sustainability; the ecological constraint. These subsequently became powerful terms in the lexicon of international development policy and politics, particularly in the work of the UN's 1992 Environment Conference in Rio, the 1995 World Summit for Social Development and the 1996 World Food Summit.

Chambers and Conway (1992) and its precursors

The origination of sustainable livelihood as a concept is widely attributed to Robert Chambers at the Institute of Development Studies (IDS). The key reference is the 1992 discussion paper he co-authored with Gordon Conway (Chambers and Conway 1992). Here they offered a working definition similar to the definition subsequently adopted by DFID:[75]

A livelihood comprises the capabilities, assets (stores, resources, claims and access) and activities required for a means of living; a livelihood is sustainable which can cope with and recover from stress and shocks, maintain or enhance its capabilities and assets, and provide sustainable livelihood opportunities for the next generation; and which contributes net benefits to other livelihoods at the local and global levels and in the short and long-term. (Chambers and Conway 1992: 7)

The paper explicitly recognized that it was both reacting against and building on earlier thinking. It criticized many previous analyses of production, employment and income as industrial and reductionist, which 'do not fit or capture the complex and diverse realities of most rural life' (Chambers and Conway 1992: 4). It presented sustainable livelihoods as linking the three extant concepts of capability, equity and sustainability. For each of these, there was a tradition of research extending back through the 1980s and even earlier in some cases. For example, reference is made in the paper to the work of Sen (1981), Jodha (1988) and Schumacher (1973) in relation to capability and to that of Pearce et al. (1989), Lele (1991) and Swift (1989) in relation to sustainability, for which Chambers and Conway emphasized the social as well as the environmental dimension.

In the paper, Chambers and Conway offered a framework for development thinking that was both normative and practical. Their concluding policy prescriptions were presented under three headings (Chambers and Conway 1992: 31).

- Enhancing capability – in facing change and unpredictability, people are versatile, quick to adapt and able to exploit diverse resources and opportunities.
- Improving equity – priority should be given to the capabilities, assets and access of the poorer, including minorities and women.
- Increasing social sustainability – the vulnerability of the poor should be minimized by reducing external stress and shocks and providing safety nets.

The final paragraphs of the paper restated its purpose:

In this paper we have tried to open up and explore concepts, analogies and relationships to fit future needs. In doing so, we have rejected some conventional professional wisdom. In the spirit of exploration, we have also allowed ourselves the liberty of speculation, of seeing where a line of thinking would lead. In consequence, the paper raises more questions than it answers. It also puts forward combinations of working concepts, categories and hypotheses for testing for practical utility. (Chambers and Conway 1992: 34)

Donor practices in the early 1990s

By the early 1990s, certain donor agencies had seen sufficient merit in sustainable livelihoods to begin employing SLA in their work. From 1993, Koos Neefjes in Oxfam was promoting sustainable livelihoods as a component in formulating its overall aims, improving project strategies, and in staff training. Oxfam later published reports on ideas, experiences and achievements of country projects in the livelihoods field. In a strategic policy statement, Oxfam maintained the 'right to sustainable livelihoods' as one of its five overall aims (Oxfam 1998e; Neefjes 2000). In 1994, CARE International adopted 'household livelihoods security' as a programme framework in its relief and development work. The following year, after the World Summit for Social Development, the UNDP adopted the promotion of sustainable livelihoods as one of its five mandates. It has pursued this in two ways: as an analytical and planning methodology (Helmore and Singh 2001) and in the design and delivery of its country programmes (Roe 1998).

The approach to operating SLA in these agencies was later compared with that subsequently adopted by DFID (Carney et al. 1999). The conclusion was that all four agencies shared an asset-based approach and all stressed the need for effective micro/macro policy and practice links; but they differed in their understanding of sustainability, their stress on empowerment and the role of technology.

Empirical sustainable livelihoods research leading to the 1996 SLA programme

In the early 1990s, empirical research on sustainable livelihoods also proceeded in a number of places worldwide. For example, in 1993 the International Institute for Sustainable Development (IISD) in Canada, where Naresh Singh was appointed Director of a new Poverty and Sustainable Development programme, undertook case studies in a number of African countries funded by the UNDP (Singh and Kalala 1995; Rennie and Singh 1996).[76] A year later, the Society for International Development (SID), with financial support from the Netherlands' government, began a three-year, multi-country project on Sustainable Livelihoods and People's Everyday Economics 'to contribute to the search for alternatives to mainstream development strategies, support ongoing civil society-led experiments in countries of the South, and develop further the theory of the sustainable livelihoods approach to sustainable development' (Amalric 1998: 1). It involved contributions from researchers and NGOs, case studies in 19 countries, regional workshops in Bangladesh, Tanzania and Colombia, and two international round tables.

IDS continued work on sustainable livelihoods through the 1990s, both through individual[77] and group projects. The IDS Environment Group, for example, won an award in 1996 under the Economic and Social Research Council's Global Environmental Change programme for work on environmental entitlements, which established a new focus on institutional processes governing access to resources – an important precursor for later sustainable livelihoods work at IDS (Leach et al. 1997a,b, 1999).

The International Institute for Environment and Development (IIED) continued work on its Sustainable Agriculture and Rural Livelihoods programme, established in 1986. Through a succession of projects, initially under Gordon Conway's direction, it has undertaken many case studies, publishing a 'Policies that Work' series of reports and developing a mode of research for participatory learning and action (Pretty et al. 1995). Sustainable livelihoods research was also undertaken by John Farrington, Diana Carney and Caroline Ashley at the Overseas Development Institute (ODI) (Farrington et al. 1999) and by Frank Ellis at the University of East Anglia (Ellis 1998a,b).

It was in this context of developing sustainable livelihoods practice and research that DFID's predecessor – the Overseas Development Administration (ODA) – decided in 1995-96 to invest in a major research programme on sustainable livelihoods.[78] The topic had emerged as a priority for research under the Administration's Economic and Social Research programme (ESCOR), following a wide-ranging consultation both inside ODA and outside in the research and practice communities, conducted by Sean Conlin, Head of ESCOR. Research centres already active in this field were invited to submit a 'capability statement' and subsequently four received invitations to tender.

This competition was won by IDS at the University of Sussex, in partnership with Sussex's Poverty Research Unit and IIED. Their project had an institutional focus, addressing the questions: What institutional arrangements enable some poor people to achieve sustainable, secure livelihoods when others fail? What policies support both groups? Fieldwork in the IDS project was undertaken in Bangladesh, Ethiopia and Mali with local collaborators (Brock and Coulibaly 1999; Carswell et al. 2000; Shankland 2000; Toufique 2000). The Overseas Development Group (ODG) at the University of East Anglia was a runner-up in the ESCOR bid and components of its proposal were also funded, including work on livelihood diversification (Ellis, 1998b, 2000a,b).

In 2000, a further three large-scale research awards were made in the sustainable livelihoods area by DFID's Policy Research Programme, following a competitive tender process in which 11 institutions or consortia were invited to bid. These were won by the ODI (John Farrington) for work in South Asia; ODG (Frank Ellis) for work in East Africa and Malawi; and IDS Sussex (Ian Scoones and Melissa Leach) for work in southern Africa. These projects were respectively called Livelihood Futures (ODI), LADDER (ODG), and Policy Reforms around Land, Water and Wild Resources (IDS). In addition, part funding was provided to a fourth project, based at Leeds University (John Soussan), for additional work in South Asia.

Collaboration has characterized this research as much as competition. Members of some research teams were part of more than one bidding consortium. Also much inter-institutional collaboration is found in the funded projects. Additionally there has been an expanded participation in the work by researchers from the countries where the research is being undertaken.

The 1997 White Paper

The November 1997 White Paper (DFID 1997) made the elimination of poverty in poorer countries the overriding aim of UK policy for international development. It also reaffirmed the UK's commitment to the International Development Targets endorsed *inter alia* by the Development Assistance Committee of the Organisation for Economic Cooperation and Development (OECD).[79] In pursuit of these goals, the White Paper adopted the creation of sustainable livelihoods for poor people as one of three priority policy objectives, alongside promoting human development and conserving the environment.

Although the White Paper offered no formal definition of sustainable livelihood, it expressed a range of views and offered a number of prescriptions that spelled out its meaning.

- All people have the same basic needs: fresh air to breathe, clean water to drink, uncontaminated food to eat, and livelihoods that allow them to earn their keep and raise healthy, educated children (DFID 1997: paragraph 1.7).
- Poor people have assets in their own skills, in their social institutions, in their values and cultures and in their detailed and sophisticated knowledge of their own environment (DFID 1997: paragraph 1.11).
- Given the necessary support, the poor can be the means as well as the beneficiaries of sustainable development (DFID 1997: paragraph 1.12).
- In order to benefit and promote the participation of the poor, economic growth must incorporate a sound and open macro-economic framework in which resources are used productively and which facilitates the development of income- and employment-generating activities that specifically include poor people, particularly women, since the majority of the poor are women (DFID 1997: paragraph 1.17).
- The State must also provide a framework of law and regulation within which people can exercise their rights; it is the poor everywhere who pay the price where these conditions are not in place (DFID 1997: paragraph 1.19).

In the White Paper, sustainable livelihood was presented as a policy objective rather than a specific programme. It was to be delivered through a wide range of policies and actions (DFID 1997: Statement of Purpose, panel 3): sound policies and pro-poor economic growth; the development of efficient and well-regulated markets; access of poor people to land, resources and markets; good governance and the realization of human rights; the prevention and resolution of conflicts; and the removal of gender discrimination. After 1998, the Department's annual reports always included a chapter on policies and actions that promote sustainable livelihoods, in which DFID's work directed towards the 1997 White Paper objective was reported.

The sustainable rural livelihoods framework (1998)

In June 1998, IDS published a working paper providing an analytical framework for sustainable rural livelihoods (Scoones 1998). Figure 6.1 (see page 140) shows the framework diagram from this paper. What it expressed was the question:

Given a particular context *(of policy setting, politics, history, agro-ecology and socio-economic conditions), what combination of* livelihood resources *(different kinds of capital) result in the ability to follow what combination of* livelihood strategies *(agricultural intensification/ extensification, livelihood diversification and migration) with what* outcomes? *Of particular interest in this framework are the* institutional processes *(embedded in a matrix of formal and informal institutions and organisations) which mediate the ability to carry out such strategies and achieve (or not) such outcomes.* (Scoones 1998: 3, emphasis in original)

The framework therefore highlighted five interacting elements: contexts, resources, institutions, strategies and outcomes.

In elaborating on these, the paper acknowledged the existing research from which it had derived its ideas. The framework originated from IDS brainstorming in 1996, during preparation of their bid for DFID's research programme on sustainable livelihoods. ODG's bid contained a different version, with some similarities to the IDS framework but independently developed from the same set of ideas. These frameworks were discussed in 1998 by the DFID Rural Livelihoods Advisory Group of which Scoones was a member (see 'Natural Resources Department's SLA initiative' below). A framework diagram was eventually adopted by the group, discussed at the NRAC conference and published by DFID (Carney 1998; see Figure 6.2, page 141).

Natural Resources Department's SLA initiative

In January 1998, the Natural Resources Policy and Advisory Department (NRPAD) in DFID, under Michael Scott, initiated a consultation on SLA. The consultation extended both within DFID (at headquarters and in regional offices) and outside (with NGOs, other donor agencies, researchers and consultants). A Rural Livelihoods Advisory Group was also established, comprising a mix of DFID officials and outsiders from the UK research community, plus Oxfam. Michael Scott was the chair and Diana Carney, then a researcher at the ODI, was secretary. Its prime objective was to implement the sustainable livelihoods concept

Figure 6.1 *IDS's sustainable livelihoods framework*

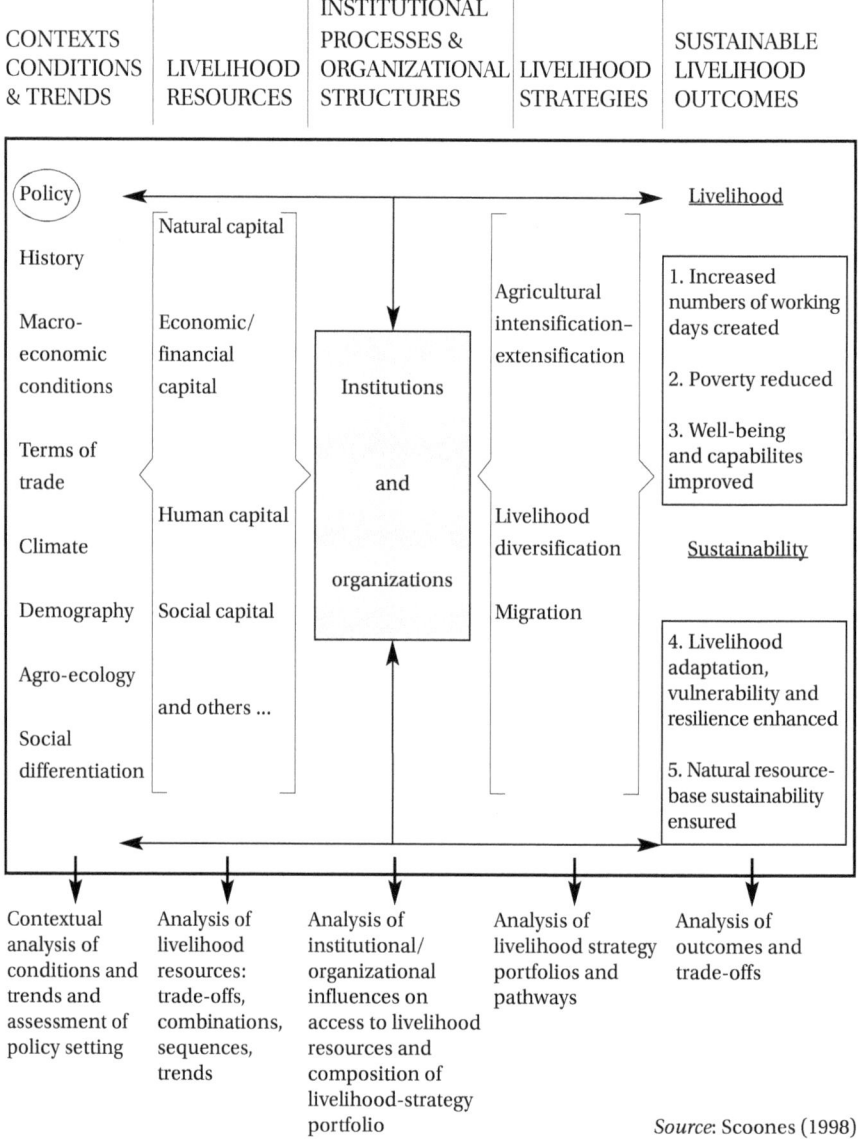

Source: Scoones (1998)

to which the White Paper had committed UK policy. The group produced papers that were presented at the DFID natural resources advisers' conference in July 1998 (Carney 1998).

In April 1999, all this work was brought within the ambit of a newly created Sustainable Livelihoods Support Office (SLSO) within DFID. Jane Clark was appointed head of the SLSO. The office had four advisers with different programme expertise and 'link persons' in other DFID departments.

Figure 6.2 DFID's sustainable livelihoods framework

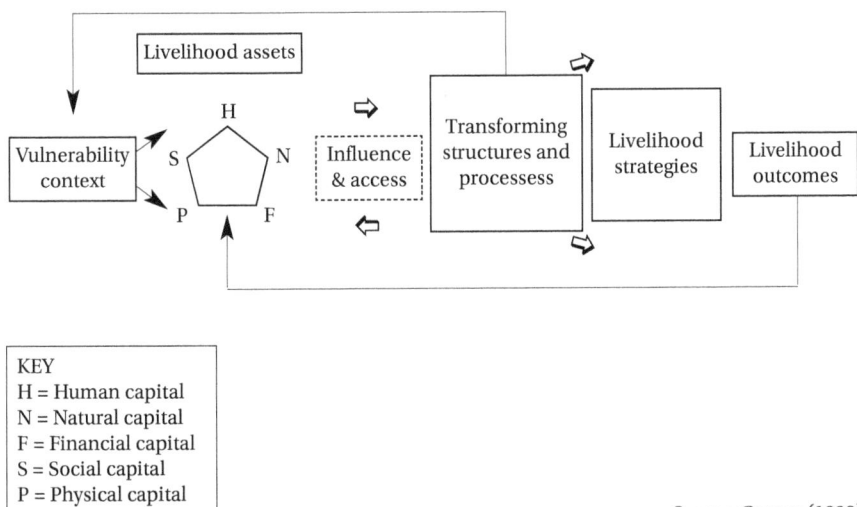

Source: Carney (1998)

In the subsequent years, the SLSO actively promoted SLA in a number of ways.

- Preparation of a series of sustainable livelihoods guidance sheets to summarize and share emerging thinking on SLA – the first, which provided an overview, was published in April 1999, and others followed on conceptual framework, uses, methods, policy reform, comparing development approaches, SLA in practice, and on references and sources (DFID 1999d, 2000d, 2001). French, Spanish and Portuguese translations are available.
- Creation of the Livelihoods Connect website (www.livelihoods.org), managed for DFID by IDS, with reference material; news of publications, policy developments and events; an open noticeboard; links to organizations; and an email update service for subscribers.
- Provision of distance-learning materials for practitioners, based on the guidance sheets and available from the Livelihoods Connect website.
- In succession to the earlier virtual resource centre, the establishment of the Sustainable Livelihoods Resource Group (SLRG) – a group of researchers and consultants with call-down contracts to act as advisers to DFID, either individually or through the formation of subgroups.
- Promoting and supporting the application of SLA in DFID's country programmes – SLSO estimates that up to £200 million has been spent in SLA-relevant aid (estimate by Jane Clark in interview).
- Running workshops and conferences – for example, a series of forums to introduce SLA to consultants; in-country training of

DFID and partner organizations; a regional workshop in Bangladesh in May 2001.
- Publishing promotional reports on SLA, many authored by researchers and consultants, on topics such as the lessons from early experience (Ashley and Carney 1999); comparison of different agencies' approaches to SL (Carney et al. 1999); the contribution of SLA to poverty reduction (DFID 1999c); a review of current SLA thinking and practice (DFID 2000a); and an explanation of DFID's livelihoods approach (DFID 2000b).
- Commissioning further research under the DFID Policy Research Programme with a focus on the implementation of SLA policies (see 'Empirical sustainable livelihoods research leading to the 1996 SLA programme' above).

The annual three-day meetings of DFID's natural resources advisers provided regular opportunities to reflect on progress with SLA, exchange experiences and develop ideas. Outsiders from the practice or research communities were always involved, often as presenters or discussion leaders. Papers from the conferences are often published (e.g. Carney 1998; Ashley and Carney 1999). In 2001 Diana Carney conducted a more thoroughgoing review for DFID, involving consultation with the research, policy and practice communities and subsequent discussions at a meeting in October 2001 (Carney 2002).

Inter-agency working

DFID operates in a global context of NGOs, other donor agencies and multilateral institutions. The 1997 White Paper made a commitment to:

> *work closely with other donors and development agencies to build partnerships with developing countries to strengthen the commitment to the elimination of poverty, and use our influence to help mobilise the political will to achieve the International Development Targets.* (DFID 1997: section 2 summary)

Following the 1997 White Paper, DFID actively promoted SLA with other agencies. This was pursued through:

- Inclusive policy-development work, consulting widely with NGOs, other donor agencies and partner organizations, as DFID reflected on experience with SLA and developed SL thinking – often engaging external consultants in this work.
- Joint initiatives – a good example is the March 2000 inter-agency forum on implementing sustainable livelihoods approaches. This was organized by the Food and Agriculture Organization of the UN (FAO), part-funded by DFID and attended by representatives of CARE International, the World Food Programme (WFP), UNDP

and the International Fund for Agricultural Development (IFAD) (FAO 2000). As a follow-up, DFID has funded an FAO Livelihoods Support Programme seeking to improve the impact of FAO interventions through the application of SLA.
- Facilitating job mobility of UK researchers, policy makers and practitioners for permanent posts, short-term contracts or secondments with various multilateral organizations including the World Bank, FAO and IFAD.

Late 1990s research, connecting the macro and micro

In the late 1990s, a new strand of work by researchers began exploring the interconnections between practical analyses and actions to promote sustainable livelihoods on the ground and the broader questions of development policy. The rationale was that:

there remains a wide gap between bottom-up livelihoods analysis and top-down policy analysis with the findings of the former generally being seen as too context-specific to guide policy making, and the findings of the latter generally being seen as too highly aggregated to reflect the complexity of livelihoods. (Shankland 2000: summary)

Some of this new work was emerging from existing empirical research, some was more the product of conceptual thinking and much of it was commissioned by DFID. Examples of topics covered by work of this kind include:

- Policy analysis and the sustainable livelihoods framework – the final report from the IDS SLA research (Shankland 2000);
- Rights and sustainable livelihoods – a background paper commissioned by DFID for the World Development Report 2000/01 on sustainable development (Moser and Norton n.d.);
- Creation of a Policy Institutions and Processes (PIP) sub-group of the SLRG, led by Frank Ellis of ODG, that prepared short papers and held a workshop in 2000; later synthesized into a single document by Hobley (2001);
- The use of SLA in poverty-reduction strategies – a discussion paper commissioned by DFID (Norton and Foster 2001);
- The implications of SLA for organizational change and policy processes – a paper drawing on the discussions at the March 2000 inter-agency forum (Hobley, n.d.) and other IDS papers (Keeley 2001; Pasteur 2001);
- Technological change and market development in SLA – work by the Intermediate Technology Development Group (Albu 2002);
- Working papers emerging from the four PRP-funded livelihood research projects described above and running from April 2000 to March 2003; these projects provided new insights into the research application of SLA in a poverty-reduction context.

Much of this recent work has used the sustainable livelihoods framework as its point of departure; exploring, interpreting and even modifying its components and relationships. SLA remained a work in progress and such continuing research helped to develop its potential.

The 2000 White Paper

In December 2000, a second White Paper on international development was published entitled 'Eliminating world poverty: making globalisation work for the poor'. The Secretary of State declared in its foreword:

> *this second White Paper on International Development stands alongside our first...[that] committed us to focus all our development effort on the reduction of poverty and the mobilisation of the international system to meet the International Development Targets....This second White Paper analyses the nature of globalisation. It sets out an agenda for managing the process in a way that could ensure that the new wealth, technology and knowledge being generated brings substantial benefits to the one in five of humanity who live in extreme poverty.* (DFID 2000e: foreword)

While this second White Paper was intended to complement the 1997 White Paper, it was not explicit about how its new analyses and commitments related to the existing policy objectives of *inter alia* creating sustainable livelihoods for poor people. Implicitly it raises the issue – pursued in the most recent research – of what macro-policy framework is needed to support sustainable livelihoods. This was the new challenge for SLA.

The key research/policy/practice interactions

A range of actors, including researchers, practitioners and policy makers, drive the story of how SLA developed. Sometimes they worked alone within their own research, policy or practice communities; sometimes they crossed the boundaries of those communities and engaged with others – through writings, discussions and collaborations of varying degrees of formality. This section pinpoints the key stages at which important interactions between research, policy and/or practice seem to have occurred. As can be seen now, what was important about these interactions was that they set a new course for, or gave a new impetus to, the development of SLA.

Emergence of the SL paradigm

The emergence of the sustainable livelihoods concept had all the qualities of a classic 'paradigm shift' – defined as 'a fundamental change in approach or underlying assumptions'.[80] In interviews, researchers, practitioners and policy makers often attested to the role of the 1992

IDS discussion paper (Chambers and Conway 1992) in changing their perceptions of the nature of rural development and the priorities for policy and practice. Some could clearly recall when and where they first read or heard of the concept. This shift came at a time when previous dominant theories and practices – particularly those associated with integrated rural development – were losing their intellectual and political attraction. Sustainable livelihoods offered a fresh approach.

Part of its attraction was that it captured and synthesized diverse strands of evolving thought and action. It has been seen as having conceptual, practical and organizational roots (Ashley and Carney 1999: 4). Conceptually, it drew on changing views of poverty, recognizing the diversity of aspirations, the importance of assets and communities, and the constraints and opportunities provided by institutional structures and processes. In practical terms, it placed people – rather than resources, facilities or organizations – as the focus of concern and action; and emphasized that development must be participatory and improvements must be sustainable. Organizationally, it had evolved within research institutes, NGOs and donor agencies and was not exclusive to one or the other.

While the Chambers and Conway paper gave powerful expression to the concept, it had been in circulation for some time. It seems to have first been presented five years before in the report of an agriculture advisory panel of the Brundtland Commission, of which Chambers was the UK member. The panel had argued for agricultural systems that focused as much attention on people as on technology; as much on resources as on production; and as much on the long term as on the short term (World Commission on Environment and Development 1987b). The sustainable livelihoods concept had also been pursued at a 1987 conference organized by IIED from which papers were published (Conroy and Litvinoff 1988).

Nevertheless, it was through the 1992 IDS paper that the concept gained widespread currency. It provided an appealing presentation by well-known thinkers from an institution of high repute. It built on well-established research traditions in different fields and chimed with an evolving political philosophy of a more people-centred approach to development. It was the right statement at the right time.

Adoption of sustainable livelihoods in practice and research

This can be appreciated by the speed at which a number of agencies picked up the sustainable livelihoods concept. Members of staff at Oxfam, CARE and UNDP were attracted by it and adopted variations in their work. This happened explicitly from 1993 onwards, but seems to have been foreshadowed by earlier internal debates and practices. It appears they may also have been tuning in to the emerging concept before the 1992 IDS paper appeared in print. In embracing sustainable livelihoods, NGOs were building on their long-standing commitment to participatory approaches to development. The concept not only aligned with their existing values and beliefs, but it also gave the NGOs powerful new analyses and arguments with which to promote those values and beliefs.

For the researchers, the sustainable livelihoods concept provided a rich new agenda. It quickly became an international focus for both empirical and theoretical work – in IISD in Canada, in the Rome-based SID, as well as in the UK at IIED, ODI, UEA and IDS. For them, as for the donor agencies, it had the appeal of both continuity and change. It built on established perspectives but reconfigured them in a new and attractive paradigm. It was this new intellectual direction in the research community that ODA identified when looking in 1995–96 for new major research initiatives to support.

But while the agencies provided fertile ground for SLA to take root, it required individuals in these organizations to sow the seed. Naresh Singh was instrumental in forging links between UNDP and IISD, where he became Director of the Poverty and Sustainable Development Programme in 1993; he later became the UNDP's principal adviser on these issues. Koos Neefjes played a similar role at Oxfam, as did Tim Frankenberger at CARE International. The prime mover in ODA was Sean Conlin, who saw in sustainable livelihoods the potential for a major new priority for the ESCOR research programme.

Political endorsement: the 1997 White Paper

It was quite clear that development policy was due for a shake-up when Labour gained power in May 1997. Clare Short, the new Secretary of State for International Development, showed strong commitment to pro-poor strategies and, like all the new ministers, she was keen on issuing an early White Paper. Even so, the prominence given to sustainable livelihoods in the November 1997 White Paper took the practice and the research communities by surprise. Its status as one of the three main policy objectives was universally welcomed, however it remained unexplained to those outside DFID.

An important part of the background to this development was the need to reorient UK policy towards the international development targets for 2015. Among these targets was one for halving the proportion of people living in extreme poverty and another for reversing current trends in the loss of environmental resources. In 1996 Western donor countries, grouped together in the OECD's Development Assistance Committee (DAC), had endorsed the targets. Sustainable livelihoods as an approach to meeting these targets was discussed within DAC and particularly in its Environment Working Committee, of which Andrew Bennett of ODA was a member and for which Richard Sandbrook of IIED was an adviser.[81] Implementing the targets became the *leitmotiv* of the White Paper.

Within the UK, the process of White Paper preparation was inclusive. Submissions were encouraged from outside organizations between the election in May and White Paper publication in November. Oxfam,

IIED and IDS all made such submissions. There were also round-table meetings with ministers and officials to which researchers and practitioners were invited.[82] There had also been earlier discussion on sustainable livelihoods within DFID in the course of the consultative processes, through which the 1996 brief for the ESCOR research programme was defined.

Thus, through both international and domestic contacts, the sustainable livelihoods concept was clearly 'in the air' in DFID at the time of work on the White Paper, but doubtless so were many other ideas. What seems to have been particularly attractive about sustainable livelihoods to the White Paper authors was its value as a coherent organizing principle for bringing a range of multi-sectoral actions to bear on the primary goal of reducing poverty. It was attractive politically because of its emphasis on the asset base, because of its inherent dynamism and because of its support for self-reliance – qualities that resonated with New Labour's philosophy. In terms of presentation, it sounded pro-active – as one interviewee remarked: 'you experience a life, but you make a livelihood'. However it is also clear that, at this stage, thinking about SLA within DFID had not really proceded much beyond the embrace of the philosophy and the adoption of the language.

Operationalizing SLA

The White Paper's new policy priorities did not map neatly onto the existing pattern of policy responsibilities or professional competences within DFID. Nor was there seemingly any impetus from the top of DFID to reorganize around them. The political endorsement of SLA in the White Paper was a necessary but not a sufficient condition for change in DFID's programmes.

It was in this context that the then Natural Resources Policy and Advisory Department, and its head Michael Scott, saw an opportunity to reorient its work towards DFID's new commitment to sustainable livelihoods. Scott was finding their traditional approaches, which focused on resources and technologies, less and less convincing in the field. Much of the work was also embedded in rural development programmes that had fallen out of favour politically. He saw SLA as an opportunity to make his team's work more people-centred and to move it into the mainstream of DFID work.

This change had a mixed response from DFID natural resource colleagues – some felt it devalued their technical expertise, while others found it intellectually liberating and organizationally empowering. Outsiders from IDS, ODI, UEA and Oxfam were brought into the policy development process. In particular, Diana Carney of ODI was given a powerful role as secretary (and principal report author) of the Rural Livelihoods Advisory Group that was established in 1998. Later, the SLSO was created as a separate entity to uncouple SLA from natural resource interests alone, and to reach across to all DFID programme areas and beyond them to the wider development-assistance community.

This whole post-White Paper initiative was therefore designed to bring outside experience and thinking into DFID's policy and practice on SLA.

Throughout this process, the sustainable livelihoods framework provided a powerful focus in adopting SLA. Ian Scoones offered it as a working idea to the Advisory Group and Frank Ellis had independently developed another version. DFID took it up with enthusiasm, adapting it somewhat along the way to become the version that appeared in the first sustainable livelihoods guidance sheet (see Figure 6.2, page 141).[83] The framework has proved a powerful tool in all DFID's subsequent work – in promoting SLA within the Department at headquarters and in its regional offices and to partner organizations; as a focus for discussions with other donor agencies (Carney et al. 1999); and as an agenda for further policy development and research.

Testing the context, evidence, links framework

It is clear that both research and researchers have influenced the development of policy and practice in SLA. This has happened in various ways and at various stages of the narrative. To what extent can all this be explained in the terms of the context, evidence, links framework presented in Chapter 2?

The context of politics and institutions

Time and place have played their part in the SLA case. They have often provided a favourable context at a particular stage in the development of SLA. From the early 1980s to the mid-1990s, there was clearly a shift in thinking towards a more people-centred approach to international development. NGOs had pioneered this shift, researchers provided analytical support for it, and in time government agencies also came to accept it – the Brundtland Commission report in 1987 and the first UNDP Human Development Report in 1990 were evidence of this. This approach later found particular expression in the international development targets, which focused on human well-being and sustainability rather than economic growth. This provided a context in which novel, crosscutting ideas that addressed this new agenda, such as sustainable livelihoods, found a welcome audience.

There were also more specific examples of context favouring the SLA. There were clearly people and agencies, working in increasingly participatory ways in rural development in the early 1990s, for whom the Chambers and Conway thesis (Chambers and Conway 1992) articulated their ideas and practices. In the mid-1990s, DFID was in the market for new research priorities for its ESCOR programme. After the 1997 election, there was a new administration and a new minister seeking new approaches that would deliver on goals for international development. DFID officials had a pressing need to produce a coherent and rigorous statement of policy for a White Paper – a need that the sustainable livelihoods concept helped to meet. After the publication of the White Paper, its commitment to SLA chimed with the ambition of the Natural Resource Policy and Advisory Department to redefine its role. Most recently the interest of researchers in exploring the institutional constraints on SLA has found application through the commitment in the 2000 White Paper to find ways of 'making globalisation work for the poor' (DFID 2000e).

However it is important to recognize that such favourable contexts rarely offer a *tabula rasa*. The new knowledge created by research usually enters a world of policy or practice already occupied by – even pre-occupied with – other knowledge, which informs existing thought and action. Such working knowledge may have been derived from previous research or other sources. To be adopted by policy makers or practitioners, new research findings must compete for attention with this existing knowledge and sometimes displace it in their thinking. The SLA case shows this is achieved most readily by reaching those who are at the cutting edge of policy or practice and actively looking for new ideas – donor organizations in the early 1990s, DFID at the time of the 1997 White Paper, and the Natural Resources Department thereafter.

Two contextual influences can be separated out in the SLA case. First is an underlying, progressively more favourable climate for the adoption in policy thinking of increasingly participatory, poverty-focused approaches to international development. The scope of this contextual shift was international, focused particularly in global institutions and forums – the UN and its agencies, OECD, the international NGOs – and it happened through the late 1980s and early 1990s. However, it found little expression in UK policy until the change of government in 1997. Second, there was a context favourable to the development of the specific SLA concept in both research and practice, and through their interaction. Practitioners seeking new approaches to development work, and researchers funded to reflect this practice, characterized this favourable context. It was only after the 1997 White Paper, with the urgent need to implement its SLA commitment, that these two contexts connected.

The communication and credibility of evidence

The evidence to support the SLA concept accumulated over a decade before the policy shift of the 1997 White Paper. It derived from both theory and practice and, importantly, from the iteration between the two, made possible by the intimate networks connecting researchers and practitioners in this field. The SLA concept therefore had the advantage of being both intellectually attractive and empirically tested – characteristics that were attractive to the White Paper authors. Nonetheless its adoption as a DFID policy was not actively promoted by any alliance of institutions or individuals. There was no SLA political campaign. Rather the concept was brought to the attention of DFID policy makers by a variety of routes and media. It then progressively became part of the policy discourse in the mid-1990s, initially for the international development targets to which the UK subscribed as an OECD member and subsequently for the 1997 White Paper.

It is notable how modest in size the two key research documents were in the SLA narrative. The Chambers and Conway 1992 paper ran to 34 pages and Scoones' 1998 paper to 22 pages – both very readable and easily reproducible. They both used powerful modes of expression. In the 1992 paper it was the term 'sustainable livelihoods'. Chambers claims to have calculatedly conjoined the two words, making a new phrase in order to arouse curiosity, to challenge conventional thinking and to insert a new idea into established discourse.[84] In Scoones' 1998 paper it was the diagram of the sustainable rural livelihoods framework that grabbed attention. Its principal virtue was its economy in expressing ideas about a complex set of relationships – really 'a picture worth a thousand words'. Subsequently, it also proved valuable in mapping the various interests with whom DFID and the SLSO would have to deal if they were to promote SLA.

The SLSO has recognized the continuing importance of effective communication in promoting and developing SLA. For political and lay audiences, it has published reports that use clear prose and graphics to present SLA in lay terms, often employing brief case studies to bring the arguments to life (DFID 1999c, 2000a–c). For practitioner audiences, it has created the sustainable livelihoods guidance sheets as a loose-leaf handbook (DFID 1999d, 2000e, 2001). It has also exploited the potential of the internet by creating (with IDS as its agent) the Livelihoods Connect website as an open and accessible resource for all who wish to keep up to date and to exchange views and experiences on SLA.

But the SLA case also shows the importance of personal contact in the transfer of knowledge between research, policy and practice. Personal contact has two key characteristics. First, it is interactive and two-way, allowing question and answer and discussion – most apparent in face-to-face meetings but clearly also in telephone or email communication. Second, it is individualized, and so the knowledge transfer can be tailored precisely to the expertise and interests of those involved. Personal interaction can take place in many ways – through contact (sometimes arranged, sometimes chance) between people working in different settings or brought together in the same setting through job mobility (sometimes secondments, sometimes job changes). Many of the key influences of research on policy and practice in the SLA narrative were strongly shaped by these kinds of personal contact.

Even the most strongly targeted and personalized interaction between research, policy and practice may not achieve influence with a single shot. The SLA narrative had several strands to it – with many actors playing diverse roles, having different perspectives, or engaged in many interactions at successive stages. This multiplicity was one reason for the success of research in shaping policy and practice in this case. This is comparable to the law of requisite variety in cybernetics (Ashby 1956): that a regulating system needs to generate as many states as can the regulated system. So where the context of policy and practice is complex, as in the SLA case, the means adopted by research to influence it must be equally complex. Thus a single communication of a research finding, for example spoken at a conference or written in a publication, will never be sufficient. It must be communicated many times and in many different ways to many people to strengthen its chances of influence.

The legitimacy and influence of links between actors and networks

While researchers, policy makers and practitioners have all played parts in the SLA narrative, these terms are insufficient to define the variety of roles in their many interactions. Once sustainable livelihoods had been created as a concept, people playing a variety of roles facilitated its adoption in practice and policy, for example:

- as testers – applying it empirically and reporting the results;
- as developers – expanding and extending the concept to enhance its relevance;
- as champions – promoting and supporting commitment to the sustainable livelihoods concept;
- as communicators – expressing it in ways that enhanced its appeal to different audiences;
- as interpreters – relating it to different issues and contexts;
- as advocates – building more support.

There are many examples of these roles being played in the SLA case. Chambers and Conway had a talent for communication as well as for thought. Naresh Singh at IISD/UNDP and Koos Neefjes at Oxfam were acting as testers, developers and champions of sustainable livelihoods in those organizations. Sean Conlin championed further research. Diana Carney, as secretary of the Rural Livelihoods Advisory Group, was skilful as both interpreter and communicator. Michael Scott acted as a champion for SLA within DFID after the 1997 White Paper. The frameworks described by Ian Scoones and Frank Ellis were important development work. Advocacy has also been an important part of the SLSO's remit. As these examples show, these different roles were not always discrete and indeed were often combined. Particular roles were not usually exclusive just to researchers, policy makers or practitioners; that is, the same kinds of actor played different roles and different actors could play the same role. In the course of the development of SLA, the roles often recurred.

These roles were shared among a fairly small community of people involved in the development of SLA – as researchers, policy makers or practitioners. They are mostly specialists with long careers in this field – this certainly is truer of officials in DFID than of those in many other government departments. Consequently they know of each other, mostly know each other, and are in frequent communication. In recent years the SLSO has actively fostered the development of this community, both nationally and internationally, and has drawn researchers into policy development work, particularly through the Sustainable Livelihoods Resource Group. This intimacy has fostered awareness, mutual respect and trust, which have eased the communication of ideas and experience between practice, policy and research. It does also mean though that it has become more difficult for researchers outside this community to wield influence.

It is also notable how job changes have been a feature of the SLA narrative – examples are Singh moving between IISD and UNDP; Carney between ODI and DFID (as an adviser) and then into consultancy; Scoones from IIED to IDS; Moorehead (née Davies) between IDS and DFID; and Conway between Imperial College, IIED, Ford Foundation, Sussex University and the Rockefeller Foundation. As they moved (and continue to move) from one organization to another, they took their knowledge and experience of sustainable livelihoods' thought and practice with them.

The networks in which these actors played their roles had a particular configuration. A conventional view is that research informs policy and that policy is implemented through practice. This linear, one-way relationship can be expressed thus:

Research ⟶ Policy ⟶ Practice

So policy is the appropriate target for influential research. The SLA narrative reveals a rather different pattern of relationships. Research impacted on practice – in the early 1990s, as much as on policy – in the 1997 White Paper. Also the relationships were not just one way. Chambers and Conway remarked that 'livelihoods, and sustainable livelihoods, are concepts which have evolved more from open-ended fieldwork than from the closed concerns of surveys and statistics' (Chambers and Conway 1992: 25). Similar interactions between practice and research operated in the work of the UNDP, IISD and IIED. At a later stage the policy commitments flowing from the 1997 White Paper had a marked influence on the researchers' agenda. So in the SLA case, the conventional view of research informing policy which frames practice (Research → Policy → Practice) could be better represented as a triangle where all components have two-way interactions with each other, as shown below:

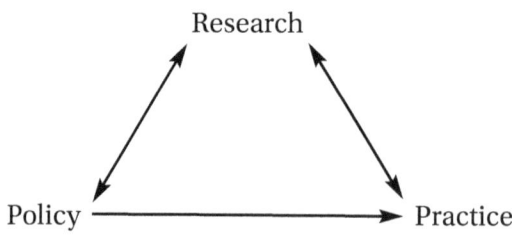

Conclusions

The SLA case is a remarkable story of research influencing policy. Over less than a decade, between 1987 and 1997, an idea that originated from researchers, conceptualizing both emergent theory and practice, was adopted as a guiding principle of UK development policy. It is easier to provide a narrative of how this happened than an explanation of why it happened. The proximate causes of each development – especially the four key interactions analysed under the heading 'The key research/policy/practice interactions' – can be readily identified. The ultimate causation is less apparent.

Nevertheless the 'context, evidence, links' framework helps to explain much. In summary:

- There was a context of practice imperatives and research opportunities that provided favourable ground for the development of the SLA; and, for its translation into policy, there was a progressively more favourable context for its acceptance and then finally the major opportunity of the 1997 White Paper.
- There was an intimate network of actors including researchers and practitioners who, in various roles, nurtured the idea in its early years and then later shared it with their policy contacts – albeit in an undirected way.
- Finally, the idea itself was credible and attractive as evidence, both intellectually and practically, and was powerfully and repeatedly communicated between researchers, practitioners and policy makers.

However, this still leaves two other important factors in the SLA case that are not addressed in the framework: **time** and **chance**. The SLA idea took a decade to travel from its origin in research and practice to its policy destination.[85] That was partly the consequence of waiting for the right conjunctions of context, actors and evidence that enabled each of the key interactions to speed the idea on its journey. In this case, the impact of research on policy did not happen in one leap, but through a number of steps forward. The decade-long lapse may also be because ideas travel slowly. Ideas compete for the attention of practitioners and policy makers, so they have to be persuaded to discard old ideas – and the policies and practices derived from them – as well as to embrace new ideas. This rarely happens through instant conversion; more often it happens through a progressive change in perceptions that takes time for people to recognize and acknowledge. A decade may not be a long time in policy development.

There must also be recognition of the serendipity that characterized some episodes in the SLA story. The 1992 Chambers and Conway paper was conceived when the two long-standing friends found themselves with time for long discussions while both working in India in 1991. Richard Sandbook was advising the OECD in 1996 when the international development targets were on the DAC's agenda. Andrew Bennett of the ODA was also involved at that time. Ian Scoones' recruitment to DFID's Rural Livelihoods Advisory Group, which adopted his tentative idea for a sustainable livelihoods framework, resulted from a chance encounter with Michael Scott. It can be argued that if one such chance connection had not occurred, then – within the close networks characterizing the field – another with similar effect might have done, but one cannot be certain of that.

So the SLA case study suggests that, while the 'context, evidence, links' framework captures most of what happened, it is perhaps too mechanical, too determinate to provide a full explanation. It would fit the SLA case better if the framework incorporated the distinction between **necessary** and **sufficient** conditions in historical interpretations of events. That is, the framework identifies the necessary conditions for the successful impact of research on policy – if they were not met then there would have been no chance of effective impact. However, they alone could not guarantee impact. Actual impact required other, sufficient conditions to be met. In the SLA case, these were the elapse of time and chance encounters. In other cases, these sufficient conditions may be different.

Part III
Synthesis and conclusion

Chapter Seven
Crosscutting issues and implications: promoting more informed international development policy

JULIUS COURT, INGIE HOVLAND and JOHN YOUNG

In this final chapter we draw conclusions from the research exercise. We wish to revisit the question posed in the introduction: Why are some of the ideas that circulate in the research–policy networks picked up and acted on, while others are ignored and disappear? The four comparative case studies provide a good basis for more comprehensive reflection around this problem. The first section of this chapter therefore draws out crosscutting issues from the case studies, facilitated by the analytical tools provided by the conceptual framework. The following section discusses various issues that have emerged through the research process that need to be addressed further; these emerging issues also provide an opportunity to reflect on the possibilities and limitations of the integrated framework itself. The third section moves on to the implications this has for researchers, practitioners, policy makers and others who wish to be aware of and contribute to improved research–policy linkages through their own work. Given the particularly robust nature of the findings for the evidence domain of our framework, the final section makes some specific recommendations for researchers in terms of enhancing the policy influence of their work.

Synthesis of crosscutting issues from the case studies[86]

This section starts with some broad points about what our case studies reveal about the existing models of research–policy linkage. We then structure our discussion around the three arenas in the RAPID framework: context: politics and institutions; evidence: approach and credibility; links: influence and legitimacy. As we go along, we indicate where our analysis supports some of the key strands of theory in the literature.

The first point is that while many of our cases focus on specific policy change, they also do highlight the **indirect** influence of research on policy. In this way, they greatly support the work of Carol Weiss on 'percolation', 'enlightenment' and 'knowledge creep'. In all the cases, there were examples where ideas had gradually filtered through networks of research, policy and practice. The PRSP case emphasizes how academic research through the 1970s, 1980s and 1990s had an indirect influence by shifting the international-development discourse towards poverty reduction, participation and aid effectiveness. This research highlighted problems with development practices and set the stage for the policy reviews of the 1990s. The SLA case is also one where research 'filtered' into the policy arena – and then was substantially assisted to influence a specific policy orientation.

The cases also support the arguments of Gladwell: that changes in context, key individuals and communications can lead to a 'tipping point' where a relatively minor occurrence galvanizes trends that have been building up 'beneath the surface'. All the cases included here tended, to different degrees, to have a general context where it was increasingly apparent that change was needed, and where specific issues then spurred the policy change. In the Sphere case, the tipping point came when general concerns about accountability were accentuated dramatically by the response of humanitarian agencies to the Rwanda crisis. In the PRSP case, there was a creeping concern about a 'problem' with development policy. It was the need to reform HIPC, not in itself such a massive issue, that provided the trigger for a tipping point for the adoption of the PRSPs, which represented a much broader shift in international development policy.

In the Kenya case, the tipping point came when evidence about the gradual spread of para-vets contributed sufficiently to the alarm of the Kenya Veterinary Board (KVB) to lead them to publish a letter in the national press, threatening to punish livestock owners and veterinarians involved in para-vet programmes. Up to this point, there had been a long period where community animal-health workers (CAHWs) schemes gradually proliferated, generating powerful evidence of their value, and providing an issue around which different groups of stakeholders, supporters and antagonists could form formal and informal networks. The letter brought the work of all the different actors, including the KVB itself, into focus and resulted in a process where all stakeholders came together to develop a new policy framework with the emphasis in favour of the CAHW approach.

The cases do support some of the existing theory about research–policy links. However, they also highlight (particularly in the Kenya case) that care must be taken when applying models developed in the OECD to developing countries. There is a need to take a broader framework than one that might be used in the OECD. The social, economic and political contexts may be different and more varied and basic assumptions about political and academic freedoms may not apply.

Context: politics and institutions

Comparison across the four case studies certainly supports the literature and the findings of other studies (Court and Young 2003) that the political institutional context is the most important arena affecting the uptake of research into policy. Power relations, political contestation, institutional pressures and vested interests matter critically in all the cases. The attitudes and incentives among officials and the local historical context also greatly influence policy processes. In certain political contexts, research may be completely ignored.

The cases highlight the importance of changes in the wider political environment for the agenda-setting process and policy formulation. This is clearly reflected in the sustainable livelihoods case. SLA was in tune with wider international shifts towards sustainable human development rather than economic growth. There was also an imperative at the institutional level as DFID strove to redefine its role and mark the change of government in 1997. These broader shifts are also key strands in the PRSP case (with pressure on the IFIs to change policy from governments and civil society) and in the Sphere case (with donor concerns about NGO performance). The cases very much support the work of Kingdon (1984), who highlights the importance of 'political streams' such as government changes and public opinion.

The case studies in this book describe situations where there have been quite dramatic changes in policy – PRSPs, the Sphere Project and the SLA approach. These are what Lindquist might term 'fundamental' decision-making processes (in contrast to routine, incremental and emergent processes).[87] They reflect what Kingdon (1984) calls policy windows, where new and more radical solutions are needed. Policy windows provide opportunities where research can have a substantial impact, but they tend to occur suddenly by chance or due to an external crisis. For example, the crisis of Rwanda was the critical factor that led to a policy change in the humanitarian arena.

The degree of demand from the policy maker is one of the main issues that distinguish cases of research uptake from those that have little impact. Demand was critical to the emergence of Sphere. By the early 1990s, there was no longer an unquestioning acceptance of the activities of humanitarian agencies in emergency situations. However, it was the scale and intensity of the humanitarian crisis in Rwanda in 1994 – and the spotlight on the response by agencies – which created the demand for major changes. The same is true in the PRSP case. The 1997 Asia crisis and the continuing weak economic performance in sub-Saharan Africa led to a widespread sense of there being 'a problem' within international development policy, and spurred questions about the roles of the IMF and World Bank. There was a backdrop of major external pressure building up around the debt issue, particularly from the NGO movement such as Jubilee 2000 and from the US government, to ensure that resources freed up by debt relief would be 'well spent'. The degree of demand for a new solution became too great to ignore.

It is not just demand for the solution to a problem that matters, however, but also consensus on the nature of the solution. This was most notable perhaps in the Sphere case study, where high-profile failures in Rwanda and pressures for reform – plus the credible solution proposed – made building a consensus much easier. The PRSP case study concludes that the most important contextual factor was the convergence of debates and controversies in the field of international development. The case-study notes that:

The simultaneous recognition of similar sets of problems and similar ideas for solutions by various actors in the international development field in the late 1990s is probably the reason why the PRSP idea, which was a substantial challenge to current practice, took hold relatively easily and rapidly.

The lack of consensus on legislation for the animal-health sector in Kenya was glaring. Due to the troubled political context, the need for change – and the widespread use of an approach that provided a solution – was not enough to spur legislative reform. The resistance from vested interests in Kenya prevented any formal change in the law despite the evidence that new approaches were effective. The animal health policy process had become the sort of complex, highly politicized process described by Sutton (1999) and Keeley and Scoones (2003), with increasingly polarized views developing in the different camps, and no mechanism for dialogue and resolution. Personalities and personal relationships were at least as important as any formal relationships and structures in hindering consensus.

The cases also support the work of Clay and Schaffer (1984) on how political structures and interests at many different levels affect the room for manoeuvre of policy makers. The PRSP case describes how the room for manoeuvre of staff is limited by the need to ensure that policies 'get through the Board', and so members of staff adapt their behaviour accordingly. The case highlights that the policy problems, the Asia crisis and ESAF review created an increased room for manoeuvre in the IFIs in the late 1990s that led to the ability to look for new solutions. The Sphere case highlights how the Rwanda crisis created a lot of room for manoeuvre within the humanitarian aid system:

'Discomfort and disaffection with NGO performance had been around for a few years beforehand, but became much more urgent and widespread as a consequence of the crisis.'

The Kenya case highlights that the reduced Veterinary Department budgets from the mid-1980s to mid-1990s left little room for manoeuvre.

Policy is not just about statements and laws; it is also about implementation. Our cases certainly support the work of Lipsky (1980) on how 'street-level bureaucrats' have an enormous influence on how policies are implemented. Street-level bureaucrats are the employees of an organization who are responsible for implementation and, Lipsky argues, ultimately decide how policy is to be translated into practice. All the cases indicate that paying attention to how the policies will be put into practice is an important element of policy change.

The Kenya case provides a powerful demonstration, where practitioners adopted effective community-based approaches to animal healthcare across the arid northern region despite the fact that they were actually illegal. Vets in the field, finding themselves with virtually no operational budgets, adopted the new approaches as the only way they could continue to provide any services at all. Interestingly, the Kenya case highlights how street-level bureaucrats may be forced to deal with new problems before high-level policy makers, and therefore go through the process of policy adaptation earlier.

The PRSP case describes how the different structures at the World Bank and IMF (with the World Bank being less conservative, rigid and hierarchical) lead to greater potential for Bank staff to interpret and adapt policies as they are implemented. The Sphere case demonstrated how the street-level bureaucrats selectively implemented the recommendations from the evaluations. Whereas the recommendations on performance were welcomed, there was resistance to strengthening the accountability of humanitarian agencies, specifically NGOs, through some form of accreditation or regulation of NGOs. Regulation or accreditation was more than the operational NGOs responsible for making the decision were prepared to accept.

Finally, it is interesting that all four cases give an indication that new actors – in this case NGOs – are playing an unexpectedly significant role in developing policy making. In the Sphere case, the main actors and instigators of policy reflection were NGOs themselves. In the Kenya case, ITDG, church groups and local Kenyan actors played a key role. In the PRSP case, there was increasingly sophisticated analysis by development charities and the advocacy coalition around the debt campaign, led by Jubilee 2000. The SLA case highlighted a range of think tanks, NGOs and foundations. Many would argue that this is a positive step in its own right, facilitated by the fact that policy making regimes are becoming more open. The cases suggest that the increase in actors tends to translate into greater use of evidence in development policy making. But more work is needed to better assess where, how and to what degree these new actors actually make a difference.

Evidence: credibility and communication

The findings for this set of issues appear particularly robust. The case studies support a number of key findings that are also emphasized in other studies (Court and Young 2003). Three sets of issues emerge regarding the research or evidence – the key dimensions seem to be relevance, credibility and providing useful solutions.

First, research appears to have a much greater impact when it is topically relevant. For an impact in the short term, research needs to relate to the policy issue of the day. In the Sphere case, a key reason why Study 3 of the Joint Evaluation had an immediate impact on policy makers was because it was directly related to a crisis that had dominated news reports. In the PRSP and SLA cases, the nature of the policy shift reflected the findings of growing bodies of academic research on poverty, aid effectiveness, participation and livelihoods – all topics centrally relevant to development assistance. The action research in the Kenya case focused on a critical issue to the welfare of those living in arid parts of northern Kenya.

Second, the perceived quality of the research is very important for policy uptake. All the cases emphasize the issue of credibility. In the SLA case, the credibility of some of the key researchers and their clarity in expressing complex processes, combined with the diverse sources of the evidence that helped foster uptake within DFID. In the Sphere case, the Joint Rwanda Evaluation was seen as a 'veritable Rolls Royce of humanitarian evaluation with unprecedented scope and unprecedented resources available'. The independence of the evaluation ensured that the sometimes-unpopular findings were protected from censure. The PRSP case highlights the rigorous economic research needed to influence policy in the IFIs.

But credibility also depends on the user. In the PRSP case:

'One of the key sources of the credibility of much of this research was the fact that it was directly commissioned by the policy makers in the IFIs. In very general terms, external research is regarded as less credible by both IFIs than internally produced or commissioned research. The least credible research is that which questions the paradigm and which is not written in a language that is accessible or relevant to IFI staff.'

The Kenya case highlights the ways different audiences attach credibility to research: NGOs and donors valued NGO studies, but government staff considered NGO studies suspect because they perceived them to be biased. Reports from government vets in the field were highly valued by government staff. While most of the formal academic research was not considered, the Hübl study was highly regarded by everyone – due to the composition of the study team and the approach, which included a wide degree of stakeholder participation.

Third, it is clear from the studies that the operational usefulness of the research is critical. Research that had an operational orientation or action research seemed to have a great impact. The fact that researchers in the Rwanda evaluation had practical experience was emphasized. Critical in the PRSP case was the applied policy research focusing on recommendations for the IFIs and on providing workable solutions.

The Kenya and SLA cases highlight that it was important that a new approach had been piloted and that researchers and communicators could clearly demonstrate the value of the new option. In the PRSP case, applied policy research in the late 1990s – the HIPC review for example – focused on providing policy recommendations and operational solutions. In addition, the positive experience of undertaking the Poverty Eradication Action Plan (PEAP) in Uganda had a strong influence in convincing policy makers in the IFIs of the value and feasibility of PRSP-type strategies.

Operational usefulness enables research to provide solutions to a problem. The CAHW approach in Kenya was the solution for how to provide services in arid areas in a climate of minimal funding. The PRSP was the solution to a variety of problems faced by the IFIs and donor governments. As the case study notes:

In summary, the PRSP was an operational solution that solved several internal problems and provided an answer to external pressures, particularly for the IFIs but also within different bilateral organizations.

The Sphere process was the solution to the conundrum of the accountability of humanitarian agencies. The SLA provided the answer to DFID's search for an innovative approach to development assistance. As formulated in the marketing literature (e.g. Lambin 1996), people buy products that provide a solution to a problem.

But it is not just the content of the evidence that matters. How findings are communicated is crucial, since policy makers cannot be influenced by research unless they are actually in some way aware of its existence. Interestingly, the issue of credibility does not just concern the quality of the research but also the way that research is packaged to make it palatable to policy makers. The evidence from the case studies supports much of the existing literature on communication, showing that nature of communications efforts and the format of the research outputs matter critically for policy impact.

It is hard to underemphasize the issue of defining the message and target audience. The Sphere case specifically emphasized that the Joint Rwanda Evaluation's:

'findings and recommendations were clearly presented, and were often targeted at particular groups of actors ... Study 3 put across its recommendations in a concise and simplified way, but they were backed up by a great deal of detail.'

In the PRSP case, research was considered most credible when it was communicated in a language that was accessible and relevant to World Bank and IMF staff and other donor agencies. In the SLA case, DFID staff had recognized the importance of communicating in different ways for different audiences. For non-specialists, reports used clear prose and graphics as well as brief case studies, whereas technical guidance sheets were prepared for practitioners.

The cases also demonstrate the power of visual images. As has often been emphasized in the literature, frequently 'seeing is believing' (Philo 1996). In the Kenya case, evidence generated by operational CAHW schemes, communicated directly to visitors by livestock owners and the animal health staff involved in them, seems to have been much more important than research reports. The case study notes:

The visible evidence, on the ground and as described by farmers and local veterinary personnel, had high legitimacy and was extremely convincing for visitors.

Early on, this evidence contributed to the rising popularity of such programmes with donors and field veterinarians.

The cases also provide evidence to support the literature (Mattelart and Mattelart 1998) that it is best to take an interactive approach to communication. It seems that continuous interaction leads to greater chances of successful communication than a simple or linear approach. This appears to be most evident in the SLA case, where key individuals had extensive discussions over periods of time. Evidence of the conceptual and practical use of the SLA approach gradually accumulated over the decade preceding the 1997 White Paper as the idea was passed back and forth within networks, leading to its rapid and widespread adoption from 1997 onwards. The importance of interaction between researchers and policy makers is also emphasized in all the other cases.

What is interesting is that the cases indicate how evidence can help to change the policy context. The PRSP case clearly indicated that the research evidence helped create a policy context where the prevailing narrative was 'there is a problem with development policy'. This evidence and campaigns using it helped influence the political contexts in a number of countries and at international level. The same is also true for the Kenya case. NGOs generated good evidence that decentralized animal programmes provided an effective, cost-efficient and safe service which was convincing to many field veterinarians on the ground in northern Kenya (and donors) and the approach spread. This caused alarm within the KVB, the letter in the national press and the ensuing crisis. The outcome however was that the letter enabled the evidence to be discussed and eventually resulted in the new policy context.

Links: influence and legitimacy

Much of the literature on bridging research and policy emphasizes that the links between researchers and policy makers are critical. Key issues include feedback, dialogue and collaboration between researchers and policy makers; the role of networks and policy communities; and issues of trust, legitimacy and participation. However, it is also apparent that there are many issues that remain unanswered in this arena. This section focuses on relevant issues in this area that emerge from the four case studies.

The case studies highlight how networks play a vital role in policy change. As such they support the work of Kickert et al. (1997) and Robinson et al. (1999) who regard policy making as a series of negotiations that can be completed through formal and informal networks. The Sphere case is probably the best example here. It highlights how the links between researchers and policy makers were:

'institutionalized in the structure put in place for the Joint Rwanda Evaluation ... Thus, a critical and cooperative link was established right at the beginning between those who commissioned the 'research', and the policy makers at whom the findings were directed.'

These links served to maximize the sense of ownership and buy-in to the evaluation process and the implementation of the findings.

The other three cases also demonstrate the importance of networks. The PRSP case study describes the 'high level of contact' and 'multitude of links' among policy makers, researchers and NGOs. As one informant noted, 'none of the players is more than two handshakes away from any of the others'. The case emphasized the role of the SPA, not so much for its direct influence but as a valuable forum where policy makers met and discussed ideas that were emerging. The Kenya case highlights that the first ITDG vets' workshop in 1988, which brought together decentralized animal health (DAH) practitioners from several projects around the country, marked a significant increase in interactions between researchers/practitioners and policy makers in Kenya, and ITDG's international DAH workshop strengthened the emerging international network of practitioners and links between policy makers and practitioners.

The cases show the ways in which networks can facilitate knowledge sharing, coordination and cooperation. But a key question that remains is 'what are the characteristics of networks that best enable them to act as a bridge between research and policy?' Haas (1991) describes how 'epistemic communities' – colleagues who share a similar approach or a similar position on an issue and maintain contact with each other across their various locations and fields – create new channels for information and discussion of new perspectives. Such communities are believed to be particularly effective if they include a few prominent and respected individuals. Epistemic communities did seem to be important in the SLA, PRSP and Sphere cases.

The critical role of certain individuals emerges from the analysis in this book as an important aspect of bridging research and policy. Many of these individuals correspond to Gladwell's (2000) classification of salesmen, networkers and 'mavens' (people who collect information). For example, the Sphere case describes two key policy entrepreneurs as salesmen and networkers; two other people played critical connector roles. The PRSP case highlights the heads of the World Bank and IMF policy departments, the IMF Deputy Managing Director and the DFID Secretary of State as important 'connectors' and 'salesmen'.

The cases also repeatedly draw attention to the issue of legitimacy. The point is that researchers' links to the populations and communities that will be affected by the policies can also be important as a basis for legitimacy (Fine et al. 2000). Recent work for the Rockefeller Foundation (Figueroa et al. 2002) emphasizes that social change will be more sustainable if the affected community owns not just the physical inputs and outputs of policy implementation, but also the process and content of the communication involved. The issue of legitimacy is most emphasized in the Kenya para-vet case. The case demonstrates that although it takes a great deal of time and work with local communities to develop effective and sustainable examples of new approaches, this is essential to prove their effectiveness and to acquire the legitimacy to advocate for change. In the Joint Rwanda Evaluation and Sphere process, great effort was given to inclusion, and the legitimacy this conferred seems to have contributed enormously to the project's impact. The case also highlights the role (and legitimacy) that umbrella NGOs had in influencing the policy change.

Two of the cases particularly emphasize the importance of three-way feedback processes between researchers, policy makers and practice. The SLA case does this most emphatically, highlighting the role of a number of individuals and institutions who worked as 'testers, developers, champions, communicators, interpreters and advocates' of SLA to facilitate its adoption within DFID. Similarly the PRSP case highlights the interactions between academic researchers, policy researchers, donors, the Boards of the IFIs and street-level bureaucrats within the Bank and IMF.

Finally, it is worth noting that all the cases involve an element of the transnational interactions of researchers, policy makers and donors, and the utilization of research by international policy communities. This is most noticeable in the PRSP case, which focused on an international policy process but also emphasized the role of the Jubilee debt-relief campaign, very much a transnational advocacy network as described by Keck and Sikkink (1998). The humanitarian sector portrayed in the Sphere case represents a global public policy network (Reinicke and Deng 2000). In the Kenya case, it was an international NGO, ITDG, which facilitated the transfer of an idea across sectors and continents. While these were not cases of pure knowledge networks, the set of associations in each case clearly were crucial to the transfer of knowledge internationally.

Research-policy linkages: emerging issues

The comparison across the four case studies, facilitated by the framework, also throws up a range of further issues. These provide additional and interesting perspectives both on the nature of research-policy linkages in general, and on the challenges and opportunities of using the integrated framework itself. Most of them remain in need of more systematic research. In this section, they have been grouped around the following keywords: dynamic relationships, external influences, democratic systems, Southern institutions and networks.

The dynamic nature of the framework and of the research-policy relationship

One of the first observations to be made when comparing the four case studies, was that the configuration of the three spheres in the framework seemed to vary according to the case. In the PRSP case, for example, there was a great overlap between the links sphere, where policy makers and some researchers and NGOs were in frequent contact with each other, and a political context where similar sets of problems and ideas for solutions were emerging from various actors simultaneously. This was in contrast to the case of livestock services in Kenya, where the links between livestock owners and veterinarians were advancing successful DAH practice on the ground, but were far removed from the underlying political context of policy making and legislation, which was largely unaware of its existence. The analytical framework then, should be viewed as a trio of floating spheres of variable size and degree of overlap, rather than a solid mesh with context, evidence and links held as equally important, and equally overlapping, in every case.

This reveals an aspect of the framework that was emphasized by the case study authors when comparing across the cases: it is a challenge - and a potential strength of the framework - that the three spheres have to be seen in dynamic relationship to each other. First, this emphasis on the dynamic aspect of the framework means that the diagram of three equal and evenly overlapping circles is only an ideal model. The framework can only be used meaningfully if the researcher adapts it to the particular case in question. In a sense this requires that the researcher abandons the perfect symmetry and the diagram itself, in order to discover the factors that are important in her or his case -

whatever sphere these factors might belong to and whatever way they might stand in relationship to each other.

Second, the emphasis on dynamism is meant to apply not only in relation to different contexts but also to changes over time. Applying the framework at different points during a policy process will highlight different issues. For example, the adoption of the SLA in the 1997 White Paper occurred more than a decade after the conceptualization of the SLA approach. Time is also a particular issue in two of the other cases – in terms of the filtering of academic research over three decades in the PRSP case, and the extensive time lag in Kenya between the initiation of a new approach and its formal policy adoption (still pending). A diagram with highly flexible and moving shapes, preferably portrayed in 3D, would better reflect this emphasis on dynamic change – both across contexts and through time.

Third, the dynamic relationship between the spheres in the framework highlights the integrated nature of research–policy linkages in general. In the preliminary phase of mapping out the RAPID project on bridging research and policy, it soon became evident that any attempt to understand the nature of the relationship between research and policy in development would touch on a great number of questions raised in various parts of the social sciences – ranging from the big debates on structure versus agency, or nature versus nurture, right down to the question of how two people communicate with each other.

In order to take this into account, it became necessary to devise an integrated framework – rather than a framework with separate components that could be seen in isolation from each other, or a framework that was set up in a step-by-step manner where each step could be analysed independently of the next. There may be greater research challenges associated with using an integrated framework, but when addressing research–policy linkages a framework that is able to take account of complex interactions has proved indispensable. This has been neatly summed up in the SLA case study, where Solesbury notes:

in the SLA case, the conventional view of research informing policy which frames practice (Research → Policy → Practice) could be better represented as a triangle where all components have two-way interactions with each other, as shown below:

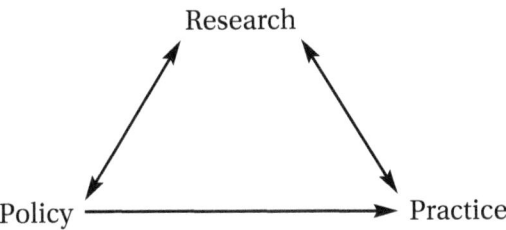

More systematic research on this three-way relationship is still needed, both within sectors and across countries. Ongoing work by the GDN[88] should be a valuable contribution to the field; it includes a range of studies of research–policy linkages, emphasizing both rigour and standardization of analytical approaches across the cases, as well as creative in-depth examination of specific research–policy processes.

External influences and transnational processes

In all four case studies, a set of factors emerged that had decisive influence on the policy change in question and that also generally affected the spheres of context, evidence and links. This set of factors can loosely be grouped under the heading 'external influences'. It includes, for example, donor actions on research–policy interactions, the impact of international politics, and the specific research-funding or lending instruments used by the IFIs. In the PRSP case study, which reflects on the dynamics of an international policy process, it becomes clear that pressures felt by the World Bank and IMF have an impact not only on the IFIs themselves but also on most bilateral donors and, in turn, on all loan- or aid-receiving national governments. In other words, the effect of changes within the IFIs is an external influence that can have a substantial and wide-reaching impact on national policy processes. The effect of this external influence will be greater for loan-receiving governments in the South than for others.

The role of such external influences seems so important – especially in relation to research–policy linkages in Southern and international development processes – that this set of factors might be regarded as a fourth dimension of the framework (see Figure 7.1).

External influences also have a direct effect on the production and dissemination of research within international development. Broad incentives, such as EU access or the PRSP process, can have a substantial impact on the demand for research by policy makers (Court and Young 2003). Trends towards democratization and liberalization and donor support for civil society are also generating demand for comparative analysis and for evidence-based recommendations. Donors are funding both research and communications and networking activities. DFID has drawn up a strategy for the development research that it wishes to fund (Surr et al. 2002). In this situation, new questions emerge. For example, what is to count as legitimate research demand? Whose interests will guide research funding? And how will donor funding of research be evaluated?

The increasing importance of international policy processes also throws up a set of new research questions concerning transnational knowledge networks. As mentioned above, all the cases involve fascinating elements of the transnational interactions of researchers, policy makers and donors. For example, the Kenya case involved the translation of a Chinese idea (barefoot doctors) into a different sector (animal health) in a completely different part of the world (arid Kenya). How did this series of transnational interactions come about? Was there something about this sector that made it open to an idea transmitted across borders? And why did it occur in arid Kenya rather than

Figure 7.1 The RAPID framework

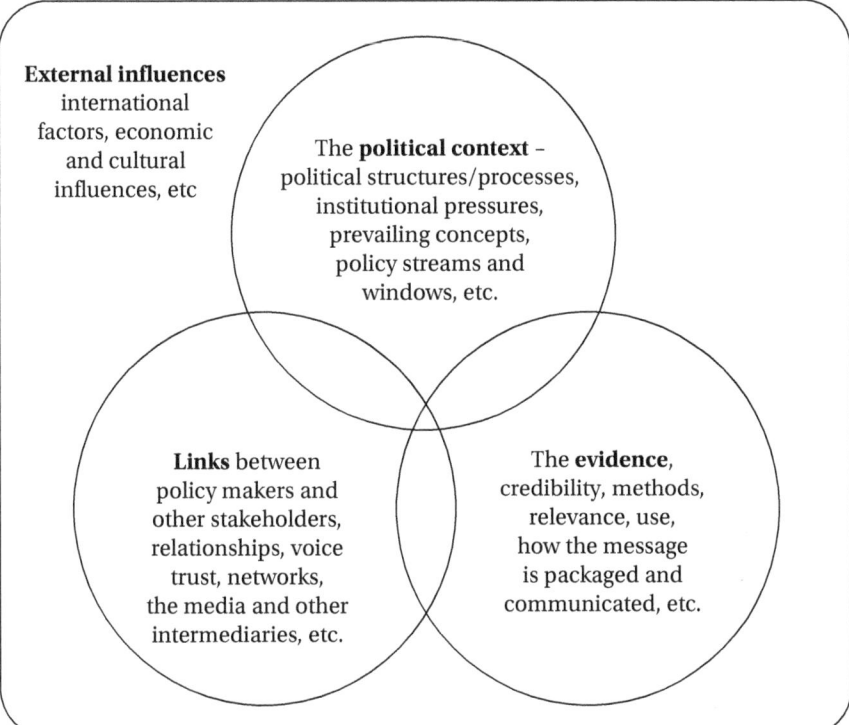

somewhere else? In a globalizing world, transnational knowledge sharing is increasingly important, but our knowledge of the dynamics in this field remains limited (Stone and Maxwell, 2004). More effort to understand more systematically the formal and informal processes at work here would be valuable.

The role of democratic systems

Our work supports others' findings that political context has a critical impact on the uptake of research into policy. There remains, however, very little evidence from the democracy and governance literature about the impact of democracy and good governance on the uptake of research into policy in the South. Much of the existing theory is from OECD countries and is based on assumptions of political and civil freedoms – especially academic and media freedoms. There is surprisingly little systematic evidence from contexts where these freedoms cannot be taken for granted.

We are left with some key questions: Do countries or organizations with good governance (accountability, transparency and responsiveness) use research more than others? It might be suggested that democratic countries share a greater incentive – and seem more likely – to use research in policy processes. The reasons democracies would be more effective at taking up research into policy include factors on both the supply and demand side (and the relationship between them). In terms of the supply of evidence, open political systems allow evidence to be freely gathered, assessed and communicated. In terms of demand, democracies imply a greater accountability of governments and therefore a greater incentive to improve policy and performance. Democratic contexts also imply that policy-making processes are, in general, more transparent and accessible to the public. In contrast, autocratic regimes tend to limit the gathering and communication of evidence and have weak accountability mechanisms.[89]

In addition to general democracy and governance ratings, some other specific issues are relevant here. Academic freedom is an issue that is likely to be critical for research–policy linkages at specific policy level as well as the national level.[90] For example, it is more feasible to conduct economic research in some countries than it is to undertake research on democracy or human rights. In recent years, Human Rights Watch has set up an academic freedom programme to 'monitor, expose, and mobilize concerted action to challenge threats to academic freedom worldwide'[91] However, there is no systematic data available yet on this issue.

Second, media freedom would presumably be a key factor influencing the communication of ideas into policy and practice. Freedom of information may be valued in its own right, but information and press freedoms have also been linked persuasively by Amartya Sen to the state's willingness to intervene in famine prevention, particularly in India (Sen 1999).[92] Each year since 1980, Freedom House has conducted an annual press freedom survey to track trends in media freedom worldwide.[93] The work provides numerical rankings and rates each country's media as 'free', 'partly free' or 'not free'. Country narratives examine the legal environment for the media, political pressures that influence reporting, and economic factors that affect access to information. In addition, Reporters Without Borders creates a Press Freedom Index that might be used. The index measures 'the amount of freedom journalists and the media have in each country and the efforts made by governments to see that press freedom is respected.'[94]

Third, civil society plays a part in most political systems – it is where people become familiar and interested in public issues and how rules tend to affect the articulation of interests from society. Theories of social capital emphasize the importance of local associations in building trust and confidence both in institutions and among people (Putnam 1993). Key issues here include the conditions under which citizens can express their opinions, organize themselves for collective action and compete for influence. There is also much evidence to suggest civil society is an important link between research and policy (Court and Young 2003). Recent evidence suggests that civil society is important in affecting the impact of agricultural research on poverty reduction – relevant issues emerged related to trust, NGOs and informal social groups (Meinzen-Dick et al. 2003). There is new specific data for some countries as part of the Civil Society Index being developed by CIVICUS – the index generates measures for the structure, environment, values and impact of civil society at the national level.[95]

The role of Southern institutions in international development research–policy processes

Given the importance of external influences on Southern policy contexts, a further question that becomes pertinent concerns the effects of uneven access to international research–policy networks for Southern institutions. Much of the research on development issues is undertaken in the North, raising issues of perceived relevance and legitimacy. Perhaps even more importantly, there is an imbalance between the relatively low priority given to research-capacity building in Southern institutions in comparison to the research budgets spent on Northern-based institutions.

A consequence of this imbalance is the fact that Northern-based civil society institutions, including various research institutions and development NGOs, have more ready access than their Southern counterparts to knowledge about international development policy processes. They are also more likely to be able to participate in networks with Northern and international-level policy makers, and have greater chances of influencing international development policy. On the other hand, a substantial amount of the development research that is undertaken in the poorest countries is funded by international donors, which also raises a range of problematic issues around ownership, whose priorities are taken into account, use of external consultants and, again, perceived legitimacy. As policy processes become increasingly global, this arena will increase in importance.

How do networks work?

The growing importance of transnational knowledge networks also highlights a question that emerged from the comparative case studies concerning the nature of networks in general. In short, it is obvious that networks work, but how and why do they do this? Out of the three spheres in the framework (context, evidence, links), our understanding of the links arena remains the most limited. Although it is relatively simple to draw a 'family tree' of the key individuals and partnerships involved in a particular policy episode, it is harder to understand how more diffuse networks influence the research–policy process. The current theoretical literature provides myriad typologies of 'formal and informal networks', 'epistemic communities' and 'downward links', all of which seem to be evident and important in the case studies. They do not, however, add up to a comprehensive analytic tool for understanding what makes links function. What are the characteristics of networks that enable them to act as a bridge between research and policy? And where, how, and to what degree do networks actually make a difference to policy making? Networks have not been evaluated regularly until quite recently – which means there is a lack of comprehensive data on their roles and effects. Different assessment models are being developed to address this issue (Church et al. 2003; Provan and Milward 2001), but the area remains in need of further research.

In the literature on network management, the starting point is often a view of policy making as negotiation over 'public action'. Networks are seen as a relatively efficient means of handling such negotiations, and keywords are therefore 'competition', 'coordination' and 'cooperation' (Kickert et al. 1997; Robinson et al. 1999). The 'public management' aspect of links is sometimes evident in the case studies: for example the Sphere case, where policy makers were able to use their links with NGOs to put indirect pressure on them to 'get their act together'. However, many of the links described in the cases do not share this characteristic. They are better explained by an alternative stream of literature that emphasizes the informal nature of networks, arguing that they are not mainly a means of 'public management' but rather a potent means of challenging public management through generating multiple unofficial and creative policy 'interpretations' (Stacey 1995). Over time these informal ideas become institutionalized – as happened most obviously in the PRSP and SLA cases. Once informal ideas have become recognized as official policy, however, the networks will already have started generating new unofficial ideas.

This perspective – associated with chaos theory – is more prone to emphasize the informal and non-linear aspect of negotiation processes over ideas, rather than the official narratives of competition, coordination and cooperation. The 'nonlinearity' of networks is an important part of any creative institutional process (Stacey 1995). The case study that emphasized this most clearly is the SLA case, which notes, akin to the findings of Clay and Schaffer (1984), that chance plays a role through a number of 'lucky encounters, overlapping diaries, and external decisions'. Network coordinators may be unable to manage the way such chance encounters are played out, but they can perhaps provide as favourable conditions for exchange as possible – for example, through tolerating informal processes, or by creating a web of interlocking relationships between a wide range of actors. The role of donor agencies may be to provide long-term funding to networks, so as to enable sustainable capacity building and some degree of experimentation (Söderbaum 2001), thus leading to improved research–policy linkages.

Implications: recommendations for improved research–policy linkages

So what should researchers, practitioners, policy makers and others do if they wish to improve research–policy linkages in order to contribute towards evidence-based and pro-poor policy making? The material in this book suggests preliminary recommendations that confirm and elaborate on the hypotheses presented in the introduction.

1. Research is more likely to contribute to evidence-based and pro-poor policy making if it recognizes and acknowledges the political and institutional limits and pressures of policy makers, and resonates with their ideological assumptions, or sufficient pressure is exerted to challenge those limits.

The case studies confirm this hypothesis. In fact, the comparison across the case studies suggests that **context** is key. Political context – especially the level of demand for change, the nature of contestation and openness to new ideas – has emerged as critical in terms of policy change and usually has a degree of impact over and above other factors. Importantly however, it is exceptionally clear that whilst the political context at the moment of policy shift is a critical factor, the cases do not suggest that this context is immovable, unstoppable or deterministic of policy outcomes.

This is probably most clearly expressed in the PRSP case study, where use of evidence did indeed change the policy context. The NGO campaigns on debt relief drew on research that spoke the language of policy makers but which strongly challenged their viewpoints. The conflict that was created proved effective in changing the domestic political context in a number of countries, and put pressure on the G7 to insist on changes in debt-relief policy – thus additionally altering the international policy context.

In the Sphere and SLA cases, talented policy-entrepreneurs seized on the significant policy windows that occurred in 1994 (Rwanda crisis) and 1997 (DFID White Paper). In both cases, these policy-entrepreneurs were able to maximize the impact of their research through an understanding of the policy context and the need to engage with this critical stage of the policy process. In the Kenya case, this element is missing. The authors suggest that more effort by ITDG to understand the policy context for DAH programmes – the legal and policy framework, the key actors, their attitudes and influences, and reform processes and programmes (for example, the ASMP) – might have contributed to more rapid policy change.

2. Research is more likely to contribute to evidence-based and pro-poor policy making if outputs are based on local involvement and credible evidence, and are communicated via the most appropriate communicators, channels, style, format and timing.

The case studies suggest that research is more likely to be influential when it is regarded as rigorous. The PRSP case highlights the increased credibility gained by NGO research on debt relief as their analyses became increasingly more sophisticated. In the Sphere case study, the credibility of the evidence was high, due to the status of the researchers and the formal structure that had been set up for the evaluation, and this credibility was a very important factor. Similarly, in the SLA case, researchers already known for their thorough work presented the idea.

The cases underline that rigorous and credible evidence is not necessarily synonymous with pure academic research. Academic research is more likely to have an indirect 'percolation' effect on policy language and the policy environment over time, while applied or policy-oriented research is more likely to have a direct and more immediate influence on policy. Interestingly, the cases also show that action research can play an important role in convincing policy makers at decisive stages of the policy process.

In the PRSP case, applied policy-oriented research or evidence that translated academic findings into the policy context was directly useful for policy makers, and was therefore picked up and used relatively quickly. And, as mentioned above, the demonstration effect of the PEAP in Uganda did much to assure policy makers at a critical stage that PRSP-type programmes were feasible in practice. In the Sphere case study, the research that was influential was also directly oriented to policy. It was conceived as an evaluation study, and was commissioned by the policy makers, which all contributed to the results being taken seriously and having a major impact.

In the Kenya case, formal research seems to have contributed relatively little to the policy process, and research reports even less so (with the exception of the Hübl study). Evidence generated by operational CAHW schemes and communicated directly to visitors seems to have been much more important. Based on this, it is possible to suggest that more effort earlier on to get government staff, especially those opposed to the idea, to visit working CAHW schemes might have provided the necessary link between action research and policy makers that was missing in the Kenya case.

The case studies emphasize the importance of the 'packaging' and communication of the evidence. The SLA idea was attractive as evidence, both intellectually and practically, and was powerfully and repeatedly communicated between researchers, practitioners and policy makers. The PRSP idea was packaged in the language of the policy makers – specifically, the policy makers in the World Bank, IMF and large bilateral donors. The cases also support recent shifts within the field of development communication, which have moved away from the assumption that 'more information = more development', towards the importance of understanding the relationship between communication processes and wider political (and economic) processes (Hovland 2003). The PRSP and Sphere cases in particular emphasize that the amount of information is less important for impact than the strategic use of this information.

The relative importance of local involvement for improved research–policy linkages is harder to assess. Both the PRSP and Sphere case studies observe that local involvement was limited and was not prioritized. The Kenya case study concludes that:

taking the time to develop strong relationships with local communities, and working with them to develop effective and sustainable community-based services, is essential to prove the effectiveness of an approach, and acquire the fundamental legitimacy to advocate for change. That takes time.

On the whole, the case studies seem to demonstrate the difficult balance between acknowledging the legitimacy conferred on research and policy by local involvement on the one hand, and on the other hand being realistic about the high political levels at which international development policy is shaped and the importance of networks that operate at these levels.

3. Research is more likely to contribute to evidence-based and pro-poor policy making if researchers and policy makers share particular types of networks and develop chains of legitimacy for particular policy areas.

All four case studies conclude that researchers are more likely to be influential if they interact with policy makers. In the PRSP case, those researchers who were involved in one of the networks around HIPC, ESAF, SPA, PREM or debt relief were more likely to have an impact than researchers outside these circles. In the Sphere case, shared networks were formalized in the structure of the Rwanda evaluation, although the networks also went beyond this temporary structure. In relation to the Sphere Project, it is also worth noting the prominent role of two central 'policy entrepreneurs'. These persons acted as both connectors and salesmen (Gladwell 2000), as well as having an eye for policy windows to take forward their ideas, thus serving as two personified links who connected several different actors. Similarly, in the process leading up to the adoption of the SLA approach there was an intimate network of actors, including researchers and practitioners who, in various roles, nurtured the idea in its early years and then later shared it with their policy contacts – albeit in an undirected way.

The importance of effective connections and networks is also underlined by the Kenya case, where the lack of such connections served as a hindrance. The case study concludes that a carefully managed process to try to influence Dr Wamukoya's attitudes when he was appointed Director of Veterinary Services might have helped him to see the benefits of the CAHW approach, but nobody in the research/practitioner camp had the necessary connections to do so at the time. In addition, it is pointed out that if the vets' workshops had continued to include senior policy makers, rather then government vet practitioners, and a communication strategy to target tailor-made communication materials at policy makers had been used, this may have accelerated the policy process considerably in Kenya in the mid-1990s.

Towards a practical framework for researchers

The case studies, then, support the conditions outlined in the original three hypotheses. However, these three conditions are not always met in practice. Although researchers can often control the credibility of their evidence and ensure they interact with and communicate well with policy makers, they may have limited capacity to influence the political context within which they work, especially in less democratic

Table 7.1 Practical recommendations

What stakeholders need to know	What stakeholders need to do	How to do it
Political context Who are the policy makers? Is there policy maker demand for new ideas? What are the sources/ strengths of resistance? What is the policy-making process? What are the opportunities and timing for input into formal processes?	**Political context** Get to know policy makers, their agendas and the constraints they operate under Spot potential supporters and opponents Keep an eye on the horizon and prepare for opportunities in regular policy processes Look out for and react to sudden policy windows	**Political context** Work with policy makers Seek commissions Line up research programmes with high-profile policy events Reserve resources to be able to move quickly to react to policy windows Allow sufficient time and resources
Evidence What is the current theory? What are the prevailing narratives? How divergent is the new evidence? What sort of evidence will convince policy makers?	**Evidence** Establish credibility over the long term Provide practical solutions to problems Establish legitimacy Build a convincing case and present clear policy options Package new ideas in familiar theories or narratives Communicate effectively	**Evidence** Build up respected programmes of high-quality work Use action research and pilot projects to demonstrate the benefits of new approaches Use participatory approaches to help with legitimacy and implementation Clear strategy and resources for communication from the start Use real communication – 'seeing is believing'
Links Who are the key stakeholders in the policy discourse? What links and networks exist between them? Who are the intermediaries and what influence do they have? Whose side are they on?	**Links** Get to know the other stakeholders Establish a presence in existing networks Build coalitions with like-minded stakeholders Build new policy networks	**Links** Partnerships between researchers, policy makers and communities Identify key networkers and salesmen Use informal contacts

countries. Resources are also limited, and researchers need to make choices about what they do.

So what should researchers and others with a stake in development research and policy do if they wish to improve research–policy linkages? The themes drawn out in this volume provide preliminary recommendations in three areas – things you need to know, things you need to do and ways you can do it. Specific recommendations would depend on the context, but some of the general issues are summarised in Table 7.1.

First, there are some things stakeholders need to know about the political context, issue area (evidence), and key actors and networks (links). On political context: Is there political interest in change? Is there room for manoeuvre? How do policy makers perceive the problem? On evidence: Is it there? Is it relevant? Is it practically useful? Are the concepts familiar or new? Does it need repackaging? On links: Who are the key individuals? Are there existing networks? How best to transfer information (for example, media and/or campaigns). But, understanding context, evidence and links is only the first part of the process.

Second, there are some things they need to do in each of these areas. In the political context, researchers need to get to know the policy makers, identify friends and foes, prepare for regular policy opportunities, and look for policy windows. A key issue is also to make sure the evidence is credible. This has much more to do with long-term reputation than the scientific credibility of an individual piece of research. Researchers should make the most of the existing links by getting to know the other actors, work through existing networks and build coalitions and partnerships.

Third, some evidence is emerging about the most effective way of working. One of the best ways of working with policy makers is to seek commissions. Researchers should establish an approach that combines a strategic focus on current issues with the ability to respond rapidly to unexpected opportunities. Using action research and pilot projects to generate legitimacy seems to be particularly powerful. Researchers also need to network with others, such as good salesmen, who can convince the sceptics. They may also need to employ informal 'shadow networks' as well as more formal channels.

Final remarks

We hope that this volume contributes to a deeper understanding of the critical factors, and the interaction between them, that influence why some of the ideas that circulate in the research–policy arenas are picked up and acted on, while others are ignored and disappear. And we hope that the analysis of the theory and the comparison across four in-depth case studies provides some useful insights and ideas – both analytical and practical – for researchers, practitioners, policy makers and others who wish to further more evidence-based and pro-poor policy in their own work.

At the same time, despite the conceptual and empirical insights gained in this field, it seems there will also always be an element of unpredictability and surprise. Policies that were expected to change slowly may suddenly go through dramatic shifts. Research that has had low impact over several years may suddenly be picked up at the right moment and have decisive impact as a new policy is being formulated. As emphasized throughout the volume, the interplay of factors in a given situation of policy change (or stasis), and the role of research in this process, is so complex that it cannot be reduced to a linear equation (research–policy–practice). Rather, research–policy linkages are 'nonlinear', dynamic and complex processes. And this complexity – challenging as it may be to navigate for actors and organizations – is at the same time a condition for creativity. The field of research–policy linkages provides valuable insights into international-development policy processes because it presents opportunities to critically review old ideas that persist and to consider how new ideas may come to the fore. There are ways you can maximize the impact of research on policy and practice in international development.

German philosopher Immanuel Kant identified three aspects of knowledge: knowledge as critical reflection, knowledge as action, and knowledge as hope. The knowledge that has been the topic of this book – knowledge of research–policy linkages in international development – contains an element of all these three aspects. First, it is meant to provide a space for critical reflection and strategic consideration. Second, this cannot happen isolated from action in the world; knowledge of research–policy linkages will influence and impact on political decisions, actions and interactions. And third, the use of this knowledge is meant to contribute to policy making that is better equipped to work towards achieving the overarching goals and hopes of international development: to reduce poverty, alleviate suffering and save lives.

Endnotes

CHAPTER ONE

1. For further details on the Tanzania Essential Health Interventions Project (TEHIP) project, see: *http://web.idrc.ca*
2. Transnational dimensions of research and policy communities have also been neglected, but are addressed in Stone and Maxwell (2004).
3. Democracy is defined as a political system with institutionalized procedures for open and competitive political participation, where chief executives are chosen in competitive elections and where substantial limits are imposed on the powers of the chief executive.
4. Estimates included in speech by World Bank President James Wolfensohn in 1999. (*www.worldbank.org/html/extdr/am99/jdw-sp/jdwsp-en.htm*)
5. This was based on and remains similar to the OECD definition: 'creative work undertaken on a systematic basis in order to increase the stock of knowledge, including knowledge of man, culture and society, and the use of this stock of knowledge to devise new applications' (OECD 1981).
6. Personal communication, Peter Walker to Margie Buchanan-Smith.

CHAPTER TWO

7. As quoted by Nutley et al. (2002) – see Box 9 in that paper for details.

CHAPTER THREE

8. The term 'World Bank' is used throughout this chapter to refer to the International Bank for Reconstruction and Development (IBRD) and the International Development Association (IDA), both of the World Bank Group.
9. The research for this case study is based on accounts given by key actors of events of three or four years ago, and a literature review, particularly of policy documents, official statements, as well as some internal and 'grey' material. Interviews were conducted mainly in Washington and London in the period August to October 2002. The original *Working Paper* (Christiansen with Hovland 2003) provides a list of the interviewees as well as a chronological presentation of events.
10. As of February 2003, the period covered by the process of generating a PRSP can be two to five years.
11. See *www.imf.org/external/np/pdr/prsp/poverty1.htm#III*
12. These were Albania, Bolivia, Burkina Faso, Ethiopia, Gambia, Guinea, Guyana, Honduras, Malawi, Mauritania, Mozambique,

CHAPTER THREE

Nicaragua, Niger, Rwanda, Senegal, Tajikistan, Tanzania, Uganda, Vietnam, Yemen and Zambia. Kenya and Ghana both had a complete PRSP that had not gone to the Board. Cambodia and Kyrgyz Republic were next in line.

13 As of March 2003, the eight countries that reached completion point were Benin, Bolivia, Burkina Faso, Mali, Mauritania, Mozambique, Tanzania and Uganda.
14 For more assessments and reviews of PRSPs, see Booth (2001) and the PRSP Monitoring and Synthesis Project (*www.prspsynthesis.org*).
15 Other influential documents included a set of strategic policy statements from bilateral donors (e.g. DFID 1997; SIDA 1997; SDC 2000); as well as guidelines from OECD-DAC (2001) and UNDP publications that packaged poverty reduction as human development.
16 Participation is in this context associated with a number of other concepts drawn from political science and policy studies, most notably the concepts of transparency (a major concern of World Bank economist Joseph Stiglitz, for example), accountability (Jenkins and Goetz 1999), democracy (Moore and Putzel 1999), ownership and empowerment (World Bank 2000/01).
17 Studies that looked at this include those by the World Bank (1988, 1998) and research by Mosley (1987), Gupta and Islam (1983) and Cassen et al. (1986).
18 In response, there was also a proliferation of conditions that were meant to try and overcome the criticisms. While the impact varied from country to country, in the most extreme cases this resulted in loans with more than 200 conditions ranging from the standard specifications on macro-economic, trade, finance and privatization changes to detailed conditions on the protection of specific forest resources and the rights of indigenous people.
19 Key work in this area includes Killick (1991), Helleiner (2000), Helleiner et al. (1995) and Mosley et al. (1995); and the work by Dollar and his collaborators such as Burnside and Dollar (1997), Dollar and Kraay (2001) and Collier and Dollar (1999). Thomas (2003) summarizes the major critiques of conditionality.
20 Influential documents in this area include Johnson and Wasty (1993), Haggard and Kaufman (1992), Tarp and Hjertholm (2000) and Dollar and Svensson (2000). Critiques of ownership were also voiced (e.g. Killick et al. 1998), and as one interviewee for this study put it: 'we did not need Dollar and Kraay to tell us ownership of policies mattered, the question was how to tell if there was enough, and how to make it better'.
21 Key influential internal World Bank critiques were the Wapenhans Report (Wapenhans 1992) and 'Assessing Aid' (World Bank 1998).
22 Adapted from Lawson et al. (2002).

23 The UN system also attempted some internal coordination through the UNDAF (UNDAF Guidelines, April 1999, see *www.un.org.np/res_cor/un_reform/undaf/UNDAF_guide.pdf*).
24 For a more thorough discussion of each of the key players, see the original *Working Paper* (Christiansen with Hovland 2003).
25 The term IFIs will be used throughout this paper to denote the World Bank and the IMF only.
26 For further discussions, see Coyle (2001), Stern with Ferreira (1997) and Wade (1997).
27 A key difference between the two research departments reflects the issues discussed above in relation to the policy processes. The World Bank has a disclaimer policy, which means that the research conducted is not the official view of the organization, and publication is under the name of the researchers themselves. This puts staff in a position where they potentially face complicated and possibly contradictory incentives: Are they serving the academic community or the World Bank? Research in the IMF, on the other hand, is the official line of the organization, and is only published after middle-management signs it off.
28 Source: *www.spa-psa.org*
29 The Utstein Group was originally set up as a group of female Development Ministers, including those from Sweden, Netherlands, Germany and the UK, with Norway joining more recently. The term 'like-minded' is less formal but usually refers more or less to the same group – plus or minus Canada and Germany, depending on the issue.
30 The IDTs were presented in May 1996 in the DAC document 'Shaping the 21st century: The contribution of development cooperation' (*www.oecd.org/dataoecd/23/35/2508761.pdf*). For a discussion of their role, see Poston et al. (2003).
31 See especially DFID (1999a,b), Grant (1999), Spray (1999), and Spray and Grant (1998).
32 Examples of the NGO publications that developed include Christian Aid (1997), DRI (1999), Jubilee 2000 Coalition (1997), and Oxfam (1997, 1998a–d, 1999a–e, 2000a–e, 2001a–d).
33 For further discussion of the PEAP process and the domestic politics behind it, see Piron (2003).
34 For a more detailed discussion of the CDF, see the World Bank's final report on the multi-stakeholder evaluation (World Bank 2003)
35 Kwesi Botchwey (Harvard Institute for International Development), Paul Collier (Oxford University), Jan Willem Gunning (Free University of Amsterdam) and Koichi Hamada (Yale University).
36 For further information on HIPC1 and prior debt relief, see Daseking and Powell (1999).
37 The rest eventually reached completion point on HIPC2 terms, with the exception of Cote d'Ivoire because of the deterioration of the political situation in the country.

CHAPTER THREE

38 Ending up, via Oxfam, as articles in the *Financial Times* and *The Economist* in particular.
39 See the two volumes on the HIPC Debt Initiative (1999a,b) and the series of joint IMF and World Bank papers from 1999.
40 Available at *www.worldbank.org/hipc/hipc-review/Linkage.pdf*
41 Available at *http://poverty.worldbank.org/library/view/3910*
42 See *www.brettonwoodsproject.org/article.shtml?cmd[126]=x-126-15645* and *www.brettonwoodsproject.org/article.shtml?cmd[126]=x-126-15595* and *www.brettonwoodsproject.org/article.shtml?cmd[126]=x-126-16340*
43 Despite the fact that the Addis Ababa meeting was the main mechanism during the consultation process for input from the 'South', especially Southern governments, still only around half of the participants were from Southern institutions. It is also worth noting that all the presentations at the meeting were made by Northern organizations, apart from the presentation on the Uganda experience (HIPC Debt Initiative 1999a). In the compendium of comments (HIPC Debt Initiative 1999b), containing around 20 submissions, there are only three substantive comments from Southern institutions.
44 For example, it is possible to have IDA lending from the World Bank, but not a low-income-country loan from the IMF's Poverty PRGF.

CHAPTER FOUR: *How the Sphere Project came into being*

45 Other initiatives include the Active Learning Network for Accountability and Performance in Humanitarian Action (ALNAP), and the Humanitarian Ombudsman Project which later became the Humanitarian Accountability Project (HAP).
46 The attempt to map out the origin of Sphere in this case study is based on accounts given by key actors and review of the relevant literature. Interviews with key informants were mainly conducted in the period October to December 2002, and a list of these is provided in the original *ODI Working Paper* (Buchanan-Smith 2003).
47 For example, Borton describes it as 'closer to a commissioned multi-disciplinary research study than a conventional evaluation' (Borton 2001: 74).
48 This is in contrast to the portrayal of some emergencies in the 1980s, such as the Ethiopia emergency in the mid-1980s when drought was emphasized rather than the political causes of the famine.
49 Duffield (1994) describes humanitarian space as negotiated access, where the agreement of warring parties has been secured for the movement of neutral humanitarian aid.

50 For instance, one NGO reportedly hired a crew to take photos of the famine in Ethiopia that were then sold to the media. This was regarded as distasteful practice by many other NGOs.
51 Oxfam did have written policies, but lacked a statement of the fundamental principles.
52 SCHR is an alliance for voluntary action of CARE International, Caritas Internationalis, IFRC, International Save the Children Alliance, Lutheran World Federation, MSF International, Oxfam International, and the World Council of Churches. ICRC joined in 2001.
53 *The People in Aid Code of Best Practice in the Management and Support of Aid Personnel*, first published by RRN, ODI, in 1997.
54 See also Leader (1999) for a full review of these and other 'code of conduct' initiatives.
55 Most of this section and the next on the international humanitarian response is based on Study 3 of the Rwanda evaluation (Borton et al. 1996), discussed at greater length in the 'Rwanda evaluation' section.
56 It should be made clear, however, that failure to prevent the genocide, which claimed most lives, was a political, diplomatic and military failure, rather than a failure of the humanitarian operation.
57 Australia, Austria, Belgium, Canada, Denmark, France (until it left in December 1995), Finland, Germany, Ireland, Italy, Japan, Luxembourg, Netherlands, New Zealand, Norway, Spain, Sweden, Switzerland, UK, USA, Commission of the EU, OECD/DAC, IOM, UN/DHA, UNDP, UNHCHR, UNHCR, UNICEF, WFP, WHO, IBRD, ICRC, IFRC, ICVA, Doctors of the World, InterAction, SCHR and VOICE.
58 Quote taken from a memo from InterAction to Peter Walker and Karen Donovan in February 1996.
59 After this meeting, InterAction canvassed the views of its members, who agreed to this collaborative action.
60 The concept of a charter seems to have been at least partially influenced by developments in the commercial and public sector at the time. In the UK, for example, charters were being drafted in different sectors to define the rights of consumers or service users.
61 It is also interesting to note that the US State Department initially opposed Sphere 'as an attempt by NGOs to create international law' (personal communication), until they were persuaded that this was an attempt to implement existing international law, at which point it became a strong supporter of and donor to Sphere.
62 See, for example, a note on the InterAction Annual Forum in April 1996.
63 According to the staff of Sphere Project, opposition at field level has not been so strong, and sometimes has been retracted.
64 Any efforts to develop accreditation have been very specific: for example, related to child sponsorship within InterAction.

CHAPTER FOUR

65 Proposal for an 'International standing capacity to monitor and report on international progress in addressing the phenomenon of complex emergencies,' by Katherine Blakeslee (USAID), Niels Dabelstein (Danida) and Peter Walker (IFRC), September 1997.
66 However, the strength of the different networks varies between sectors. For example, it was strongest in the nutrition sector and weakest in the health sector. Shelter also suffered from a weak network, and from a lack of technical research and experience.
67 Statement made at an ALNAP meeting by a representative of AHA.
68 See for example, Macrae and Leader's analysis of the search for coherence between political and humanitarian responses to complex emergencies (Macrae and Leader 2000).
69 As quoted by Crewe and Harrison (1998).

CHAPTER FIVE

70 The research for this case study, carried out in collaboration with the Department of Veterinary Services (DVS) and Intermediate Technology Development Group East Africa (ITDG), is based on identification of key actors, critical events, and a review of the relevant literature. Two individuals who had been involved in the decentralized animal healthcare story in Kenya, Jacob Wanyama (ITDG) and Julius Kajume (DVS), were contracted to organize a mini-workshop in Nairobi to develop the timeline and identify the key documents and actors. Participants in the mini-workshop identified 27 key informants from government, private sector and non-government agencies, who were interviewed in Nairobi and at an international conference on 'Primary Animal Health Care in the 21st Century: Shaping the Rules, Policies and Institutions' held in Mombasa, Kenya in October 2002. The original *ODI Working Paper* (Young et al. 2003) provides a full list and brief information about each of the key informants.

CHAPTER SIX

71 The research for this case study is based on identification of key events, texts and interviews with key actors. A list of the interviewees is provided in the working paper (Solesbury 2003). The work originated in a DFID consultancy project evaluating the policy impact of its economic and social research, undertaken in 2001.
72 Some people prefer the plural 'sustainable livelihoods approaches' but in this paper, for convenience, the singular is used and usually abbreviated as SLA. This term refers to the policies and practices that DFID adopted. The term sustainable livelihood(s) is used in this paper for the underlying concept or philosophy.
73 It is recognized that the origins of the sustainable livelihood

concept extend back more than 20 years and into more literature, especially from non-UK sources, than it has been possible to examine here. However the focus for this paper is on what is believed to have been most influential on UK policy and practice.

74 The distinction between policy, practice and research is not always clear in the SLA narrative; we have characterized the relevant documents as either 'policy' or 'research' documents dependent on the position of the contributor as policy maker or policy adviser (usually in DFID), practitioner (in executive development agencies and/or in the field), or researcher (academic or consultant).

75 For example DFID (1999d), see the opening quote in the introduction to this chapter

76 This and later work provides the basis for Helmore and Singh (2001).

77 For example, Robert Chambers (Chambers 1995), Susanna Davies (Davies 1996) and Ian Scoones (Scoones 1996).

78 This was in the context of a shift of departmental-research funding towards supporting a smaller number of larger research programmes that would be competitively tendered – the Sustainable Livelihoods programme was one of these.

79 The international development targets cover extreme poverty, universal primary education, gender equality, infant mortality, reproductive healthcare, sustainable development, and resource conservation.

80 Definition from the *New Oxford Dictionary of English* (1998) and referenced to the writing of Thomas Kuhn, in particular *The Structure of Scientific Revolutions* (1962).

81 The Environment Working Committee had appointed IIED, IUCN (International Union for the Conservation of Nature) and WRI (World Resource Institute) as its advisers.

82 There had also been such meetings with Labour politicians and advisers before the 1997 general election.

83 In Scoones' view, expressed in interview, DFID's adaptation shifted the focal point of the framework from institutions to assets, which perhaps was necessary to ease its adoption by natural resource interests; later DFID would re-emphasize the institutional dimension.

84 Other more recent examples of such tropes are 'social capital' and 'ethical investment'.

85 Such elapses of time are not uncommon for the adoption of many kinds of social or technological innovation.

CHAPTER SEVEN

86 An earlier version of this section appeared in Court and Young (2004).
87 It is important to note that the process of collecting cases probably underemphasizes the importance of routine and incremental decisions and overemphasizes the importance of fundamental or emergent ones.
88 See *www.gdnet.org/rapnet*
89 For example, a case study from Uruguay charted the negative effect the dictatorship had on the use of research in health policy (Salvatella et al. 2000).
90 For various pertinent aspects of academic freedom, see *www.aaup.org*
91 See *http://hrw.org/advocacy/academic*
92 It is also worth noting that de Waal argues, perhaps equally persuasively, that state commitment to famine prevention is less the result of media freedoms than a political contract between the state and its citizens in which famine prevention is at the core (de Waal 1997).
93 See *www.freedomhouse.org/research/pressurvey.htm*
94 See *www.rsf.org/article.php3?id_article=4118*
95 See *www.civicus.org*

Bibliography

African Rights (1994) 'Humanitarianism Unbound? Current Dilemmas Facing Multi-mandate Relief Operations in Political Emergencies', *African Rights Discussion Paper 4*, African Rights, London.

Albu, M. (2002) *Understanding Livelihoods that Involve Micro-enterprise: Putting Markets and Technological Capabilities into the SL Framework*, ITDG, London.

Amalric, F. (1998) *The Sustainable Livelihoods Approach: General Report of the Sustainable Livelihoods Project 1995–1997*, SID, Rome.

Anderson. J M. (1975) *Public Policy-making*, Praeger, New York.

Appleton, S. (1998) 'Changes in Poverty in Uganda 1992–1996,' *Working Paper Series No. 79*, Centre for the Study of African Economies, Oxford.

Appleton, S. (2001) 'Poverty in Uganda 1999/2000: Preliminary Estimates from the Uganda National Household Survey', University of Nottingham, Mimeo.

Ashby, W.R. (1956) *An Introduction to Cybernetics*, Chapman and Hall, London and New York.

Ashley, C. and Carney, D. (1999) *Sustainable Livelihoods: Lessons from Early Experience*, DFID, London.

Berkout, F. and Scoones, I. (1999) 'Knowing How to Change: Environmental Policy Learning and Transfer', *Development Research Insights 30: 1–2*, June 1999.

Boone, P. (1994a) *The Impact of Foreign Aid on Savings and Growth*, Centre for Economic Performance, London School of Economics, London.

Boone, P. (1994b) *Politics and the Effectiveness of Foreign Aid*, Centre for Economic Performance, London School of Economics, London.

Booth, D. (2001) 'PRSP Institutionalisation Study – Third Report', *Report for the Strategic Partnership with Africa*, May, ODI, London.

Borton, J. (2001) 'Doing Study 3 of the Joint Evaluation of Emergency Assistance to Rwanda: The Team Leader's Perspective', *Evaluating International Humanitarian Action. Reflections from Practitioners*, Wood, A., Apthorpe, R. and Borton, J. (eds), Zed Books, London and New York.

Borton, J., Brusset, E., Hallam, A., Collins, S., Pottier, J., de Lame, D., Chalinder, A., Shoham, J., Lee, L., Connaughton, R., Ishøyet, T., Telford, J., Goetz, F., Shepherd, G., Hilsum, L., Jones, B., Turton, D., Jackson, L., Shellard, N. and Walsh, A. (1996) *The International Response to Conflict and Genocide: Lessons from the Rwanda Experience. Joint Evaluation of Emergency Assistance to Rwanda. Study 3. Humanitarian Aid and Effects*, Steering Committee of the Joint Evaluation of Emergency Assistance to Rwanda, Copenhagen.

Brock, K. and Coulibaly, N. (1999) 'Sustainable Rural Livelihoods in Mali', *Research Report 35*, IDS, Brighton, UK.

Brown, L.D. and Fox, J. (2001) 'Transnational Civil Society Coalitions and the World Bank: Lessons from Project and Policy Influence Campaigns', *Global Citizen Action*, Edwards, M. and Gaventa, J. (eds.), Lynne Rienner, Boulder, USA.

Buchanan-Smith, M. (2003) 'How the Sphere Project Came into Being: A Case Study of Policy-making in the Humanitarian Aid Sector and the Relative Influence of Research', *ODI Working Paper 215*, ODI, London.

Burnside, C. and Dollar, D. (1997) *Aid, Policies and Growth*, Macroeconomics and Growth Division, Policy Research Department, World Bank, Washington, DC.

Camroux, D. (1994) 'The Asia Pacific Policy Community in Malaysia', *Pacific Review*, 7(4): 421–35.

Carney, D. (2002) *Sustainable Livelihoods Approaches: Progress and Possibilities for Change*, DFID, London.

Carney, D. (ed.) (1998) *Sustainable Livelihoods Approaches: What Contribution Can We Make?*, DFID, London.

Carney, D., Drinkwater, M., Rusinow, T., Neefjes, K., Wanmali, S. and Singh, N. (1999) *Livelihoods Approaches Compared*, DFID, London.

Carswell, G., de Haan, A., Dea, D., Konde, A., Shankland, A. and Sinclair, A. (2000) 'Sustainable Livelihoods in Southern Ethiopia', *Research Report 44*, IDS, Brighton, UK.

Cassen, R. et al. (1986) *Does Aid Work? Report to an Intergovernmental Task Force*, Clarendon Press, Oxford.

Castells, M. (1993) 'The Informational Economy and the New International Division of Labour', *The New Global Economy in the Information Age*, Carnoy, M., Castells, M., Cohen, S.S. and Cardoso, F.H. (eds.), Macmillan, London.

Chambers, R. (1983) *Rural Development: Putting the Last First*, Longman, New York.

Chambers, R. (1993) *Challenging the Professions*, ITDG Publishing, London.

Chambers, R. (1994) 'The Origins and Practice of Participatory Rural Appraisal', *World Development* 22 (7): 953–69.

Chambers, R. (1995) 'Poverty and Livelihoods: Whose Reality Counts?', *IDS Discussion Paper 347*, IDS, Brighton, UK.

Chambers, R. (1997) *Whose Reality Counts? Putting the First Last*, ITDG Publishing, London.

Chambers, R. and Conway, G.R. (1992) 'Sustainable Rural Livelihoods: Practical Concepts for the 21st Century', *Discussion Paper 296*, IDS, Brighton, UK.

Chapman, J. and Fisher, T. (1999) 'The Thoughtful Activist. A Toolkit for Enhancing NGO Campaigning and Advocacy' (draft), New Economics Foundation, London.

Chomsky, N. (1987) 'The Manufacture of Consent', *The Chomsky Reader*, Peck, J. (ed.), Serpent's Tail, London.

Christian Aid (1997) 'Change the DEBT Rules, Basic Policy Paper', draft PS/9, Christian Aid, London.
Christian Aid (2004) *The Politics of Poverty: Aid in the New Cold War*, Christian Aid, London.
Christiansen, K. with Hovland, I. (2003) 'The PRSP Initiative: Multilateral Policy Change and the Relative Role of Research', *ODI Working Paper 216*, ODI, London.
Church, M. et al. (2003) 'Participation, Relationships and Dynamic Change: New Thinking on Evaluating the Work of International Networks' *DPU Working Paper No. 121*, Development Planning Unit (DPU), University College London (www.ucl.ac.uk/dpu/WP121.pdf).
Clay, E.J. and Schaffer, B.B. (1984) *Room for Manoeuvre: An Exploration of Public Policy in Agricultural and Rural Development*, Heinemann, London.
Collier, P. (1997) 'The Failure of Conditionality', *Perspectives on Aid and Development*, Gwin, C. and Nelson, J.M. (eds), Overseas Development Council, Washington, DC.
Collier, P. and Dollar, D. (1999) 'Aid Allocation and Poverty Reduction,' *Policy Research Working Paper No. 2041*, World Bank, Washington.
Conroy, C. and Litvinoff, M. (eds) (1988) *The Greening of Aid: Sustainable Livelihoods in Practice*, Earthscan, London.
Court, J. and Young, J. (2003) 'Bridging Research and Policy: Insights from 50 Case Studies', *ODI Working Paper 213*, ODI, London (www.odi.org.uk/publications).
Coyle, E. (2001) 'Consensus and Dissent in Washington: Negotiating Change in the World Bank and IMF', MPhil thesis, Centre of International Studies, University of Cambridge, Cambridge.
Crewe, E. and Harrison, E. (1998) *Whose Development? An Ethnography of Aid*, Zed Books, London.
Crewe, E. and Young, J. (2002) 'Bridging Research and Policy: Context, Evidence and Links', *ODI Working Paper 173*, ODI, London.
Dabelstein, N. (1996) 'Evaluating the International Humanitarian System: Rationale, Process and Management of the Joint Evaluation of the International Response to the Rwanda Genocide', *Disasters Journal*, 20(4): 286–94.
Darroch, R.A., Mulvany, P. and Pillai, E.T.S. (1982) 'International Workshop for Trainers of Animal Health Auxiliaries and Livestock Farmers', *Workshop Report*, Peradeniya, Sri Lanka, Commonwealth Secretariat, London.
Daseking, C. and Powell, R. (1999) 'From Toronto Terms to HIPC Initiative: A Brief History of Debt Relief for Low-Income Countries', *International Monetary Fund Working Paper 99/142*, IMF, Washington, DC.
Davies, S. (1996) *Adaptable Livelihoods: Coping with Food Insecurity in the Malian Sahel*, Macmillan, London.
De Haan, C. and Bekure, S. (1991) 'Animal Health Services in Sub-Saharan Africa: Initial Experiences With Alternative Approaches', *World Bank Technical Paper 134*, World Bank, Washington, DC.

De Haan, C. and Nissen, N.J. (1985) 'Animal Health Services in Sub-Saharan Africa', *World Bank Technical Paper 44*, World Bank, Washington DC.

De Vibe M., Hovland, I. and Young, J. (2002) 'Bridging Research and Policy: An Annotated Bibliography', *ODI Working Paper 174*, ODI, London.

De Waal, A. (1997) *Famine Crimes: Politics and the Disaster Relief Industry in Africa*, James Currey in association with African Rights, Indiana.

Demery, L. and Walton, M. (1998) *Are Poverty Reduction and Other 21st Century Social Goals Attainable?*, World Bank, Washington, DC.

DFID (1997) *Eliminating World Poverty: A Challenge for the 21st Century*, White Paper on International Development, Cm 3789, DFID, London.

DFID (1999a) *Fiscal Implications of Debt and Debt Relief*, Economist Group, DFID, London.

DFID (1999b) *Debt Relief and Poverty Reduction: A UK Submission to Phase 2 of the HIPC Review*, HM Treasury and DFID, London.

DFID (1999c) *Sustainable Livelihoods and Poverty Elimination*, DFID, London.

DFID (1999d, 2000d, 2001) *Sustainable Livelihoods Guidance Sheets*, Nos. 1–8, DFID, London (also available on www.livelihoods.org).

DFID (2000a) *Sustainable Livelihoods – Current Thinking and Practice*, DFID, London.

DFID (2000b) *Sustainable Livelihoods – Building on Strengths*, DFID, London.

DFID (2000c) *Achieving Sustainability: Poverty Elimination and the Environment, Strategies for Achieving the International Development Targets*, DFID, London.

DFID (2000e) *Eliminating World Poverty: Making Globalisation Work for the Poor*, White Paper on International Development, Cm 5006, DFID, London.

Dollar, D. and Svensson, J. (2000) 'What Explains the Success or Failure of Structural Adjustment Programs?', *Economic Journal* 110: 894–917.

Dollar, D. and Kraay, A. (2001) 'Growth is Good for the Poor', *World Bank Working Paper No. 2587*, World Bank, Washington, DC.

DRI (1999) *HIPC Debt Strategy: The Newsletter of the HIPC Debt Strategy and Analysis Capacity Building Programme*, Issue 1, Debt Relief International, London.

Duffield (1994) 'Complex Emergencies and the Crisis of Developmentalism', *IDS Bulletin*, 25(4), IDS, Brighton, UK

DVS (2000) 'Memorandum of Understanding' with SNV for delivering livestock services in Northern Kenya, DVS, Nairobi, Kenya.

Edwards, M. (2001) 'Introduction', *Global Citizen Action*, Edwards, M. and Gaventa, J. (eds), Lynne Rienner, Boulder, USA.

Edwards, M. (2004) *Civil Society*, Polity Press, Cambridge.

Elliot, P. (1995) 'Intellectuals, the 'Information Society' and the Disappearance of the Public Space', *Approaches to Media: A Reader*, Boyd-Barret, O. and Newbold, C. (eds.), Arnold, London.
Ellis, F. (1998a) 'Survey Article: Household Strategies and Rural Livelihood Diversification', *Journal of Development Studies* 35(1): 1–38.
Ellis, F. (1998b) 'Livelihood Diversification and Sustainable Rural Livelihoods', *Sustainable Rural Livelihoods: What Contribution Can We Make?*, Carney, D. (ed.), DFID, London.
Ellis, F. (2000a) *Rural Livelihoods and Diversity in Developing Countries*, Oxford University Press, Oxford.
Ellis, F. (2000b) *Mixing It: Rural Livelihoods and Diversity in Developing Countries*, Oxford University Press, Oxford.
Eriksson, J. (1996) *The International Response to Conflict and Genocide: Lessons from the Rwanda Experience. Synthesis Report*, Steering Committee of the Joint Evaluation of Emergency Assistance to Rwanda, Copenhagen.
FAO (2000) *Inter-agency Experiences and Lessons: from the Forum on Operationalising Sustainable Livelihoods Approaches*, FAO, Rome.
Farrington, J., Carney, D., Ashley, C. and Turton, C. (1999) 'Sustainable livelihoods in practice: early application of concepts in rural areas', *Natural Resources Perspectives 42*, ODI, London.
Ferguson, J. (1990) *The Anti-politics Machine; Development, De-politicisation and Bureaucratic Power in Lesotho*, Cambridge University Press, Cambridge.
Figueroa, M.E. et al. (2002) 'Communication for Social Change: An Integrated Model for Measuring the Process and Its Outcomes', *The Communication for Social Change Working Paper Series* No. 1, Rockefeller Foundation, New York (www.comminit.com/stcfscindicators/sld-5997.html).
Fine, M., Weis, L., Weseen, S. and Wong, L. (2000) 'For Whom? Qualitative Research, Representations, and Social Responsibilities', *Handbook of Qualitative Research* (2nd ed.), Denzin, N. and Lincoln, Y. (eds), Sage Publications, Thousand Oaks, USA.
Foster, M. (2000) 'New Approaches to Development Cooperation: What can we learn from experience with implementing sector wide approaches?', *CAPE Working Paper 140*, Centre for Aid and Public Expenditure (CAPE), ODI, London.
Foster, M., Healey, J., Matthew, M. and White, H. (1999) *Linking HPIC II Debt Relief with Poverty Reduction and Wider Aid Issues: Some Reflections and Suggestions*, Centre for Aid and Public Expenditure (CAPE), ODI, London.
Franco, J. (1994) 'Beyond Ethnocentricism: Gender, Power and Third World Intelligentsia', *Colonial Discourses and Post-colonial Theory: A Reader*, Williams, P. and Chrisman, L. (eds.) Harvester Wheatsheaf, New York.
Freedom House (2003) *Freedom in the World*, Freedom House, Washington DC.

Garrett, J.L. and Islam, Y. (1998) 'Policy Research and the Policy Process: Do the Twain Ever Meet?' *Gatekeeper Series* 74, IIED, London.

Gaventa, J. (2001) 'Global Citizen Action: Lessons and Challenges', *Global Citizen Action*, Edwards, M. and Gaventa, J. (eds), Lynne Rienner, Boulder, USA.

Gladwell, M. (2000) *The Tipping Point: How Little Things Can Make a Big Difference*, Little, Brown & Co, London.

Government of Kenya (1965) 'African socialism', *Sessional Paper* No. 1 of 1965, Government Printers, Nairobi.

Government of Kenya (1986) 'Economic management for renewed growth', *Sessional Paper* No. 1 of 1986, Government Printers, Nairobi.

Grant, P. (1999) *Maximising the Poverty Reduction Impact of Debt Relief*, DFID, London.

Grindle, M.S. (ed.) (1980) *Politics and Policy Implementation in the Third World*, Princeton University Press, Princeton.

Grindle, M. and Thomas, J. (1991) *Public Choices and Policy Change: The Political Economy of Reform in Developing Countries*, Johns Hopkins University Press, Baltimore, USA.

Gupta, K.L. and Islam, M.A. (1983) *Foreign Capital, Savings and Growth: An International Cross-Sectional Study*, Reidel, Dordrecht.

Gurr, E., Marshall, M.G. and Kholsa, A. (2001) *A Global Survey of Armed Conflicts, Self-determination Movements and Democracy*, Center for International Development and Conflict Management, University of Maryland, Maryland.

Haas, E.B. (1991) *When Knowledge is Power: Three Models of Change in International Organizations*, University of California Press, California.

Haggard, S. and Kaufman, R.R. (eds) (1992) *The Politics of Economic Adjustment*, Princeton University Press, Princeton, NJ, USA.

Hailey, J. and Smillie, I. (2001) *Managing for Change: Leadership and Strategy in Asian NGOs*, Earthscan, London.

Harper, C. (2001) 'Do Facts Matter?', *Global Citizen Action*, Edwards, M. and Gaventa, J. (eds.), Lynne Rienner, Boulder, USA.

Helleiner, G.K. (2000) 'External Conditionality, Local Ownership and Development', *Transforming Development: Foreign Aid for a Changing World*, Freedman, J. (ed.), University of Toronto Press, Toronto.

Helleiner, G.K., Killick, T., Lipumba, N., Ndulu, B.J. and Svendsen, K.E. (1995) *Report of the Group of Independent Advisers on Development Cooperation Issues between Tanzania and its Aid Donors*, Royal Danish Ministry of Foreign Affairs, Copenhagen.

Helmore, K. and Singh, N. (2001) *Sustainable Livelihoods: Building on the Wealth of the Poor*, Kumarian Press, Connecticut, USA.

HIPC Debt Initiative (1999a) '1999 Review, Phase II, Volume 1', *Proceedings of the HIPC Review Seminar*, hosted by UN ECA, Addis Ababa, Ethiopia, 29–30 July, IMF/World Bank, Washington, DC.

HIPC Debt Initiative (1999b) '1999 Review, Phase II, Volumes 2', *Compendium of the Comments and Contributions*, IMF/World Bank, Washington, DC.
Hobart, M. (1993) *An Anthropological Critique of Development: The Growth of Ignorance*, Routledge, London.
Hobley, M. (2001) 'Unpacking the PIP box', unpublished paper prepared for DFID.
Hobley, M. (n.d.) 'Transformation of Organisations for Poverty Eradication: the Implications of Sustainable Livelihoods Approaches', unpublished paper prepared for DFID.
Hovland, I. (2003) 'Communication of Research for Poverty Reduction: A Literature Review', *ODI Working Paper* 227, ODI, London (www.odi.org.uk/publications).
Hübl, K., Gathuma, J.M. and Kajume, J.K. (1998) *Improved Delivery of Animal Health Services in Kenya*, Vol. 1, Ministry of Agriculture and Rural Development, Nairobi, Kenya.
Hudson, A. (2000) 'Making the Connection: Legitimacy Claims, and Northern NGO's International Advocacy', *New Roles and Relevance: Development NGOs and the Challenge of Change*, Lewis, D. and Wallace, T. (eds), Kumarian Press, Bloomfield, USA.
Hyden, G., Court, J. and Mease, K. (2004) *Making Sense of Governance: Empirical Evidence from 16 Transitional Societies*, Lynne Rienner, Boulder, USA.
IMF (1998a) *External Evaluation of the ESAF*, Report by a Group of Independent Experts, IMF, Washington, DC.
IMF (1998b) *Distilling the Lessons from the ESAF Reviews*, IMF, Washington, DC.
IMF (1999) *Proposals to Strengthen the Initiative for the Heavily Indebted Poor Countries (HIPCs)*, IMF, Washington, DC.
IMF/World Bank (1999a) *Heavily Indebted Poor Countries (HIPC) Initiative – Strengthening the Link between Debt Relief and Poverty Reduction*, IMF, Washington, DC (http://www.worldbank.org/hipc/hipc-review/Linkage.pdf).
IMF/World Bank (1999b) *Modifications to the Heavily Indebted Poor Countries Initiatives*, IMF, Washington, DC.
IMF/World Bank (1999c) *Poverty Reduction Strategy Papers – Operational Issues*, IMF, Washington, DC.
ITDG (1987) 'Livestock Keeping in Lower Meru', internal report, ITDG, UK.
ITDG (1991) 'Vets Workshop, Baragoi, Samburu, November 1991', *ITDG Report*, ITDG, Nairobi, Kenya.
ITDG (1993) 'Vets Workshop, Hunters Lodge, Ukambani, April 1993', *ITDG Report*, ITDG, Nairobi, Kenya.
ITDG (1994) '4th Annual Vets' Workshop, Isiolo, July 1994', *ITDG Report*, ITDG, Nairobi, Kenya.
ITDG (1999) 'Proceedings of the 8th Decentralised Animal Health Workshop, May 1999', *ITDG Report*, ITDG, Nairobi, Kenya.

ITDG (2000a) 'Proceedings of the 9th Decentralised Animal Health Workshop, Theme: Strengthening Animal Health Service Delivery in Arid and Semi-Arid Lands, June 2000', *ITDG Report*, ITDG, Nairobi, Kenya.

ITDG (2000b) *Community-Based Animal Health Care in East Africa: Experiences and case studies with particular reference to Kenya*, ITDG/EA, Nairobi, Kenya.

ITDG (2000c) *The Role of Community-based Animal Health Care in Rural Development: ITDG EAs Experience*, ITDG/EA, Nairobi, Kenya.

Jagerskog, A. (2002) 'The Sanctioned Discourse – A crucial factor for understanding water policy in the Jordan River Basin', *Occasional Paper* 41, Department for Water and Environmental Studies, Linköping University, Sweden.

James, L., Heffernan, C. and Sidahmed, E. (1999) *IFAD and the Delivery of Veterinary Services to the Rural Poor*, IFAD, Rome.

JEFF (1997) *The Joint Evaluation of Emergency Assistance to Rwanda: A Review of Follow-up and Impact Fifteen Months after Publication*, report by JEFF in conformity with a decision by the Joint Evaluation Steering Committee at its final meeting on 14 February 1997 in Copenhagen, ODI, London.

Jenkins, R. and Goetz, A.M. (1999) 'Accounts and Accountability: Theoretical Implications of the Right-to-information Movement in India', *Third World Quarterly* 20(3): 603–22.

Jodha, N.S. (1988) 'Poverty in India: A Minority View', *Economic and Political Weekly*, Special 23, November, pp 2421–8.

Johnson, J. H. and Wasty, S.S. (1993) 'Borrower Ownership of Adjustment Programs and the Political Economy of Reform', *World Bank Discussion Paper* No. 199, World Bank, Washington, DC.

Jubilee 2000 Coalition (1997) *Consultation on the White Paper on International Development – Submission on International Debt*, Jubilee 2000, London.

Kajume, J. (1998) 'Community Based Animal Health Services Delivery Strategy: Justified or Not?', 8th DAH Workshop, Meru, ITDG, Nairobi, Kenya.

Kasiye, F. and Silkin, T. (2002) *Veterinary Policies in the Horn of Africa*, OAU/IBAR PACE project , Nairobi, Kenya.

Keck, M. and Sikkink, K. (1998) *Activists Beyond Borders; Advocacy Networks in International Politics*, Cornell University Press, Ithaca, USA.

Keeley, J. (2001) *Influencing Policy Processes for Sustainable Livelihoods: Strategies for Change*, IDS, Brighton, UK.

Keeley, J. and Scoones, I. (1999) 'Understanding Environmental Policy Processes: A Review', *IDS Working Paper* 89, IDS, Brighton, UK (http://server.ntd.co.uk/ids/bookshop/details.asp?id=494)

Keeley, J. and Scoones, I. (2000) 'Knowledge, Power and Politics: the Environmental Policy-making Process in Ethiopia', *Journal of Modern African Studies*, 38(1): 89–120.

Keeley, J. and Scoones, I. (2003) *Understanding Environmental Policy Processes in Africa: Cases from Ethiopia, Mali and Zimbabwe*, Earthscan, London.
Keen, D. (1994) *The Benefits of Famine: A Political Economy of Famine in South-Western Sudan, 1983–1989*, Princeton University Press, Princeton, USA.
Kickert, W. et al. (1997) 'A Management Perspective on Policy Networks', *Managing Complex Networks*, Kickert, W., Klijn, E.H. and Koppenjan, J.F.M. (eds), Sage, London.
Killick, A. (1991) 'The Developmental Effectiveness of Aid to Africa', *Country Economics Working Paper* 646, World Bank, Washington, DC.
Killick, A. with Gunatilaka, R. and Marr, A. (1998) *Aid and the Political Economy of Policy Change*, Routledge, London and New York.
Kimanzi, R.S. (1997) 'Welcoming Remarks at the Graduation Ceremony for the AHITI, Ndomba, Kirinyaga, April 1997', personal copy of speech.
Kingdon, J.W. (1984) *Agendas, Alternatives, and Public Policies*, Harper Collins, New York.
Kitson, A., Harvey, G., and McCormack, B. (1998) 'Enabling the implementation of evidence-based practice: A conceptual framework', *Quality in Health Care* 7(3): 149-159.
Kotler, P., Armstrong, G., Saunders, J. and Wong, V. (1999) *Principles of Marketing* (2nd ed.), Prentice Hall, UK.
Kuhn, T.S. (1970) *The Structure of Scientific Revolutions*, University of Chicago Press, Chicago, USA.
KVA (2000) 'Minutes of the KVA Annual General Meeting', Mombasa, April 2000, KVA, Nairobi, Kenya.
KVA (2002a) 'Workshop Proceedings: Delivery of Quality Veterinary Services to Preserve Animal Health in ASAL areas', Silver Springs Hotel, Nairobi, September 2002, KVA, Nairobi, Kenya.
KVA (2002b) 'Letter to the Permanent Secretary MoA&RD and DVS, 6 March 2002', KVA, Nairobi, Kenya.
KVB (2002a) *Minimum Standards and Guidelines for Training of Community-based Animal Health Workers in Kenya*, KVB, Uthiru, Kenya.
KVB (2002b) 'The Veterinary Practitioners Bill (2002)', draft, KVB, Nairobi, Kenya.
Lambin, J. (1996) *Strategic Marketing Management*, McGraw-Hill, UK.
Lawson, A., Booth, D., Harding, A., Hoole, D. and Naschold, F. (2002) 'General Budget Support Evaluability Study, Phase 1, Final Synthesis Report', Report to UK DFID, Oxford Policy Management and ODI, Oxford and London.
Leach, M., Mearns, R. and Scoones, I. (eds) (1997a) 'Community-based Sustainable Development: Consensus or Conflict?', *IDS Bulletin* 28(4).

Leach, M., Mearns, R. and Scoones, I. (1997b) 'Environmental entitlements: a conceptual framework for understanding the institutional dynamics of environmental change', *IDS Discussion Paper* 359, IDS, Brighton, UK.

Leach, M., Mearns, R. and Scoones, I. (1999) 'Environmental Entitlements: Dynamics and Institutions in Community-based Natural Resource Management', *World Development* 27: 225–47.

Leader, N. (1999) 'Codes of Conduct: Who Needs Them?', *Relief and Rehabilitation Network Newsletter* 13, ODI, London.

Lefebvre, R.C. (2001) 'Theories and Models in Social Marketing', *Handbook of Marketing and Society*, Bloom, P.N. and Gundlach, G.T. (eds), Sage, London.

Lele, S.M. (1991) 'Sustainable Development: A Critical Review', *World Development* 16(6): 607–21.

Lindquist, E.A. (1988) 'What Do Decision-Models Tell Us About Information Use?', *Knowledge in Society* 1(2): 86–111.

Lindquist, E.A. (2001) *Discerning Policy Influence: Framework for a Strategic Evaluation of IDRC-Supported Research*, IDRC, Canada.

Lipsky, M. (1980) *Street-level Bureaucracy; Dilemmas of the Individual in Public Services*, Russell Sage Foundation, New York.

Lipton, M. and Maxwell, S. (1992) 'The New Poverty Agenda: An Overview', *IDS Discussion Paper* 306, IDS, Brighton, UK.

MacArthur, A. and van Trotsenburg, A. (1999) 'The HIPC Initiative: Delivering Debt Relief to Poor Countries', World Bank and IMF, Washington, DC.

Macrae, J. (ed.) (2002) 'The New Humanitarianisms: a Review of Trends in Global Humanitarian Action', *HPG Report* 11, ODI, London.

Macrae, J. and Leader, N. (2000) 'Shifting Sands: The Search for 'Coherence' between Political and Humanitarian Responses to Complex Emergencies', *HPG Report* 8, ODI, London.

Martin, M. (2001) *The Impact of Community Animal Health Services on Farmers in Low-Income Countries: A Literature Review*, VetAid, UK.

Mattelart, A. and Mattelart, M. (1998) *Theories of Communication, A Short Introduction*, Sage, London.

McPherson, P.K. (1994) 'Accounting for the Value of Information', *Aslib Proceedings* 46(9): 203–15.

Meinzen-Dick, R., Adato, M., Haddad, L. and Hazell, P. (2003) *Impacts of Agricultural Research on Poverty: Findings of an Integrated Economic and Social Analysis*, IFPRI, Washington, DC.

Minear, L. (1988) *Helping People in an Age of Conflict: Toward a New Professionalism in US Voluntary Humanitarian Assistance*, InterAction, New York and Washington, DC.

Minear, L. and Weiss, T. (1993) *Humanitarian Action in Times of War. A Handbook for Practitioners*, Lynne Rienner, Boulder and London.

Ministry of Agriculture and Rural Development (2002) *Policies and Strategies for the delivery of veterinary services in Kenya*, DVS and KVB, Nairobi, Kenya.

Molas, J., Tang, P. and Morrow, S. (2000) 'Assessing the Non-academic Impact of Grant-funded Socio-economic Research: Results from a Pilot Study', *Research Evaluation*, 9(3): 172, December.

Moore, M. and Putzel, J. (1999) 'Thinking strategically about politics and poverty', *IDS Working Paper* 101, IDS, Brighton, UK.

Moser, C. and Norton, A. (n.d.) 'Rights and Sustainable Livelihoods', mimeo, ODI, London.

Mosley, P. (1987) 'Conditionality as a Bargaining Process: Structural Adjustment Lending, 1980–1986', *Princeton Essays in International Finance* 168, Princeton University, Princeton, NJ, USA.

Mosley, P., Harrigan, J. and Toye, J. (1995) *Aid and Power: The World Bank and Policy-Based Lending in the 1980s*, 2nd ed., Routledge, London.

Mosse, D. (2003) 'Good Policy is Unimplementable? Reflections on the Ethnography of Aid Policy and Practice', paper presented at the EIDOS Workshop Order and Disjuncture: The Organisation of Aid and Development, SOAS, London, 26–28 September 2003.

National Center for the Dissemination of Disability Research (1996) *Review of the Literature on Dissemination and Knowledge Utilization*, NCDDR, USA.

Neefjes, K. (2000) *Environments and Livelihoods: Strategies for Sustainability*, Oxfam, Oxford, UK.

Neilson, S. (2001) *Knowledge Utilization and Public Policy Processes: A Literature Review*, Evaluation Unit, IDRC, Canada.

Norton, A. and Foster, M. (2001) *The Potential of Using Sustainable Livelihoods Approaches in Poverty Reduction Strategy Papers*, ODI, London.

Nutley, S. Walter, I. and Davies, H. (2002) 'From Knowing to Doing: A Framework for Understanding the Evidence-into-practice Agenda', *Discussion Paper 1*, Research Unit for Research Utilisation, University of St Andrews, UK.

OECD (1981) *The Measurement of Scientific and Technical Activities: Proposed Standard Practice for Surveys of Research and Experimental Development (Frascati Manual)*, OECD, Paris, France.

OECD-DAC (2001) *The DAC Guidelines: Poverty Reduction*, DAC, OECD, Paris, France.

Orbinski, J. (1998) 'On the Meaning of the Sphere Standards to States and Other Humanitarian Actors', speech delivered to Sphere launch, London, December 3.

Oxfam (1997) *Debt for Poverty Reduction – A New Contract*, Briefing Paper, Oxfam Publishing, Oxford.

Oxfam (1998a) *Debt Relief and Poverty Reduction: Strengthening the Linkage*, Position Paper, Oxfam Publishing, Oxford.

Oxfam (1998b) *The HIPC Review Paper: A Wasted Opportunity*, Briefing Paper, Oxfam Publishing, Oxford.

Oxfam (1998c) *Debt Relief for Nicaragua: Breaking Out of the Poverty Trap*, Policy Paper, Oxfam Publishing, Oxford.
Oxfam (1998d) *Recovery for Nicaragua and Honduras*, Briefing Paper, Oxfam Publishing, Oxford.
Oxfam (1998e) *Achieving Maximum Impact: Oxfam's Strategy for Overcoming Poverty*, Oxfam Publishing, Oxford.
Oxfam (1999a) *Oxfam International Submission to the Heavily Indebted Poor Country (HIPC) Debt Review*, Oxfam International Paper, Oxfam Publishing, Oxford.
Oxfam (1999b) *G7 Differences Threaten to Sink Debt Relief Hopes*, Briefing Paper, Oxfam Publishing, Oxford.
Oxfam (1999c) *Halfway There? G7 Must Now Make Debt Agreement Work for the Poorest*, Position Paper, Oxfam Publishing, Oxford.
Oxfam (1999d) *Debt Relief for Rwanda: An Opportunity for Peace-building and Reconstruction*, Policy Paper, Oxfam Publishing, Oxford.
Oxfam (1999e) *Outcome of the IMF/World Bank September Annual Meetings: Implications for Poverty Reduction and Debt Relief*, Policy Paper, Oxfam Publishing, Oxford.
Oxfam (1999f) *From Unsustainable Debt to Poverty Reduction: Reforming the Heavily Indebted Poor Countries Initiative*, Policy Paper prepared for Unicef, Oxfam Publishing, Oxford.
Oxfam (2000a) *Debt Relief and Poverty Reduction: Failing to Deliver*, Media Briefing, Oxfam Publishing, Oxford.
Oxfam (2000b) *Reforming the IMF*, Media Briefing, Oxfam Publishing, Oxford.
Oxfam (2000c) *Make Debt Relief Work: Proposals for the G7*, Policy Paper, Oxfam Publishing, Oxford.
Oxfam (2000d) *HIPC Leaves Poor Countries Heavily in Debt*, Briefing Paper, Oxfam Publishing, Oxford.
Oxfam (2000e) *The PRSP: Rhetoric and Reality*, Briefing Paper, Oxfam Publishing, Oxford.
Oxfam (2001a) '21st Century Debt Relief', *Parliamentary Briefing* 15, Oxfam Publishing, Oxford.
Oxfam (2001b) 'Debt Relief: Still Failing the Poor', *Parliamentary Briefing* 18, Oxfam Publishing, Oxford.
Oxfam (2001c) *Debt Relief: Still Failing the Poor*, Oxfam Publishing, Oxford.
Oxfam (2001d) *Making PRSPs Work: The Role of Poverty Assessments*, Oxfam Publishing, Oxford.
Pasteur, K. (2001) *Changing Organisations for Sustainable Livelihoods*, IDS, Brighton, UK.
Patel, S., Bolnick, J. and Mitlin, D. (2001) 'Squatting on the Global Highway: Community Exchanges for Urban Transformation', *Global Citizen Action*, Edwards, M. and Gaventa, J. (eds), Lynne Rienner, Boulder, USA.
Pearce, D., Markandya, A. and Barbier, E.B. (1989) *Blueprint for a Green Economy*, Earthscan, London.

Peterson, S.B. (1998) 'Saints, Demons, Wizards and Systems: Why Information Technology Reforms Fail or Underperform in Public Bureaucracies in Africa', *Public Administration and Development* 18(1): 37–60.

Philo, G. (1996) 'Seeing and Believing', *Media Studies: A Reader*, Marris, P. and Thornham, S. (eds), Edinburgh University Press, Edinburgh.

Piron, L.-H. (2003) 'PRSPs and Politics; Uganda Case Study', *ODI Working Paper*, ODI, London.

Poston, M., Christiansen, K. and Conway, T. (2003) *The Millennium Development Goals and the IDC: Driving and Framing the Committee's Work*, ODI, London.

Pretty, J., Gujit, I., Thompson, J. and Scoones, I. (1995) *Participatory Learning and Action: A Trainer's Guide*, IIED, London.

Price, N. (2001) 'The Performance of Social Marketing in Reaching the Poor and Vulnerable in Aids Control Programmes', *Health Policy and Planning* 16(3): 231–239.

Pross, P. (1986) *Group Politics and Public Policy*, Oxford University Press, Toronto.

Provan, K. and Milward, H.B. (2001) 'Do Networks Really Work? A Framework for Evaluating Public-Sector Organizational Networks', *Public Administration Review* 61(4): 414–23.

Putnam, R. (1993) *Making Democracy Work: Civic Traditions in Italy*, Princeton University Press, Princeton, NJ, USA.

Rai, S. (2002) 'Networking Across Borders: South Asian Research Network (SARN) on Gender, Law and Governance', paper prepared for the Global Knowledge Networks Panel, 43rd International Studies Convention, New Orleans (mimeo).

RAWOO (2001) *Utilisation of Research for Development Cooperation: Linking Knowledge Production to Development Policy and Practice*, Publication No. 21, Netherlands Development Assistance Research Council, The Hague.

Reinicke, W., Deng, F., et al. (2000) *Critical Choices: The United Nations, Networks and the Future of Global Governance*, The International Development Research Centre (IDRC), Ottawa.

Rennie, K. and Singh, N. (1996) *Participatory Research for Sustainable Livelihoods: a Guidebook for Field Projects*, IISD, Manitoba, Canada.

Robinson, D., Hewitt, T. and Harriss, J. (1999) 'Why Inter-organisational Relationships Matter', *Managing Development, Understanding Inter-organisation Relationships*, Robinson, D., Hewitt, T. and Harriss, J. (eds), Sage, London.

Roe, E. (1991) 'Development Narratives, Or Making the Best of Blueprint Development', *World Development* 19(4): 287–300.

Roe, E. (1998) *Policy Analysis and Formulation for Sustainable Livelihoods*, UNDP, New York.

RRN (1994) 'Code of Conduct for the International Red Cross and Red Crescent Movement and NGOs in Disaster Relief', *Relief and Rehabilitation Network Paper* 4, ODI, London.

Sabatier, P. and Jenkins-Smith, H.C. (1999) 'The Advocacy Coalition Framework: An Assessment', *Theories of the Policy Process*, Sabatier, P. (ed.), Westview Press, Boulder, CO.

Salvatella, R., Muzio, F. and Sánchez, D. (2000) 'Chagar Disease and Foot and Mouth Disease Eradication in Uruguay', *Lessons in Research to Action and Policy: Case Studies from Seven Countries*, Council on Health Research for Development, Geneva.

Saywell, D. and Cotton, A. (1999) *Spreading the Word: Practical Guidelines for Research Dissemination Strategies*, Water, Engineering and Development Centre, Loughborough University, UK.

Schumacher, E.F. (1973) *Small is Beautiful; A Study of Economics as if People Mattered*, Penguin, London.

Scoones, I. (1996) *Hazards and Opportunities: Farming Livelihoods in Dryland Africa: Lessons from Zimbabwe*, Zed Books, London.

Scoones, I. (1998) 'Sustainable Rural Livelihoods: A Framework for Analysis', *Working Paper* 72, IDS, Brighton, UK.

SDC (2000) *The Challenge of Eliminating World Poverty*, Swiss Agency for Development Cooperation, Berne, Switzerland.

Sen, A. (1981) *Poverty and Famines: an Essay on Entitlement and Famines*, Clarendon Press, Oxford.

Sen, A. (1999) *Development as Freedom*, Random House, New York.

Shankland, A. (2000) 'Analysing Policy for Sustainable Livelihoods', *IDS Research Report* 49, IDS, Brighton, UK.

Shepherd, A. and Bird, K. (2000) 'Did ODA Influence the World Bank?', *Evaluation of DFID Support to Poverty Reduction 1990–1997*, Evaluation Department, DFID, London.

Short, C. (1998) 'Debt Relief to Poverty Elimination', a speech made by the Secretary of State for International Development at the International Development Centre, Queen Elizabeth House, University of Oxford, 21 May (www.dfid.gov.uk).

SIDA (1997) *SIDA at Work: SIDA's Methods for Development Cooperation*, SIDA, Stockholm, Sweden.

Singh, N. and Kalala, P. (1995) *Adaptive Strategies and Sustainable Livelihoods: Community and Policy Studies for Burkino Faso, Ethiopia, Kenya, South Africa and Zimbabwe*, IISD, Manitoba, Canada.

Söderbaum, F. (2001) 'Networking and Capacity Building: the Role of Regional Research Networks in Africa', *European Journal of Development Research* 13(2): 144–63.

Solesbury, W. (2003) 'Sustainable Livelihoods: A Case Study of the Evolution of DFID Policy', ESRC UK Centre for Evidence-Based Policy and Practice, Queen Mary, University of London, *ODI Working Paper* 217, ODI, London.

Sphere (2000) *The Sphere Project: Humanitarian Charter and Minimum Standards in Disaster Response*, Oxfam Publishing, Oxford.

Spray, P. (1999) 'Jubilee 2050: World Debt and World Poverty', The Beckly Lecture.

Spray, P. and Grant, P. (1998) 'Dealing with Debt: Some Next Steps for DFID' (first and second draft), DFID, London.
Stacey, R. (1995) 'The Role of Chaos and Self-Organisation in the Development of Creative Organisations', *Chaos and Society*, Albert, A. (ed.), IOS Press, Amsterdam.
Stern, N. with Ferreira, F. (1997) 'The World Bank as "Intellectual Actor"', *The World Bank: Its First Half Century, Volume 2: Perspectives*, Kapur, D., Lewis, J.P. and Webb, R. (eds), Brookings Institution Press, Washington, DC.
Stone, D. (n.d.) 'Getting Research into Policy?', mimeo, University of Warwick, UK.
Stone, D. with Maxwell, S. and Keating, M. (2001) 'Bridging Research and Policy', an International Workshop funded by DFID, Warwick University, UK, 16–17 July.
Stone, D. and Maxwell, S. (eds) (2004) *Bridges Across Boundaries: Global Knowledge Networks and International Development*, Routledge, London.
Surr, M., Barnett, A., Duncan, A. and Speight, M. (2002) *Research for Poverty Reduction: DFID Research Policy Paper*, Development Committee Meeting, 24 October.
Sutton, R. (1999) 'The Policy Process: An Overview', *ODI Working Paper* 118, ODI, London.
Swift, J. (1989) 'Why Are Rural People Vulnerable to Famine?', *IDS Bulletin* 20(2): 8–15, IDS, Brighton, UK.
Tarp, F. and Hjertholm, P. (eds) (2000) *Foreign Aid and Development: Lessons Learned and Directions for the Future*, Routledge, London and New York.
Terry, F. (2000) 'The Limits and Risks of Regulation Mechanisms for Humanitarian Action', *Humanitarian Exchange* 17, ODI, London.
Thomas, M.S. (2003) *Can the World Bank Enforce its own Conditions?*, World Learning for International Development, Washington, DC.
Toufique, K.A. (2000) 'Sustainable Rural Livelihoods in Bangladesh: Summary of Research Findings', *Research Report* 45, IDS, Brighton, UK.
Toulmin, C. (1986) 'Pursuing National versus Local Interests: the Development Dilemma', *Development Policy Review* 4(4): 345–353.
UN (1999) *UNDAF Guidelines*, UN, New York.
UNDP (1990) *Human Development Report 1990*, Oxford University Press, Oxford.
Varey, R. J. (2002) *Marketing Communication – Principles and Practice*, Routledge, London and New York.
Volkow, N. (1998) 'Strategic Use of Information Technology requires Knowing How to Use Information', *Implementation and Evaluation of Information Systems in Developing Countries*, Avgerou, C. (ed.), Proceedings of the Fifth International Working Conference of the International Federation for Information Processing, IFIP WG 9.4, NCP, USA.

Wade, R. (1997) 'Greening the Bank: The Struggle over the Environment, 1970–1995', *The World Bank: Its First Half Century, Volume 2: Perspectives*, Kapur, D., Lewis, L.P. and Webb, R. (eds), Brookings Institution Press, Washington, DC.

Wapenhans, W.A. (1992) 'Effective Implementation: Key to Development Impact' (also known as the 'Wapenhans Report'), World Bank, Washington, DC.

Warren, D.M., Slikkerveer, L.J. and Brokensha, D. (1995) *The Cultural Dimension of Development: Indigenous Knowledge Systems*, ITDG Publishing, London.

Watzlawick, P. (1978) 'One Cannot Not Communicate', Watzlawick interviewed by C. Wilder, *Journal of Communication* 28(4).

Weiss, C. (1977) 'Research for Policy's Sake: The Enlightenment Function of Social Research', *Policy Analysis* 3(4): 531–45.

White, S.D. (1998) 'Barefoot Doctor to Village Doctor in Tiger Springs Village: A Case Study of Rural Health Care Transformations in Socialist China', *Human Organisation* 57(4): 480–90.

Williams, R. (1973) 'Base and Superstructure in Marxist Cultural Theory', *New Left Review* 82: 3–16.

Williamson, J. (1996) 'Decoding Advertisements', *Media Studies: A Reader*, Marris, P. and Thornham, S. (eds), Edinburgh University Press, Edinburgh.

Wolfensohn, J. (1999) *Proposal for a Comprehensive Development Framework*, World Bank, Washington, DC.

Woodward, S. (2001) 'Humanitarian War: A New Consensus?', *Disasters* 25(4): 331–44.

World Bank (1988) *Adjustment Lending: An Evaluation of Ten Years of Experience*, World Bank, Washington, DC.

World Bank (1998) *Assessing Aid: What Works, What Doesn't, and Why*, Oxford University Press, Oxford.

World Bank (1999) *Building Poverty Reduction Strategies in Developing Countries*, World Bank, Washington, DC (http://poverty.worldbank.org/library/view/3910).

World Bank (2000/01) *World Development Report 2000/2001: Attacking Poverty*, World Bank, Washington, DC.

World Bank (2003) *Toward Country-led Development: A Multi-partner Evaluation of the Comprehensive Development Framework*, World Bank, Washington, DC (www-wds.worldbank.org/default.jsp).

World Commission on Environment and Development (1987a) *Our Common Future: Report of the World Commission on Environment and Development*, Oxford University Press, Oxford.

World Commission on Environment and Development (1987b) *Food 2000: Global Policies for Sustainable Agriculture, Report of the Advisory Panel on Food Security, Agriculture, Forestry and Environment*, Zed Books, London.

Young, J., Kajume, J. and Wanyama, J. (2003) 'Animal Health Care in Kenya: The Road to Community-Based Animal Health Service Delivery', *ODI Working Paper* 214, ODI, London.

Index

Page numbers in *italic* refer to figures;
bold numbers refer to major references;
'n' next to the page number refers to an endnote reference

academic freedom **169-71**
academic research 11, 71, 76, 157, 161, 162, 173
access 137, 138, *140*
accountability 5, 10, 15, 16, 44, 46, *52*, n54, 55, 79, 86, 87, 88, 94, 95, 99, 101, 158, 161, 162, 169, 170
accreditation 16, 17, 80, 86, 92, 99, 102, 161
action research 6, 17, 27, 73, 103, 120, 161, 174, *176*, 177
actors 10, 11, 17, 19, 26, 28, 161, 177
    animal healthcare in Kenya **121-22**
    PRSP 53, 71
    Sphere Project 95-98
    sustainable livelihoods **151-52**, 153
Addis Ababa 65, 66
advocacy coalition 8, 12, 26, *45*, 60, 74, 101, 161, 166
Africa, strategic partnership with **57-58**
AHA xiv, 99, 110
AHT xiv, 104, 106, 115, 116
    unemployment 108
aid effectiveness 14, **54**, 61, 72, 157, 161
Akabwai, Darlington, Dr 104, 107, 108
ALNAP xiv, n79, 95
animal healthcare in Kenya **103-131**, 160, 161, 162, 163, 164, 165, 166, 168, 173, 174, 175
    budget restriction 105, 113, 123, 160
    colonial era 104
    context 17, **112-17**, *128*, 129, 130
    evidence 18, **117-20**, *128*, 129
    governmment provision 104
    chronology **104-112**
    links 19, **120-23**, *128*, 129
    overview **17-19**
    professionalism 104, 106, 109, 113, 127, 128
    unemployment 106, 108
applied research 11, 14, 34, 55, 72, 76, 162, 174
arid and semi-arid lands *see* ASAL
ASAL xiv, 17, 18, 103, 104, 105, 106, 107, 109, 110, 111, **112**, 115, 118, 160, 161, 162, 168
Asia crisis (of 1997) 13, 68, 70, 159, 160
ASMP xiv, 114, 130, 173
audience segmentation/targeting 12, 16, 41-42, 94, 100, 119, 163

Bangladesh 136, 137, 142
barefoot doctor 105, 117, 125, 168
bilateral donors 15, 58, 94, 118, 120, 125, 168, 174
Bishop, Jim 17, 96, 102
Bolivia 52, 60
Boote, Tony 63, 66, 75
Borton, John 80, 83, 85, 86, 92, 93, 96
Bredenkamp, Hugh 62, 63
Brown, Gordon 58, 71
Brundtland Commission 20, **133-134**, 145, 148
Burdon, Tony 66, 75
bureaucracy 31, 35, 56, 98
buy-in 15, 16, 80, 95, 96, 97, 164
CAHW xiv, 18, **103-131**, 158, 162, 163, 175
Camdessus, Michel 56, 61
campaign 47, 77, 163, 166, 173
capability 134, 135, *140*
capacity building 46, 84, 171, 172
CARE International 87, 136, 142, 145, 146
Carney, Diana 136, 137, 139, 140, *141*, 142, 145, 147, 148, 151, 152
CAS xiv, 62
case studies **51-154**
    overview **13-21**
Catholic Church 104, 105, 120, 131
CDF xiv, 13, *52*, 55, **62**, 69, 70
Chambers, Robert 20, 25, 54, **134-35**, 145, 148, 150, 151, 152, 153
    see also Conway, Gordon
chance 21, 153, 172
China 39, 105, 117
Chomsky, N. 34-35, 71
Chong, Dr 18, 111, 114, 128, 129
Christian Aid 6, 59, 60, 66
civil society **5**, 28, 31, 35, 44, *45*, 46, 52, 56, 76, 136, 159, 168, 170, 171
    see also CSO
Clark, Jane 140, 141
Clinton, Bill 59, 71, 74
Code of Conduct 79, 82, 86
Cold War 68, 80
collaboration 34, 38, 47, 62, 63, 113, 131, 137, 138, 142-43, 164
communication 8, 12, *27*, 30, 37, **39-43**, 46, 71, 73, 82, 99, 117, 125, 149-51, 153, **161-64**, 168, *169*, 174
    strategy 12, 19, 130, 175
community-based animal health service 17-19, **103-131**, 160
    see also CAHW
Conlin, Sean 137, 146, 151
conditionality *52*, 54, 55, 59, 61, 66, 72
conflict environments 80, 81, 82
connectors 17, **44**, 75, 101, 165, 175

consensus 62, 159, 160
contact herder 106, 118
context 7, **11**, 29, **30-37**, *36*, **158-61**, *169*, 169, 173, 175, *176*, 177
   animal healthcare in Kenya 17, **112-17**, *128*, 129, 130
   PRSP initiative 13, **68-71**, 77, 166
   Sphere 15, 80-81, **89-92**, 98-99
   sustainable livelihoods 20, **148-49**
'context, evidence, links' framework xii, **7-9**, *9*, 21, 23, **25-47**, *29*, 47, 76, *128*, 133, 148, 153, 157, 168, *169*, 171, 177
   PRSP **68-75**
Conway, Gordon 20, 21, **134-135**, 137, 145, 148, 150, 151, 152, 153
   see also Chambers, Robert
coordination 54, 55, 63, 68, 69, 71, 90, 125, 126, 164, 172
credibility 8, 9, 12, 14, 16, 22, 30, 37, 61, 63, 71, 72, 73, 76, 92, 98, 99, 101, 102, 117, **119**, 149-51, 153, 159, **161-64**, *169*, 173, 175, 177
CSO xiv, 31, 46
   see also civil society
Dabelstein, Niels 85, 94, 95
DAC xiv, 64, 74, 85, 95, 146, 154
DAH xiv, **17-19**, 103, 104, 105, 106, 107, 110, 111, 121, 124, 126, 129, 130, 164, 166
   workshop 108, 116, 117, 164
Danida 85, 95
debt cancellation 32, 39
debt relief 13, 14, 51, 53, 56, 60, 61, 62, **63-65**, 68, 69, 76, 77, 159, 166, 173, 175
Debt Round Table 60, 71
decentralized animal healthcare
   see DAH
decisions
   emergent 11, 32, **34**, 71, 99
   fundamental 11, 32, **34**, 70, 99, 159
   incremental 11, 32, **34**, 71, 99
   routine 11, **32**
DELIVERI xiv, *38*, 131
democracy n54, 166, **169-171**
   definition 5
democratization **5**, 46, 71, 168
development 143
   discourse 14, **53-55**, 157
   history, schematic *52*
   investment 3, 30
   people-centred 145, 147
   policy, more informed **157-178**
   policy 'problem' 13, 68, 159
   sustainable 134, 145
DFID x, xii, xiii, xiv, 3, 13, 19, 25, 30, 46, 55, 58, 59, 66, 115, 121, 131, 159, 163, 173
   and SLA policy **133-154**, 162, 165

disaster relief 87, 90
   see also emergency
discourse 8, 14, 26, 31, **53-55**, 72, 89, 117, 126, 129, 150, 157, *176*
discourse coalition *45*, 101
dissemination 8, 99, 102, 119, 168
'Drop the Debt' campaign 60, 63
DVO xiv, 107, 113
DVS xiv, 105, 107, 110, 111, 112, 114, 115, 116, 118, 119, 121, 123
Eastern Province, Kenya 106, 108, 116, 122
EC xiv, 108, 114, 118, 121
élite 36, 40
Ellis, Frank 137, 143, 148, 151
emergency 80, 81, 83, 96
   political causes of 80
emergent decisions 11, 32, **34**, 71, 99
empirical research 136-38, 143
empowerment 54, 136
Environment Conference 134
epistemic community 8, 12, 26, 28, *45*, 74, 165, 171
ESAF 14, **62-63**, 67, 68, 70, 72, 73, 74, 76, 77, 160, 175
ESCOR xiv, 137, 146, 147, 148
ESRC xiv, 4, 136
Ethiopia 36, n80, 107, 108, 109, 115, 121, 123, 137
EU xiv, 66, 115, 122
evidence **8**, **12**, 30, **37-43**, **161-64**, 163, *169*, 170, *176*, 177
   animal healthcare 18, **117-20**, 125-26, *128*, 129, 174
   PRSP initiative 14, **71-73**, 77
   Sphere Project 16-17, **92-95**, 99-101
   sustainable livelihoods 20, **149-51**
evidence-based policy 3-4, 9, 25, 27, 102, 168, 172, 173, 175, 177
expatriate 101, 104, 106, 114, 119, 123, 126
expert **39**, 44
external influences 9, 22, 124, 159, 162, 166, **168-69**, *169*, 171
FAO xiv, 142, 143
FARM Africa xiv, 109
Ford Foundation 21, 87, 152
Foster, M. 66, 67, 75
Francophone NGOs 80, 91
Freedom House 5, 170
fundamental decisions 11, 32, **34**, 70, 99, 159
G7 xiv, 59, 61, 65, 77
gender 32, 36, 139
genocide 83, 84, 85
giantism 33
Gladwell, M. 8, 17, 41, 44, 69, 75, 101, 158, 165, 175

global public policy 12, *45*, 166
globalization 26, 144, 149, 169
Goma, Congo 83, 93, 99
governance 31, *52*, 54, 88, 138, 169
grassroots groups 28, 36, *40*, 44, 47, 127
GTZ xiv, 106, 107, 118, 120
HAP xiv, n79, 92, 99
high-potential area 104, 112, 115
HIPC xiv, 13, 14, 59, **63-65**, 66, 69, 72, 74, 75, 76, 77, 158, 162, 175
HIPC1 xiv, 61, 64
HIPC2 xiv, 51, 59, 67, **68-69**
Hübl study 18, 110, 118, 119, 119, 121, 122, 123, 126, 128, 129, 162, 174
Human Development Report 20, **133-34**, 148
humanitarian aid agencies 15, 158, 160, 162, 166
   questioning of 15
   performance and standards 81-82, 86, 87, 90, 94, 98, 100, 102, 161
   principles 81, 82
   professionalism 79, 82, 84, 86, 99
   see also accreditation; NGO; regulation
Humanitarian Charter 15, 79, 88, 91, 95, 96, 99
ICRC xiv, 79, 81, 88, 89
ICT xiv, **6**, 26, *43*, 43
ICVA xiv, 87, 88, 96, 99
IDA xiv, 13, 51, 67
IDS xiv, 134, 136, 137, 139, *140*, 141, 143, 144, 146, 147, 152
IDT xiv, 55, 58, 64, n138, 138, 142, 144, 146, 148, 150, 154
IFAD xv, 143
IFI xv, 14, 32, 52, 57, 58, 60, 68, 71, 72, 73, 159, 160, 162, 165, 168
   conservatism 57, 69
   processes **61-65**
   self-censorship 57, 70
   see also IMF; World Bank
IFRC xv, 16, 82, 87, 89, 96, 99
IIED xv, 4, 21, 137, 146, 146, 147, 152
IISD xv, 136, 146, 151, 152
IMF xv, 13, 14, 31, 35, 51-77, **55-57**, 159, 160, 163, 165, 168, 174
   conservatism 57, 69, 70
   executive board 51, 56, 57, 63, 66, 67
   processes **61-67**
   structure 56, n57, 70
impact 4, 12, 21, 23, 25, 30, 31, 64, 102, 154, 159, 163, 165, 173, 174, 175, 178
   animal healthcare in Kenya 119-20
   Rwanda evaluation **94**, 100, 102
implementation 35, 36, 46, 52, 56, 69, 90, 96, 126, 149, 160
incremental decisions 11, 32, **34**, 71, 99

indigenous knowledge 39, 129
information and communication technology *see* ICT
insider model 40, 100
institution 22, 29, 30-31, 77, 139, **158-61**
   animal healthcare in Kenya 112-17, 123-25
   Northern 22, 39, 46, 80, 98
   PRSP 68-71
   Southern 22, 46, n66, 80, 99, 166, 168
   Sphere Project 89-92, 98-99
   sustainable livelihoods **148-49**
institutional pressure 8, 9, 22, 32, *33-34*, 46, 57, 76, 94, 102, 114, 158, *169*, 173
integrated framework **7-9**, *9*, 22, 23, 27, 30, 47, 123, 157, 166, 167
InterAction 16, 17, 82, 85, 87, 88, 89, 90, 95, 96, 102
interactive model 27, 39
interactive communication 8, 22, 97, 144-48, 151, 163, 165, 175
Intergovernmental Panel on Climate Change 45
IPRSP xv, 51, 52, 68
issue network *45*, 101, 126
ITDG xv, 17, 18, 19, 103, 105, 106, 108, 110, 115, 116, **117-19**, 120, **121**, 122, 123, 125, 126, 127, 128, 129, 130, 131, 143, 161, 164, 173
JEFF xv, 86, 87, 94, 99
job mobility 21, 143, 150, 152
Joint Evaluation of Emergency Assistance to Rwanda 16, 80, 84, 85-87, 88, 90, 92, 95, 97, 161, 163, 164, 165
   impact **94**
   management group 16, 85, 86, 95, 100, 101
   steering committee 16, 85, 87, 92, 93, 94, 95, 97, 101
JSA xv, 52, 53, 68
Jubilee 2000 13, *45*, 60, 63, 65, 71, 73, 74, 159, 161, 165
Kajume, Dr Julius 17, 18, 19, n103, 106, 107, 108, 110, 111, 114, 116, 118, 120, 121, **122**, 127, 128, 129, 130, 131
KALT xv, 108, 109, 114, 120
   threat to march 108, 115
Kenyan animal healthcare xii, 22, 32, **103-131**, 158, 160, 161, 162, 163, 164, 165, 166, 168, 173, 174, 175
   overview **17-19**
   see also animal healthcare in Kenya; ASAL; high-potential area
KFC xv, 105, 106
Kigali, Rwanda 83, 86
Kimanzi, Dr 18, 108, 110, 111, 113, 122, 127, 128, 130, 131
knowledge creep 3, 29, 157

knowledge systems 31, 166
Kosovo 80, 81
Kuhn, T. 35, 99, 124, n144
KVA xv, 18, 107, 108, 109, 111, 112, 117, 121, 122, 124, 128, 129
   Central Region branch 115, 117, 120
   executive committee 117, 120
KVAPS xv, 110, 114, 115
KVB xv, 107, 108, 109, 110, 117, 124
   advertisement 110, 114, 116
   letter 18, 115, 120, 121, 122, 124, 126, 127, 128, 129, 130, 158, 164
Labour Party (UK) 58, 71, 146, 147
legitimacy 8, 10, 12, 30, 37, 43, **46**, 73, 96, 98, 102, 123, 125-27, 131, 151-52, 163, **164-66**, 171, 174, 175, *176*, 177
Leyland, Tim 107, 108
Lindquist, E.A. 7, 32, 44, 70, 71, 99, 159
linear model 7, 25, 27, 39
links **8**, **12**, 22, 30, **43-47**, **164-66**, *169*, *176*, 177
   animal healthcare in Kenya 19, **120-23**, 126-27, *128*, 129
   PRSP initiative 14, **73-75**
   Sphere Project 16
   sustainable livelihoods 21, **151-52**
livelihood 135, 161
   assets 134, 135, 138, *140*, *141*, 145
   resources 139, *140*
   strategies 139, *140*, *141*
   see also SLA; sustainable livelihood
Livelihood Connect website 141, 150
livestock services xii, 17-19, 22, 103, 110, 117
lobby 33, 39, 109, 115
local involvement 9, 12, 39, 76, 102, 131, 165, 173, 174
low-income countries 14, 56, 57, 58, 70
LWF xv, 90, 99
Mariner, Jeff 106, 107, 113, 116
market 5, 30, 138
marketing 8, **41-43**, 44, 73, 100, 162
Masarbit, Kenya 106, 107, 109, 113
Masood Ahmed 66, 75
maven **44**, 165
MDG xv, 3, 59
media coverage 15, 83, 84, 89, 98
media freedom **169-71**
Meltzer Commission 59, 71
memorandum of understanding 120, 121
Meru, Kenya 18, 105, 106, 111, 126, 127, 128
methodology **9-12**, 92, 136
Ministry of Agriculture (Kenya) 105, 106, 112, 113, 115
minimum standards 15, 79, 87, 89, 91, 95, 99, 111
Mozambique 60

MSF xv, 87, 91
multi-stakeholder 18, 85, 111, 126, 129
Mumbai *40*
Nairobi 106, 108, 110, 115, 116, 118, 123
narrative 10, 11, 33, *36*, 37, 69, 75, 127, 133, 148, 172, *176*
Natural Resources Department
   see NRPAD
necessary conditions 21, 147, 154
Neefjes, Koos 136, 146, 151
network 9, 10, 12, 18, 28, 30, **43-46**, *45*, 73, 74, 76-77, 101, 102, 126, 127, 128, 129, 130, 149, 151-52, 153, 164, 168, *169*, **171-72**, 175, *176*, 177
NGO xv, 5, 14, 37, 57, **59-60**, 79, 81, 109, 116, 117, 125, 162, 164, 172, 173
   Francophone 80, 91
   performance and standards 81-82, 86, 87, 90, 94, 98, 100, 102, 159, 160, 161
   professionalism 79, 82, 84, 86, 99
   see also accreditation; humanitarian aid agencies; regulation
Northern institutions 22, 46, 80, 98
NRAC xv, 139, 140
NRPAD xv, 20 139, 147, 149
NSI xv, 31
OAU/IBAR xv, 106, 107, 109, 110, 111, 112, 115, 118, 119, 121, 122, 123, 126
objectivity 93, 94
ODA xii, xv, 146, 154
ODG xv, 137
ODI x, xiii, xv, 10, 29, 82, 137, 139, 147, 152
   mission statement ix
OECD xv, 3, 138, 146, 149, 150, 153, 158, 169
ombudsman n79, 86, 92, 95, 98
ownership 15, 47, 54, 55, 61, 62, 67, 77, 79, 96, 97, 118, 164, 165, 171
Oxfam 16, 60, 66, 73, 75, 89, 96, **136**, 139, 145, 146, 147
packaging 8, *9*, 41, 163, *169*, 174, 177
paradigm 8, 35, 56, 73, 99, 124, 125, 144, 146, 162
para-vet xii, 32, 117, 129, 158, 165
PARC-VAC xv, 107, 109, 110, 111, 118, 119, 121, 123
participation 14, **46**, **52**, 52, **53**, n54, 62, 72, 95, 117, 118, 126, 134, 138, 145, 146, 148, 149, 157, 161, 164, 171, *176*
partnership 52, 53, 58, 62
PEAP xv, 14, 61, 73, 162, 174
percolation 3, 7, 29, 72, 118, 157, 174
PFP xv, 13, 57, **61-62**, 70, 71
Pharmacy and Poisons Act 104, 112, 116
Pokot, Kenya 105, 110, 111

policy
  aims and methods 26
  definition 7
  see also evidence-based policy
policy community 8, 12, 28, 45, 74, 101, 129, 144, 164, 165, 176
policy entrepreneur x, 12, 17, 44, 75, 101, 165, 173, 175
policy window 9, 15, 17, 44, 69, 102, 159, 173, 175, 176, 177
politics 22, 29, **158-61**, 168
  animal healthcare in Kenya 112-17, 123-25
  PRSP 68-71
  Sphere Project 89-92, 96, 98-99
  sustainable livelihoods **148-49**
poverty reduction 14, 27, 46, 52, 53, 60, 64, 65, 70, 71, 74, 76, 103, 142, 143, 144, 157
  see also PAF; PEAP
power 33, 44, 158
  state 31
  without knowledge **25-27**
PPA xv, 52, 61
PREM xv, 66, 77, 175
PRGF xv, 13, 67, 68
private sector 52, 52, 54
privatization 17, 43, 52, 103, 105, 108, 114, 127
pro-poor 4, 6, 20, 31, 37, 46, 102, 138, 146, 172, 173, 175, 177
PRSP xii, xv, 5, 10, 22, 46, **51-77**, 52, 157, 158, 159, 160, 161, 162, 163, 164, 165, 166, 168, 172, 173, 174, 175
  context 13, **68-71**
  core principles 52-53
  evidence 14, **71-73**
  links 14, **73-75**
  overview **13-15**
public expenditure 54, 55, 58, 61, 65
public relations 61, 64, 68, 97
Purdin, Susan 17, 89, 96
quality of research 8, 12, **37-38**, 38, 99, 163, 176
radical 15, 34, 35, 75, 89, 96
RAPID xi, xii, xv, 6, 10, 166
  framework **7-9**, 9, 157, 169
refugee crisis 15, 83, 84, 85, 89, 93, 102
regulation 16, 17, 80, 84, 86, 90, 92, 95, 99, 102, 161
research
  academic see academic research
  action see action research
  aims and methods 26
  applied see applied research
  collaborative 34, 38
  definition 6
  ignored 7, 8, 12, 22, 25, 27

  quality of see quality of research
research-policy-practice 21, 152, 167
results oriented 52, 61, 62
rights based 88, 96, 99
rigorous research 76, 94, 162, 173
rinderpest 106, 107, 108, 109, 115, 118, 122
Rockefeller Foundation 21, 46, 152, 165
room for manoeuvre 8, 11, **32**, 70, 71, 113, 160, 177
routine decisions 11, **32**,
RPF xv, 83
Rural Livelihoods Advisory Group 139, 147, 148, 154
Rwanda 15, 79, 80, 81, **82-83**, 84, 85, 87, 88, 89, 100, 102, 158, 159, 160, 173
Rwanda evaluation **85-87**, 90, 91, 94, 100, 101, 102, 175
  composition 93
  impact **94**
  management group 16, 85, 93, 95, 100, 101
  steering committee 16, 85, 87, 92, 93, 95, 97, 101
salesmen 17, **44**, 75, 101, 165, 175, 176
SAP xv, 13, 17, 61, 103
  see also ESAF; SAPRI; SAPRIN; structural adjustment
SAPRI xvi, 57
  see also ESAF; structural adjustment
SAPRIN xvi, 57
SCF-UK xvi, 89, 90
SCHR xvi, n82, 82, 85, 87, 88, 90, 95
Scoones, Ian 7, 26, 28, 36, 40, 43, 126, 137, 139, 140, 148, 150, 151, 152, 154, 160
Scott, Michael 139, 147, 151, 154
self-reliance 134, 147
Sen, Amartya 135, 170
'September 11' 100
Sessional Paper No. 1 of 1965 104
Sessional Paper No. 1 of 1986 17, 105, 114, 127
Short, Clare 13, 57, 58, 59, 71, 75, 146
SID xvi, 136, 146
Singh, Naresh 136, 146, 151, 152
SLA xvi, **133-154**, 157, 161, 162, 163, 165, 172, 173, 174
  context 20
  evidence 20
  links 21
  overview 19-21
  see livelihood; sustainable livelihood
SLRG xvi, 21, 143, 152
SLSO xvi, 20, 140, 141, 150, 152
snowball effect 40, 100
SNV xvi, 110, 111, 120, 121, 126
social change 47, 69, 165

Southern institutions 22, 46, 57, n66, 80, 99, 166, 168, 169, **171**
SPA xvi, 14, **57-58**, 63, 66, 72, 74, 77, 164, 175
Sphere Project xii, **79-102**, 158, 159, 160, 161, 162, 163, 164, 165, 166, 172, 173, 174, 175
   context 15, **89-92**, 98-99
   cost and funding 90, 97
   evidence 15-16, **92-95**, 99-101
   legitimacy 98
   links 16
   management committee 89, 91, 92, 97, 101
   opposition to 90
   origins **87-88**
   overview **15-17**
stickiness factor 41, 100
Stockton, Nick 17, 87, 88, 93, 96, 97, 98, 101
Stone, D. n4, 7, 26, *27*, 39, 44, *45*, 101, 169
street-level bureaucrats 11, 35, 44, 70, 99, 124, 125, 160, 161, 165
structural adjustment 17, *52*, 54, 56, 68, 69, 103, 105, 114, 124, 127
   see also ESAF; SAP; SAPRI; SAPRIN
Study 3 15, 16, 80, 85, **86**, 91, 92, 95, 96, 100, 102, 161, 163
sub-Saharan Africa 13, 17, 54, 58, 68, 81, 117, 159
Sudan 109, 115, 121, 123
sufficient conditions 21, 147, 154
Sussex University 21, 137
sustainable development 134
sustainablility 20, 63, 64, 65, 135, 136, 148, 165
sustainable livelihoods 10
   context 20, **148-49**
   definition 133, 135
   evidence 20, **149-51**
   framework 139, *140*, *141*, 143, 144, 150
   links 21, **151-52**
   outcomes 139, *140*, *141*
   overview 19-21
   see also livelihood; SLA
Tanzania 3, 60, 110, 126, 136
Tigray, Ethiopia 36
time 21, 57, 153
   lag/lapse 10, *27*, 42, 153
tipping point 158
   animal healthcare 18, 109-10
   PRSP 14, 69
tracer study 4, 10, 29
transnational processes 26, 39, 165, 166, **168-69**, 171
transparency n54, 55, 169, 170
trust 8, 21, 38, *43*, 44, 101, 152, 164, 170
TRVTT xvi, 107, 108, 109, 118, 121, 122

Turkana, Kenya 104, 105, 110, 111
UEA xvi, 137, 146, 147
Uganda 14, 52, **60-61**, 73, 75, 76, 108, 110, 121, 123, 162, 174
UK Government 58-59, 71
umbrella organization 88, 95, 165
US Government 59, 71
UN xvi, 93, 149
UN DHA xvi, 86, 94
UNDP xvi, 20, 66, 133, 136, 142, 145, 146, 148, 151
unemployment 106, 108
UNHCR xvi, 83, 93
UNICEF xvi, 66
uptake 4, 7, 8, 159, 161, 169
Utstein Group 58, 74
vaccination 108, 109, 117, 118, 122
Veterinary Practitioners Bill 112, 117
Veterinary Public Health Division 106, 108
veterinary services 103
   budget restrictions 105, 113, 123, 160
   professionalism 104, 106, 109, 113, 127, 128
   private practice 108, 116
   see also DVS
Veterinary Surgeons Act 104, 106, 108, 112, 113, 114, 116, 117
vet scout 104, 125
vets' workshops 18, 19, 106, 107, 109, 111, 118, 119, 120, 121, 126, 127, 128, 130, 131, 164, 175
VOICE xvi, 85, 87, 88, 96
vulnerability 54, 135, *140*, *141*
Walker, Peter n15, 17, 82, 87, 88, 93, 96, 97, 98, 101
Wamukoya, Dr 18, 106, 108, 113, 127, 128, 130, 175
'war on terror' 6
WDR xvi, 53, 54, 58, 66, 70, 143
Weiss, Carol 3, 7, 28, 72, 157
whisper effect 40, 100
White Paper 30
   (1997) xii, 19, 20, 55, 58, 133, **138-39**, 140, 142, **146**, 149, 150, 152, 153, 163, 173
   (2000) **144**, 149
Wolfensohn, James n5, 13, 56, 57, 62, 70
woodfuel crisis *36*, 37
World Bank 13, 14, 31, 35, 51-77, **55-57**, 114, 117, 143, 159, 160, 163, 165, 168, 174
   executive board 51, 56, 57, 67
   processes **61-67**
   structure 56, n57
World Development Report *see* WDR
World Summit for Social Development 134, 136

www.ingramcontent.com/pod-product-compliance
Ingram Content Group UK Ltd.
Pitfield, Milton Keynes, MK11 3LW, UK
UKHW060455150426
5217IPUK00028B/2091